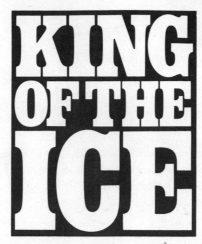

KING OF THE ICE

A study (Don Johnson)

By
Helen Corbin

FOXWEST PUBLISHING

i

KING OF THE ICE

ISBN 1-879029-01-4

Graphics/Production: Robin Fox & Associates

9 8 7 6 5 4 3 2 1

Library of Congress Catalog Number: 91-73982

For information contact the Publisher:

Foxwest Publishing
2834 North 29th Street
Suite 1
Phoenix, AZ 85008

PUBLISHED IN THE UNITED STATES OF AMERICA

Dedication
to Don

"WHOEVER IS BRAVE
IS A MAN OF GREAT SOUL." (CICERO)

Of flying it is said: Aviation in itself is not inherently dangerous. But to an even greater degree than the sea, it is terribly unforgiving of any carelessness, incapacity or neglect.

The above quotes are applicable to the man whose life story follows, Don Johnson, who spent his life flying the bush and hunting in the "Great Land."

Acknowledgements

Carpa Orloff
Mary Orloff
Rachel Rogers
Joe Sanger
Judy Travlos
Dick Rinc
Dick Gunlogson
Gary Swanson
Harlon Carter
Baron Eltz (Deceased)
Baroness Nanine Eltz
Prince Louis of Liechtenstein (Deceased)
Howard Wilson
Peter Eltz
Former Governor Egan
Bill Phifer
Warren Johnson
Danny Lynch
Steve Daniel
Harold McGready
Dwayne Johnson
Quinten Johnson
Tim Okonek
Slim Gale
Janell Gibney

Dick Remur
Nicoli Franco
Doctor Fritz Wechselberger
Margret Killigruk (Deceased)
Salmon Killigruk
Jimmy Killigruk (Deceased)
Al Bontrigger (Deceased)
Bruno Scherrer
Doctor Ron Norman
Arnold Glass
Perry Null
Doctor Goodman
Brian Hern (Deceased)
Keith Hersh
Jim Doyle
Bill Sullivan
Tom Kamph
Kath McGrady
Christina Johnson
Arlene Nelson
Nels Wilson
Robin Fox
Carol Fox
Holly Aldis
Toni Rogers

The author wishes to thank all of the above-named persons for their patience and information during the long research periods. It is also significant to acknowledge the Anchorage Public Library Historical Section, The University of Alaska and the Eltz family for their use of the Baron's diaries.

From the Author

Guns on Naval warships steaming through the Aleutians were finally silenced in 1945. Weighing anchor in Alaska, they deposited war-weary young Americans eager for discharge. Most GIs were anxious to reach the States, but a few, seeing the potential of the vast untamed territory, stayed.

The fabric of the 'New Frontier,' destined to be woven by airplanes from which the words "Bush Pilot" would emerge and become synonymous with its lore, would include the name of one of them. In the next 33 years, Don Johnson's exploits in the air would be a legend—and with that daring, hundreds of lives would be saved.

While a world hungry for peace got back to normal, hunting as a hobby would again occupy men's minds. Alaska was teeming with wildlife. This was a time before the earth grew small and fear of denuding brought laws against that pleasure. Prior to the passage of the Mammal Act in 1972 prohibiting the taking of meat except by Natives for subsistence, Don Johnson was "King of the Ice." His record polar bear, housed in the Anchorage air terminal until the earthquake of 1964 destroyed it, was, according to state authorities, the most-photographed bear in that state.

This is the story of a man who respectfully put away medals received for bravery during World War II and who, after his wounds healed, initiated polar bear hunting in the Arctic. He lived with the Inuit Eskimos for 19 winters becoming a friend and mentor. During that unique experience, he built a sheep camp in the beautiful Wrangell Mountains of southeastern Alaska, one on the Kenai Peninsula and the ultimate hunting camp called Bear Lake Lodge on the remote Aleutian Chain.

Bear Lake, reputed to be the most exclusive hunting facility in Alaska, attracted hunters from around the globe. During the ensuing years, such names as Baron Eltz of Austria; the King of Nepal; Prince Louis of Liechtenstein; General Franco of Spain and his nephew, Nicoli; Prince Gazi of Afghanistan; Prince Alverez, the Shah of Iran's brother; and Prince Bandar Bin Sultan of Saudi Arabia would share his hunts. Their friendships would take the pilot-guide worldwide on exciting unusual hunts, developing a record game collection which in 1984 was selected by the State of Alaska for permanent exhibit.

Included in the book among personal accounts of individual hunts are Don's appraisal of all major animals found in Alaska.

Those who hunt or love the land named Alaskka by the Russians, Alayeska by the Aleuts and which now is called Alaska, will surely find his story fascinating.

Foreword:

THE KING OF THE ICE
by Harlon B. Carter

This is a book about courage. The author has successfully portrayed the indomitable spirit of a man, Don Johnson, and made it understandable to those who, in their daily lives, have never experienced it. It is a story of a man's enthusiastic willingness to confront that which has existed for thousands, if not millions, of years—confrontations which he knew he might not conquer and from which, by an unforgiven error, he might not emerge.

This bush pilot, a true pioneer, answered that challenge and built a home and business in a harsh, stern and hostile land. It was as the book states, describing the lean look of the hunter in a primitive environment, "An awesome place, a place where death occurred quickly."

Man admired the beast. He treats it with respect, not because the beast has rights, but because there are decencies not to be trespassed upon by the highest order of animals—honorable men. Consequently and frequently, man seeks trophies of the hunt to enhance his memories and to make them long endure for the appreciation of others. Man respects the beast because of the difficulties and perils encountered in distant places where the beast may be found, and because, after confronting those difficulties, he has so often returned to his camp defeated, even humbled, hungry and cold.

Man gropes for a measure of achievement; hunting provides it. The book exposes the hunt in the harshest environment on earth, the Arctic, where any mistake means death and the reversal of the tables on the hunter and the hunted.

Political changes in Alaska and the increasing conflicts between the old and the new are reflected upon by the author when she states:

> "Being tough had been necessary to survive. But, a way of life was beginning to erode. It would come in the form of government interference. There would be the Mammal Act which would stop Polar Bear hunting; the sheep preserve would be taken away; statehood was already here and with it would finally come more legislation and restraints and finally, free men would allow laws against firearms."

Regrettably, it's true. As the soft mantle of civilization enfolds all of us in its placid, indulgent embrace, mankind seeks first to ignore, and then to deny, that evil exists. In his pious pretensions against crime, men seeks restraints upon inanimate objects or upon men who commit no crime.

But, from a book like this, we take heart in the assurance that we can seek and we can find Don Johnsons. There will ever be a place for them.

Contents

Chapter 1

North to Point Hope

The great Gulf of Alaska washes in a huge arc from Alexander Archipelago on the narrow, lower end adjacent to Canada, to Kodiak Island and the beginning of the Aleutian Chain before it joins the Pacific Ocean. At 10 o'clock on the curve is Kenai Peninsula.

Early in 1950 Don Johnson scanned a map after receiving results from the territorial land office of a GI homestead drawing. He had applied for, and received, 160 acres bordering Cook's Inlet. Reading on, Don decided he had better get busy. There was a log cabin to build—1,200 square feet, the letter said. A required occupancy for seven months out of the year would mean living there by June. It was still winter and crude Alaskan roads impassable.

By the end of May, Don was headed out of Fairbanks where he had gone after the Navy discharged him in 1945. Building in the "New Frontier" became a matter of cooperation. With the aid of a couple of ex-servicemen who knew more about carpentry than the flyer, the team packed up two pickup trucks loaded with lumber and tools. They were bound for the homestead in Kenai. As the crow flies it was 300 miles and at this point in time there were few roads in the territory. The trip snaked through towering mountains weeping rivers of melting snow which turned the route into a muddy bog.

Don kept a wary eye on his friends following tandem. He was excited. They were on the way to build a house for his family—his wife and a young son—then, he would level a runway for the airplane he was planning to buy. Flying hunters into the surrounding mountains and hauling fishermen on the Anchorage cannery runs seemed a good way to make a living.

A chuckle escaped him in the cab as he remembered the lights burning deep into the night in his Uncle Silvin's garage in Iowa where a Ford Bi-wing took up the whole area behind the gas station. As a boy Don had spent most of his time there tinkering with the engine and climbing in and out of the open cockpit. The rest of the Johnson clan were farmers who probably expected Don to follow that path. But, at age 14, after experiencing the rush of air in his eager face lifting off from a green pasture, the die was cast.

Damp, cold winds ripped the surface of Cook's Inlet on the peninsula as the men laid out the foundation for Don's home. Occasionally, the sun seeped through warming the crew who worked diligently; then, as evening came, crawled exhausted into the tent, anxious for a moose steak cooked over an open fire.

Between work sessions, Don was untiring in his effort to level a runway. The entire project took several months, but soon he stood smiling out of a big window in the main room at the inlet, beyond which was a spectacular view of Redoubt Volcano in the Chigmit Mountains. He was home on his own land.

By 1951 he owned a P.A. Super-Cruiser. A few well-placed ads for hunters brought results, but the income certainly wouldn't feed the family and keep the plane flying.

Down at Homer on the end of the peninsula, an oil company had established a base. They were in need of pilots to fly men and supplies to remote spots whenever weather allowed. Of course, fierce Alaskan winters were dormant employment periods, and the salmon runs occurred only in early summer. In the meantime, a few of the letters had inquired about polar bear hunts; Don decided it might be lucrative and with that in mind, he flew north to Nome near the Bering Straits. It seemed advisable to hunt during the winter months then return to Homer and work for the oil companies during warmer months.

In the beginning, Don knew little of the "Eskimos," a name coined by an early explorer meaning "eaters of raw flesh." He knew only that they were reputed to be docile hunters and whalers living in remote camps on the Northwest coast. Having an indomitable spirit, Don pushed aside all thought of the hardships surrounding the hunts, not the least of which were consuming "whiteouts." Bitter cold arctic winds would be a constant companion, but he remained undaunted.

Nome has been called the bleak arm of Alaska. It sits on the edge of a sea which remains frozen for seven months of the year. And, as it becomes liquid, it goes through a heaving fury to extricate itself from its rigid form.

Until 1898 there was no such place; in fact, perhaps 2,400 Eskimos and a handful of whites occupied the entire Seward Peninsula. But in September of that year, three Scandinavian prospectors staked claims on Anvil and Glacier creeks. The $1,800 strike ultimately made millionaires out of Lindbloom, Brinteson and Lindeberg, and the cry of gold swept inland on incoming arctic winds. Before the dead of winter 40 men had tied up 7,000 acres of the richest land. By June, 18,000 disappointed stampeders from the Klondike overran the slushy coast where nuggets were found lying on the beach.

That summer, hordes of passengers were lightered to the beach in barges while steamers and sailing vessels anchored as far as two miles offshore.

Front Street, clutched on the shores of the Bering Sea, was a straggling line of tents erected just behind the claims. No thought had been given of their proximity to hungry tongues of water which would lash the shore at whim. Eventually, the tents gave way to a row of substantial wooden and tin houses teeming with toughs, thieves and thugs as the boomtown raged.

The Nome which greeted the young pilot over 50 years later had lost its intrigue. Indian hunters and carvers plied their trades along with merchants and hotel owners. The "general sordidness" had disappeared, leaving in its wake a place where gasoline, food and a comfortable night's sleep were available.

Getting there hadn't been easy. A circuitous route took Don to Fairbanks first. Thousands of miles of raw, unoccupied territory lay beneath the wings. He knew fueling would present problems—first, he'd have to become acquainted with the natives.

After surveying the area, he realized the need for two airplanes during searches, but funds were scarce. Obviously, the flying jobs would provide needed cash for additional equipment and pilots. Eagerly, he returned to Kenai.

Within two years Don's hunting operations included rented houses in Teller on the inland side of Port Clarence, which opened onto the Bering Straits; Shishmaref on the north coast of Seward Peninsula; and Kotzebue, perched on Baldwin Peninsula. Nome had proved unsatisfactory—he kept moving north.

There were numerous problems plaguing the guide, and outfitters, seeing the potential of the hunts, were moving in. He could deal with them, but other more disturbing factors became evident as his experience grew.

From November to March merging waters of the Chukchi and Bering Seas froze in motion, one continuous petrified layer between the U.S. and Russia. Teller and Shishmaref were only a few hundred miles from their Russian counterparts hidden beneath the ice mass, making it impossible to tell where one began and the other left off.

Two of the villages were inland—sometimes as much as 50 miles on the shores of bays. Warmer air currents, colliding with arctic blasts, created thick fog and mushing on Duvag (the Eskimo word for shorefast ice which refroze nightly into a jagged crust). Game sighted near those areas was nearly impossible to hunt. Even if the pilot could find a place to land, searches in tortuous pressure ridges were futile. Kotzebue, the largest of the three where supplies were plentiful, was more desirable but with crabbing, blowing snow, constant fog and the probability of returning low on fuel, flights were dangerous. Also, ski planes often had to land and park on soft ice, sometimes crashing, sometimes sinking. There were just too many negatives. After three hard years on the ice, Don decided to move north to Point Hope.

The village, a spike of permafrost jutting into the Chukchi Sea, was on the northwest extremity of Alaska's land mass. In winter Point Hope's chit of underground sod homes became invisible — except for small, black smokestacks emitting the rancid smell of burning seal blubber. The taciturn Inuit residents, whose broad stoic countenances hid delightful warmth, were simple people of a docile nature. A hint of their whimsy escaped from blazing sloe eyes as they fished, hunted, or in frozen darkness, laughed with their women.

On the first trip Don went alone, making three passes over what appeared to be a deserted village. Within a few minutes he selected a suitable landing strip and started down.

Visitors were rare. Hearing the Cessna's powerful whine, curious Eskimos trickled out of almost indiscernible snow mounds; by the time the prop stopped, the entire tribe had assembled and quickly surrounded the plane.

Allan Rock, a 40-year-old bowhead whaler, was an elder in the Point Hope community. During the dead of winter when the Chukchi was a solid sheet and his skin boat was submerged in a snow bank, he hunted the big-bearded oogrook seals, walrus and polar bear. But frequent ice blizzards allowed time to carve wooden sleds for hunts.

On this particular day he was enjoying the warmth of his one-room sod house and polishing a brass harpoon gun. Within a few months the bowhead whales would make an entrance from the Bering Sea near Gambell on St. Lawrence Island, curve through the Bering Straits and enter the Chukchi Sea. Moving steadily, the giants' route would pass directly in front of Point Hope on their way to Barrow and the Arctic Ocean. After apprenticing in the Umniaks for five years, Allan was ready to be the skin boat's striker—the man who sits in the bow and harpoons the whale. It was a position of honor and the final step before becoming an Umealit—captain. The Inuit's cherubic face mellowed at the promise of such distinction; a powerful hand rubbed a golden glow into metal.

The sound of an airplane caught his attention. Snatching a parka, he hurried outside.

As Don was climbing out of the cockpit into blistering wind gusts, he waved a greeting to the tribesmen who were bringing oil drums for a tie-down. Others, eager to please, scurried around collecting ropes to affix to the struts. A path opened—the elder was making his way through the noisy throng to greet their visitor and within minutes the pilot had an invitation to have Labrador tea.

Herbs found on the tundra during warm summer months were dried and made into a brew which was as important to the Eskimos as coffee is to Americans. Having been up north for three winters allowed Don to develop a taste for it, and now he looked forward to a hot cup after flights.

Once their parkas were discarded, Don relaxed, anticipating a pleasant exchange. It always began with questions in halted English. "Where you been?" After that was answered the Inuit wanted to know if he had seen any of their teams returning from the seal hunts, if there was news from down the coast; and, of course, information about relatives.

Patience was the key word. Don waited, then offered treasured bits of gossip tying familiar names to the stories.

Mrs. Rock placed a box of pilot bread on the table before going to a brine-filled keg for a bowl of fresh spread. Don reached into a plastic bag, took out a large cracker-like cake, and dunked its hard crust into the steaming herbal tea. The bread man made delivery only once a year by freighter, but the pilot bread never seemed stale. Munching contentedly, he listened to the Inuit's monotone which rose a notch or two when he talked of hunting.

Seizing an opening, the pilot explained his needs, to which the Eskimo responded with an eager, guttural grunt. Although he was not fluent in English, he had learned enough words from the freighter captains to communicate. Hunting was a business, and the Inuit elder knew this white man would be good for his village.

"You use house," he offered with warmth.

Eyeing the small dwelling, Don frowned, then grinned politely. "I build more," the Eskimo quickly added.

There was a long pause while the idea germinated. Finally, Don nodded. It had taken all of an hour. He stretched and yawned casting a seductive glance at a pile of caribou skins in the corner. Since the gesture was a compliment, the Inuit returned it with a nod. His guest slid beneath fur, releasing a soothing sigh from satisfied lips as his body dented 15 pelts. Almost immediately, he was asleep.

He awoke an hour later to the tantalizing aroma of polar bear roast smothered in dried onions simmering on a cast iron stove.

Dinner was especially tasty, after which Mrs. Rock brought thick slices of muktuk. Don bit his lip before lifting a furtive, disdaining look. The bear meat had been tender with a faint flavor of coconut, the result of the bear's diet of baby seals. He had eaten his fill. There was also tea, pilot bread and the canned peaches which he'd thoughtfully remembered to bring as a gift; then, patting his midsection, he politely refused and waved the delicacy away.

Muktuk had a rich, hazelnut taste, or so it was said. Whalers cut great thick chunks of the whale's slick black hide as soon as the mammal was brought onto the beach. They considered it a gift for the family. Agvig skin is a few inches thick under which the natives leave four or five inches of blubber. Using a sharp hunting knife with a carved whalebone handle, Allan cut thick slices and finger-dunked them into a bowl of room-temperature seal oil. However, the dip was also used for raw fish and animal entrails, and there was no telling how often it was replenished.

Months later, after their friendship had been cemented and during a punishing blizzard which had lasted a week, Don gave in, but only after he and the whaler had consumed a fifth of 190-proof Everclear. They were swapping embellished stories when Allan brought the snack to the table and goaded his Caucasian friend into eating it. Don barely remember the incident the next day.

He did, however, learn to like muktuk, but never tried it with seal oil.

Breakfast was usually dried eggs and slices of walrus bacon with pilot bread and coffee. Don supplied jam and fresh eggs whenever possible. The eggs were a problem because they always froze on the trip in the bush plane. After thawing, the yolks would cook up ping-pong-ball round surrounded by flat whites. Sly guides had been known to slice the golden balls in half creating the illusion of normal servings, which Don thought was "damned dishonest."

The bathrooms at Point Hope were five-gallon honey buckets. A cover of raw plywood hugged the bucket sitting next to the cooking stove. Using it took some adjustment. 'What the hell,' Don thought, 'when in Rome. . . .'

The unpleasant reality caused some consternation with hunters accustomed to more private accommodations. Few realized that body waste would freeze in other parts of the sod house, preventing it from being dumped into big oil drums which would later be hauled on the dog sleds out onto ice pans to drift away. Permafrost subsoil had no drainage so the Inuit could never use a septic tank.

For the rest of that winter and the next three, Allan Rock's home was Don's Point Hope camp. Small crude rooms were added slowly after lumber and supplies were shipped in on the freighter, North Star. Before that service, Inuit tribes, plagued with unending storms which prohibited hunting, often died of starvation and freezing. Disease brought in by Caucasian whalers also wreaked havoc on the tribes.

Mrs. Rock charged Don $12.50 per night for hunters, which she insisted was more than enough. Later, he would convince her to charge $30; to the Eskimo that was a "king's ransom."

Clients preferred hauled-in army cots with Canadian sleeping bags in rooms which were "colder than hell." The wiser pilot-guide continued to snooze happily in the urine-cured caribou hides.

An inland lake six miles away supplied fresh water. Re-using

Polar bear just beyond the hummocks.

it was essential. After dishes (one bucket for washing, one for rinsing), it was used for clothes and finally, the mop bucket. Pots of chunk ice simmered constantly on the iron stove to be added to a huge drum of water for cooking and drinking.

During the fourth winter, a Caucasian trader named Fergeson arrived in Point Hope. He intended to build a trading post and had ordered $10,000 worth of lumber and supplies brought in. Before the huge building was completed, Fergeson was found hanging in the rafters. When Don returned and learned of it, he purchased the facility from Fergeson's widow. Now he would have a permanent camp. Immediately, Don and his cover pilot began flying in supplies and equipment, and within a few months it was a comfortable seven-room lodge.

The Eskimos had no problem with the new camp. Since Don's arrival, Point Hope had become a livelier spot. Gossip spread by mukluk telegraph brought traveling natives, pilots, poachers (who posed as hunters) and an occasional trader. Mrs. Rock became an innkeeper of some note.

Heading out to the planes at Point Hope.

Seal hunters at Point Hope.

Whale bones in the frozen tundra.

Chapter 2

Lost on the Ice Pans

Don Johnson soon learned that the Inuit were willing workers. Even though favors were traded, he usually paid them for services rendered. The men were surprisingly good mechanics. They serviced and repaired aircraft which included heating the fire-pots and refueling, often in 30-below weather. Clearing blown-in snow from the bellies of the planes was essential; in return Don brought eagerly-awaited supplies from Kenai, Kotzebue and Nome. Of course, hunters almost never took the polar bear meat, and it was sufficient to feed the entire tribe. The women washed and dried all the camp clothes for guests and pilots.

It had been Don's custom after hunts to discard bloodied surgical gloves used to skin the bears. When tribesmen finally had the courage, they asked for the gloves—which were dunked up and down on ropes through a hole in the ice and re-claimed. The Eskimos happily found uses for the white man's discards.

When Don became as much a part of the tribe as the elders, he was often invited to council meetings. They looked to him for advice, treasured the friendship he willingly gave, and were infinitely grateful for the many lives he saved.

The sea was treacherous. It was feared by hunter, pilot and tribesman alike. Sometimes 10-feet thick, it could groan and tear at whim, float miles away, then refreeze on the tide change.

Naturally, he would rescue seal hunters who were lost on the pans. It was unfortunate, but readily accepted, that seal hunters would race onto faulty ice and disappear as sled and dogs slid into black water from which there was no return. The cry of Inuit hunters cracking whips over their dogs was relished; they had returned one more time bringing home precious Misigaag (seal oil).

After a seal hunt the Inuit secured his sled, tying the huskies to a length of chain strung between two whale bones embedded in the frozen earth under the snow. Poking into a mound over a 30-foot corridor, the hunter entered the dank cavern which protected his submerged home. Their patterns were as solid as the permafrost and had been that way for a thousand years.

On occasion, Don's hunts were cancelled due to a sudden storm or a gale racing in from the Arctic Ocean. In December of 1953 on just such a night, he landed near a settlement.

His hunter, puzzled, stared over blankly. "What's happening?" he asked.

"Get out. It's not safe to go on."

They emerged into searing winds, fighting their way to the Eskimo house. The long, dark corridor was a blessed relief from the howling despot which burned their faces.

Inside, Don and the family exchanged greetings. Their cordial acceptance was apparently lost on the hunter who was busily absorbing the contents of the disheveled room. A wary eye viewed the tangled urine-cured caribou skins where the family would all huddle together during the long night. The lack of furniture surprised him. There was no kitchen. A collection of Blazo crates, piled on top of each other and filled with sundry objects, sufficed. The unsavory stench of seal blubber from the stove was suffocating and brought a feeling of nausea as he thought of the long night ahead. Outside, elements tortured the landscape; the hunter knew his choices were dismal.

"I'm not sleeping here, Don," he whispered hoarsely.

A cold stare flashed out of the fur parka. "What the hell are you going to do? It's 40-below out there. Are you nuts?"

"I don't care. I can't stand the smell." The firm announcement preceded downcast eyes.

Don's caustic chortle escaped plump, cracked lips. "Suit yourself."

Turning sharply, the hunter retreated into the corridor, inhaling deeply as he moved reluctantly into the blizzard.

It was a night like no other in his experience. The visibility was zero—a void riddled with continuous white spikes, swirling, consuming in a blinding mass. The cold burned his lungs, cutting off his breath as he tried to suck it in. Moving slowly, he passed a line of fur balls on the edge of the compound—the dogs rolled together in a trench, tied between the whale bones.

Suddenly, he smiled. 'An overturned boat!' his brain cried, 'a haven—hooray!' Bending into the fray and struggling with the heavy sleeping bag he had taken from the plane, he crawled under the gunnels, and once encased was comforted slightly. Scrunching deeply into the bag, he swore, cursing the wind, the cold and the discomfort which furthered his aggravation. Finally, he cursed his burning desire for the trophy. He would get his bear—he knew Don Johnson's reputation—but he had not anticipated this. It had cost thousands of dollars to come here to the edge of the world, a frozen hell. If he died no one would know—only God, maybe.

Hours passed—an eternity it seemed, lying on unforgiving ice. The only sound was labored breathing and the untiring wind. If day came there would be no difference; darkness was the way of it. 'Did I sleep?' he wondered. 'No. Well, maybe.' His body ached, stiff and sore, rooted into a fetal knot and now, unwilling to unbend.

Suddenly, there was a sound. The hunter's ears sharpened. It was the Eskimo calling to the dogs. The animals raged out of their pit, barking fiercely, scrambling for niggardly portions of fish entrails. Always half-starved, they growled angrily, knowing they would have a long day's work ahead before they were given the reward of a decent meal.

The hunter finally gave up and went inside, willing to give

his soul for a hot drink; he was made just as welcome as on the previous evening—a cheechakas (tenderfoot) no more.

The Point Hope lodge was adequately furnished and, except for the lack of running water, quite comfortable. There were four bedrooms in the 60-foot facility, a living room/kitchen combination, two baths with portable pots and a freezer room.

Don acquired the lodge in 1956, and until the passage of the Mammal Act in 1972, it served him well every winter for polar bear and seal hunts.

For almost 19 years, while Don flew the ice pans, his friends, the Inuit, would harness the dogs for the six-mile trip to an inland lake and willingly spend half a day chopping six or seven hundred pounds of block ice to be brought back for drinking water. One hundred pounds were dropped by the lodge where strong native arms would plop the huge cake into a 200-gallon drum inside the warm camp kitchen. By the time the hunters returned, drinking water was available. Before the sled moved off toward the village, the rest of the ice was placed onto the roof. The workers chuckled to themselves as they remembered Don's parting words: "I don't like that yellow ice, Gus." It was not uncommon for the dogs to urinate on block ice which ultimately became tea for some unsuspecting Eskimo.

Away from the camp, the hunters and guides used eight-sided Army surplus permanent tents reinforced with double-layered fabric to keep out gale-force winds. For security and protection, three feet of snow was packed against the walls. Yukon stoves were originally flown in, but wood was extremely scarce. Don decided kerosene heaters radiated enough warmth in the tight enclosures, but since they gave off some smoke, they were extinguished while the hunters slept.

Ground-sleeping on frozen subsoil presented problems which were solved with Don's ingenuity. Cardboard insulated the cold floors, over which lush caribou skins were draped. Three or four Canadian Star Wood sleeping bags, heaped on the skins, allowed the men a cozy night's sleep. Army canvas boots with soft leather soles were ideal cold-weather footwear. In fact, 20 years later,

Don noted they were still the best. One pair of light socks managed absorption over which was a pair of soft beaver socks. The hide was chewed to softness and attached to soles made from oogrooks, the big bearded seals, while tanned caribou completed the boot, which rose some 18 inches up the leg.

Heavy underwear and down covered their bodies and was worn under white canvas parkas with light quilting and a thick fur liner. The hood ruff was always about eight inches of wolverine fur, which never froze.

Dealings between Don and the Eskimos included barter. Fresh polar bear meat hauled off the ice pans, eagerly anticipated, was evenly distributed to the residents of Point Hope, providing ample food for the long winters. But life in that world was not without misery.

One evening after a particularly good meal, the men settled around the stove to discuss the hunt. Al Bontrigger was flying cover for Don. He had fixed a tasty meal after which he served drinks. An Eskimo entered, his ochre brow furrowed above an almost stoic face which cast Don a troubled stare; then, a silence developed. The pilot rose, going closer to the big man. They spoke in hushed tones; Don nodded thoughtfully, then crossed to the coat rack.

"What's wrong?" the cover pilot asked.

Sobering, the guide pulled on his fur-lined parka and gloves. "Two of the tribe are missing. They were hunting. The ice split away. It's been two days now. I've got to find them."

"Radio if you need me," Al said, getting up and retrieving his parka. The planes were cold; he would start the fire-pots to loosen the frozen oil. They left. Don pulled off the engine covers while the Eskimo rolled out the gas drums. They lit a torch to the pots. Its blue flame glowed in the Alaskan night, sending heat through long tubes which Al poked just under the oil pump, listening to the hiss. Don was already in the cockpit, switch on, waiting for a thumbs-up from Al. Soon the engine sputtered a few times, then caught.

A bitter wind rose, pummeling the frigid sea as he banked

deep, floating above a stark world—toward Russia.

The Eskimos lived on the ice in sleds—listening to singing runners while blubber hardened on their plump faces, huddling beneath caribou skins, hunting seals out on the leads. They were superstitious, carrying tufts of rabbit hair, a bear's claw, dried guillemot, a reindeer's ear. Even their dogs wore amulets. Trained to go sometimes four days without food, the huskies raced hard, dropping exhausted at each stop, molding into one fur-knot for live-saving heat until the whip drove them out again, yapping and shaking hoarfrost from their thick fur coats.

Sometimes the ice would split away in enormous sheets, floating aimlessly on the Chukchi Sea toward the Arctic Circle. However desperate their plight, an airplane was their only hope.

Knowing the ice had kept Don alive. Even in the fog, black water gave a deathly illusion. They knew it was a place from which there was no return; pilot and Eskimo alike feared it.

Don searched for hours, a lone figure soaring low, anxious to spot the bridge of ice connecting the pans. Comforted by additional gas in heavy belly tanks and extra cans in the tail section, he soared past the black path toward a floating safeguard. Lowering close to the ice, sharp eyes scanned it, ricocheting back and forth for an alien object. At last, he spotted them.

The sound of the plane alerted the hunting party. Two figures emerged from under an overturned sled, their fur-lined arms waving frantically. Broad smiles greeted the pilot as the skis raced across the frozen surface toward them. The Super-Cub shuddered, battered by the wind even with the engines running.

At the sighting, a quick radio message alerted Al who was already on his way. Three trips returned man and beast to safety. The dogs, muzzled and tied, howled under their bonds in the plane's tail section. The Eskimo valued his dogs almost as much as his life.

A potlatch would be held to celebrate the safe return of the men now recovering in the Bureau of Indian Affairs (BIA) Hospital in Kotzebue. The guest of honor—a rugged Caucasian hunter and guide, friend to the Inuit—Don Johnson.

Point Hope from the air.

It was their custom to come together under one roof—the biggest sod house in the village, where soapstone lamps provided shadowy light. The villagers sat cross-legged in a circle eating raw fish and polar bear meat, not speaking, sipping Labrador tea intermittently. The room, now pungent with seal oil, fish and sweat, was cozy. Don watched silently, accustomed to their ways, accepting the gratitude without words. His blue eyes fled to the coy flash of smiles from the women whose men he had saved. The men chewed noisily, satisfied, burping happily. It was reassuring. Later, the leader would offer his wife in friendship, and to refuse would be unthinkable and an insult never to be forgiven.

Don arriving at Bear Lake in the float plane.

Bush planes ready for hunts at Bear Lake.

Chapter 3

Bear Lake — A Beginning

R eturning from Nome in 1952, Don began flying for the oil companies and a new outfit formed to do offshore navigation called O.N.I. Between flights he took out hunting parties whose letters were trickling in from ads.

On one such trip with a California couple out to bag a moose, the weather turned sour as they were flying south over the Aleutian Chain. Ordinarily they would have continued but, after the 650-mile trip from Kenai, clouds lowered and fog developed. The woman seemed apprehensive in the air. Judging the distance to the selected hunting ground, Don decided to land in a place where he knew there was flat ground. The Tri-Pacer soared inland lowering with each mile until he was 200 feet over a wide tundra valley. He landed, coming to rest not far from a lake. The decision to land there included knowledge of the glacier ahead. Its spires, usually cloud-tipped, were completely shrouded. It was damp and cold. Pulling sleeping bags and gear from the tail section, the pilot built a fire and prepared a tasty hot meal. After supper the party bedded down in the protected valley.

At first light, Don awoke feeling refreshed and content with the world which would become his nemesis, for the winds and storms which occur there are legendary.

During the war Don had been in and out of the Aleutians regularly. The storms which had battered the Naval vessels

˜seemed unreal; that fact spurred his curiosity and some research. He learned that the hundreds of islands, atolls and archipelagoes are mainly volcanic in origin and contain numerous active or recently-active volcanoes. On the outer Pacific side are great oceanic troughs reaching depths of 3,000 to 5,000 fathoms which extend 900 miles westward from the tip of Alaska Peninsula. Here the cold winds from Siberia and the ocean currents flowing down from the Bering Sea meet warm air masses and currents moving eastward across the Pacific. Their interaction produces winds of high velocity, dense fog, rain, mist and snow. In fact, flyers who have learned to fly there become extraordinary. Their skills are constantly being developed as they operate, knowing 100-knot forces or thick cloying fog may arise without warning.

It is, however, teeming with wildlife. The Russians called the Aleutians "The Fabulous Fur Islands."

Originally, they were inhabited by a tribe called the Aleuts, who were docile native hunters until Captain Bering, a Danish officer in the Russian Navy, was dispatched by Peter the Great to see if Asia and America were united. The year was 1728.

This birth of Russian domination of Alaska also marked the brutalization of 25,000 Aleuts. By the end of the 18th Century the Aleut population had been cruelly reduced to 2,000. They were murdered, exploited and enslaved.

The Russian fur hunters—the dreaded Promyshlenniki of Siberia—had a chant: "Heaven is high, the Czar is far away." During an 80-year period 2,324,364 fur seals worth some thirty-five million dollars had been taken.

Americans were no less greedy. In 1867 Alaska was purchased from Russia for the requested figure of $7,200,000 after urging from a far-sighted congressman named Seward. It was called Seward's Ice Box. The Aleuts called the land Alayeska which means "Great Country." It was, and is, a land abounding with natural resources, both animal and mineral. At first, American seal hunters nearly denuded the rookeries in the Bering Sea. Canadian, Japanese and Russian ships aided in the slaughter until

1919 when the U.S. government prohibited pelagic sealing.

Hunting, a historic pastime in Alaska, received little or no notice from officials until statehood in 1959. Of course, at this time, 1952, Don could see the damage being done on the Kenai Peninsula. Unthinking hunters were taking sows along with male game. He knew what would ultimately happen and, since statehood wasn't even being discussed, realized the value of finding a place which had unlimited game and which, with care, would survive.

Pulling on his boots, the pilot stood up and walked to the lakeshore. Emotion grew as he absorbed the surroundings. Up ahead the glacier loomed above the water, glowing through a delicate mist centering stark black volcanic mountains against a snow mantle. Tundra flattened around him curving into a great valley rolling unevenly to the Bering Sea which was carved by a racing river. The beach was pebbled, and the glacier mirrored in the water. There was no sound except a soughing wind pushing plump, blue-gray clouds over the peaks. He knew this place was right. For a long time he stood pondering that thought. He was later quoted, "It was so pretty, I decided to stay."

Knowing there was good hunting on the mainland wasn't enough. It seemed reasonable to hunt everything. By now, the runway on the homestead was complete; he was getting regular flying jobs; there were frequent clients inquiring about the hunts; he had set trap-lines in the Kenai Range and in winter he'd go north for polar bear. He was excited. 'But this place,' he thought, scanning its vast beauty, 'this place is a hunter's paradise.' This could be the ultimate camp. The lake emptied into a roaring river and both were flush with Dolly Vardens, Pink and Silver Humpys, and down along the sea, the great king salmon which could weigh up to 70 pounds. There were birds for shotgun hunters—even the Russian emperor goose which made an annual migration from across the Bering Sea to the Aleutians. Moose roamed in herds along with caribou and their predators—the wolf, tundra fox and wolverine. And, of course, the most tempting acquisition of all— the big, brown bears. "Yes, sir. This is it." Perusing the muskeg,

Don visualized the runway not far from where he stood. "Perfect," he mumbled, almost giddy. "And, over there, a camp."

After that hunt and eager to commence, he filed a headquarters site on Bear Lake. "Bears were as thick as flies"—the name just seemed right. Alaskan law was specific: one homestead in a lifetime. The headquarters' site allowed for business properties. By 1953 it was his—all accomplished just seven years after arrival in the "New Frontier."

The first hunters were flown in and housed in 12-by-14 whitewall Rainner tents. Bear Lake was raw. In Kenai and the Wrangell Mountains logs were used for beds with 10 inches of spruce branches for mattresses. The wood and filler were easy to come by in those areas, but on the Aleutians wood was difficult to collect. The wood that was hauled in the plane was scavenged from beaches where boats which were caught in boiling seas had sunk and were bashed against rocky spits. It was needed for bitter, damp Aleutian nights where winds could rise and howl at hurricane velocity.

Heavy tin, 35-pound Yukon stoves with flat tops were used to heat, cook and warm water. With the draft closed, wood could last up to four hours but with the draft open, the stove would become cherry red and burn out quickly. Kerosene lanterns produced light up until 1955, when Don bought gasoline lamps which were fueled with white gas or Blazo. These hearty lamps were more effective and gave better light to read by but were noisy. Some of them continue to cast a glow in the small cabins near the lodge over 20 years later.

Usually, there were three tents in use: one for cooking and eating, one for clients which was as comfortable as possible, and a third for pilots, cooks and guides. Not being a stranger to deprivation, it would have been easy to build a name at the client's expense and many outfitters did just that. But Don's love of the hunt since he was a boy stalking near his father's farm drew a determination to produce the best. Arctic hunting, which he had started earlier, only increased his tenacity. Hunters sensed his doggedness and what appeared to be a lack of fear. He loved the land of Alaska; he loved the life there and blended into it naturally—for this was where he was supposed to be.

Building Bear Lake would take a long time, and the runway had to be the first priority. It was 1953 before the long strip was completed, and due to fierce weather, that job would be repeated yearly thereafter. Later, a second runway would crisscross it making approaches and landings simpler in a place where the wind had a mind of its own.

The changes occurred slowly as they must in a place where every piece of equipment, every morsel of food, every person, must be hauled by air. But Don had a distinct advantage—he was now a senior member of a bush armada. Knowing all the pilots who moved across that vast territory hauling fish, supplies, freight and people allowed the opportunity to trade favors. They were a tightly-knit bunch who relied on each other. He had earned help in many quarters and they responded.

Eventually, there would be choppers hauling beams out of a sunken ship, the beams dangling beneath their skids up over the mountains to the tundra camp. DC-3s, carrying needed tools and building supplies and fuel, would land on the new runway. And, much later, a C-182 would arrive at nearby Port Moller, opening its yawning tail to deposit an old Army truck. While all this took place, the hunts continued.

Guides, trappers, flushers, cooks, sundry friends and the man himself all worked to build the camp. Don never moved an airplane which wasn't jammed full of gear and food. Sometimes it seemed the small craft wouldn't be able to lift off. Passengers who flew with him couldn't believe what was standing beside the runway. They were even more disbelieving when he told them to get in and then added the freight.

In 1953, the government built a radar site high on a cliff overlooking Port Moller, 25 minutes away by plane from Bear Lake. Reeve Aleutian Airlines started regular runs to that spot providing the camp with an air connection. That was a real break. The season at that time was long, due to soft ice conditions at Point Hope. This gave Don a perfect reason to bring interested hunters downcamp for a brown bear.

He now had two airplanes: a P.A. Super-Cruiser and a Tri-Pacer. Knowing Don was flying regular runs into camp, people were beginning to request flights Down Chain, and as he came to be acquainted with the Aleuts there were timid comments about much-needed supplies.

That first season at Bear Lake, Don flew into camp off the Bering Sea and followed the serpentine route of the river. Over-flying the area, he saw an old Russian church, an assortment of small fishing shacks in disarray and a few homes which were obviously in use.

Outside two homes facing the sea and about a block apart were two natives. One was slight and old, perhaps in his late sixties with a sweet, weathered face who stood staring at the sea for hours on end. Down the beach in front of the other house was a younger man who did the same thing. Later that year, when the pair hiked upriver to gather spawning salmon to be smoked for winter stores and as food for the dogs, Don learned they were father and son. He never did learn why they were so captivated by the sea.

Occasionally the old man, rucksack on his back with a rifle protruding, would cross the river to the opposite bank. After beaching his skiff, he would walk 10 miles to the cannery and buy seven gallons of heavy kerosene. Without complaint, the old Aleut would return by the same route to his village home. Don began to give him a lift. Flying in from the hunts or hauling trips, the pilot would land, pick him up and drop the Eskimo and his supplies on the beach beside his home. Later, when he acquired a truck which was left on the cannery runway, he would offer the old man a ride both ways. To return the favor, and as a courtesy, the Aleut would scavenge ivory off the beach to give to the hunter.

Dead walrus and whales washed up on the shores of the coast regularly. Their tusks, oosiks and whale baleen were valuable commodities. Later, Don and his pilots would enjoy fierce com-petition on each flight to find such animals. The results of their finds turned into a lucrative business as hunters, who enjoyed collecting, arrived at camp.

Of course, the old Aleut, Yolman Orloff, and his son, Carpa, became friends and regulars at the camp. Their advice on current fishing was invaluable. They had many relatives in villages down the Chain and beside riding in the airplane, which they really enjoyed, they had a sincere desire for goods which Don could bring in from Kenai.

Unlike the Inuits, the Aleuts had been exposed to the military during the war and were still simplistic but used to sundry luxuries which were unavailable to them now that the war was over. The old airbase at Cold Bay was deserted except for a skeleton crew and a few regulars who called it home. Reeve Aleutian was flying in there sporadically. Old Quonset huts were used to house personnel and a small supply depot. It was, however, 120 airmiles away from camp and the cannery. Don began making regular runs. The natives at Nelson Lagoon, 45 minutes from the camp by plane, saw those trips as a means to acquire supplies and mail.

It was all happening very fast, but Alaska was booming. Bush planes were the "Greyhounds" of the Great Land, and Don was in on the ground floor.

Returning to Kenai, he was pleased at the mounting requests for polar bear hunts which he found in his mail. Setting up a schedule was becoming a satisfying norm. There was much to do before leaving for Point Hope, not the least of which was reconsidering the type of aircraft used in the hunts.

Bear Lake—a primitive camp in the fall of 1954.

Bear Lake Lodge, 1983.

Chapter 4

Arctic Flying and
the Frozen Wasteland

At first Don and his pilots were flying Cessna 180s, which they found unsuitable for polar bear hunting. For one thing, they were too fast for track searching. At times their weight made them difficult to maneuver on lead ice that had frozen into rough surfaces, and often too heavy for the thinner ice. He'd made up his mind to switch to Super-Cubs but, of course, there was always the problem of money.

Preparation for arctic flying between the U.S. and Russia had to be exacting. Belly tanks were mounted from which fuel was fed up to the left wing with a wobble pump. Before departure Don always set an extra 20 gallons of gas in cans in the back of the plane. After several hours of westerly flight they would follow the leads to an accessible spot, set down and immediately fill the belly tanks. This would lighten the load in the plane and allow for the long flight home against probable 40- to 50-knot headwinds. Security precautions were essential in this place where help was rarely available.

During the late '50s, Siberian winters became exceptionally bad, and communication sources for pilots were extremely limited. The planes contained old HF radios which had great distance capabilities, reaching as far as 1,500 miles. More cognizant of its northern extremity, Russia developed over 1,400 weather stations which gave explicit weather conditions each day.

27

The U.S. had less than 400 weather stations; however, there was an operator in Kotzebue who could speak Russian. He dedicated himself daily to translation, relaying lifesaving information over the radio to polar bear hunters up and down the Alaskan coast.

When the pilots were following the leads parallel to Russia, they could tune in an ADF radio directional finder, get a fix from a powerful Russian station and hopefully find the path through the whiteout back to American shores.

For Don the situation was acute. Point Hope was on a spit of land surrounded by jagged mountains. Pinpoint navigation was essential. Brute-force winds caused planes to curve in a huge arc when the pilots might have thought they were flying straight. Being able to anticipate the depth of the arc and not run out of gas was a matter of life and death. It was called crabbing, and compensating for it added a new dimension to flying.

The signals from Russia were in Morse code. An astute pilot could tell from the strength of the signal how close he was to the Russian or U.S. station. Some signals were terribly weak, but even that fact helped. They did not have a table to cross-signal the charts, which would have clearly indicated line A crossing line B. Their mental computations allowed them to judge approximate distance and direction of the signals, guiding the homeward flight.

However, for Don there was still the problem of Point Hope's geographic location. After hunts, and while returning from the Russian side of the Chukchi, he would ADF (radio navigation) Cape Lisburne many miles up the coast. Calculating the curve of the signal allowed them a fairly accurate approach, but white-outs, which occurred all too often, presented real danger.

In 1958, while hunting on the Aleutian Chain, Don spotted a buoy adrift in the Bering Sea near the beach. Since the Russians were always fishing those waters, he imagined it might be one of theirs. Already familiar with the equipment used by Aleut and American fishermen, he thought this particular one to be most unusual.

The location of the buoy was actually a happy accident. In

flight he had twisted a radio dial a little too far to the right, just beyond the normal frequency, and heard a strange signal. As he neared the buoy, the signal grew stronger. Circling and flying away from it confirmed his suspicions. He banked and returned for a closer look. A 30-foot tower swayed atop the metal float. Anxious to examine the object, Don raced back to his camp for a float plane. When he returned and landed, it was a simple matter to dismantle the tower and pull the buoy inside the cockpit. It contained a sonar system. Excited laughter erupted. This was the answer to the Point Hope problem. From that time on, the buoy sat beside the camp runway providing a direct beacon to the landing strip alongside the lodge.

By 1966 the government had outlawed HF radios, forcing pilots and fishermen to use VHF, which confused and diminished their capabilities. That dictum cost Don over $30,000 in both craft and base radios.

Arctic lands and seas total more than 7,000,000 square miles; the ice cap itself is 1,400 miles across a mammoth jagged circle of frozen waste making a complete revolution every 14 years. And, since the arctic ice sheet is the world's largest glacier, it spawns icebergs and sea ice. When the siku (sea ice) splits off, it can float four to five miles a day and often refreezes as it nears another ice mass. The first day's freeze is usually very thin, causing loss of life to unwary pilots who land on it, or to an occasional Eskimo whose sled rushes onto it during a 30- or 40-mile seal hunt.

Staying alive meant cataloging the breaks in the pilot's mind. Knowing where the splits were and how long they had been refrozen was crucial. Snow usually blew, even when blizzards weren't in progress, and thick whiteout fog often appeared suddenly and lasted for long periods—even days.

Flying in the arctic storms would have ravaged a lesser pilot, for it was not uncommon to have 50-knot headwinds returning from a hunt.

Special care was always taken during the north hunts. It was infinitely more dangerous than hunting other game anywhere else in Alaska. They carried extra gas, a three- to four-day supply of dehydrated food, sleeping bags for everyone, fire-pots, coffee, and portable landing gear for either ski, which Don had designed.

Once the party had landed, melted snow or ice was used for coffee. Knowing the "look" of the ice was important. Fresh snow or old sea ice made good coffee. New sea ice appeared cloudy or milky and was composed of fresh, frozen salt water—a real dose. The old sea ice had lost its salt content and was usable.

Flying over the ice, Don and his pilots never used a compass. When leaving Point Hope, the plan was to fly two-and-a-half hours to the west, all the while watching the wind trailing snow across the ice. That was their compass. Even during constant banking and searching for tracks, which could confuse direction, the wind pointed the way. The ADF of several Russian radio stations was added insurance.

Although his rule was no hunting if temperatures were lower than 30-below zero or the winds were more than 30 knots, occasionally a storm trapped them on the frozen sea. Being on the Chukchi overnight was a rare and dangerous experience. A tent was draped over the cowling; dropping a heavy canvas to the ice, which was linked with thick quilting, they then pulled the sleeping bags inside. Survival was the key word—death could be quick.

The hunter's fee was for a 10-day period, which in the beginning was $2,500. Of course, by the end of his 20-year career that figure would rise to $5,000. If the party filled out early Don would use the remaining days for hunting wolves or seals or fishing the frozen lakes for sheefish (tipook).

The fishing was accomplished with multiple holes in the ice, a long pole and a gill net. The whitefish is considered a rare delicacy and its acquisition a sport feat. What exotic hunter wouldn't proudly offer his dinner guests such a morsel, eager for the opportunity of discussing the hunt. Whatever was involved, Don made a sincere effort to provide his hunters a good time, not the least of which was his mischievous sense of humor.

The charter fleet.

Sometimes hunters arriving in the arctic were apprehensive about the weather. If they asked too many questions regarding accommodations, Don would usually say, "Oh, listen, we got good tents on the ice, and if the wind isn't too bad we'll be all right."

And, at least once during every hunt, when the party was enjoying a drink after dinner, Don would bring out his miniature, copper French horn. With a dour look and the usual nonchalance, the guide would offer it to some inquisitive guest, saying, "Look, I just designed this thing to call in the emperor goose." He would then embark on a long dissertation about the Russian bird and how difficult it was to hunt, all the while fingering the metal. Of course, there was always someone who would bite. By that time he had captured everyone's interest. The hunter would take the horn and blow it, at which time a plug of ashes or powder would be released over the unsuspecting man's face.

When at last the sounds of the ice breaking rolled across the arctic, Don and his cover pilot always welcomed the change of pace and headed for home. The last hunters of the season had the added bonus of flying to Anchorage with the bush pilot who almost always made unscheduled stops at Eskimo villages along the way.

Don's plane skimming ice from Point Hope to Russia.

Chapter 5

Emergency at Yakutat

O ff Shore Navigation was the name of the company which sent out ships dropping charges in previously uncharted water to obtain depth-sound readings. Shoran Navigation worked in conjunction and built two or three well-equipped survey sites setting benchmarks on the land. Special tents, costing $2,000 apiece, were constructed which could withstand 150-knot winds. Radio bases could receive and send out strong signals—offering lifesaving messages to seagoing vessels on bearing, range and tides. The entire system, the forerunner to Loran, was essential in treacherous seas and became known as O.N.I.

Flying Missions for O.N.I. during the summer months allowed Don to become part of a small air force of bush planes which included G-2 Bell helicopters and Super-Cubs.

Once the stations were in operation, planes transported fuel, drinking water, food, people and medical supplies. Since it was seasonal work, it offered needed income to pilots between hunting seasons. O.N.I. hired adventurous young men (who often got into trouble because of inexperience) to man their camps, but the pay was right and the outings exciting.

The station at Yakutat was at the 4,000-foot level in deep snow on the glacier end of Mt. Cook. Down on the narrow end of Alaska, Yakutat and the slate sea beyond were visible. And, although it was August, cold wind prevailed up on the Masaspina

Glacier.

The two men in the tent were enjoying a leisurely Sunday. Tim, the youngest and the son of an Episcopal preacher, plunked on a banjo. Scotty, his partner, hummed along while sautéing mooseburgers to go with a pile of fried potatoes he had just covered to keep warm. At 17, Tim had not yet thought of death—and yet, this was to be his last day.

By 3:30 p.m. up the coast, Don Johnson was sitting down to mugup (the Eskimo word for early supper) in O.N.I.'s barracks. The phone rang. Hoping the call wouldn't disrupt the meal, he went to answer. The business was erratic, and the words coming over the wire forced a sigh. Don prepared to fly.

"There's an emergency at Yakutat, Don," the caller had said. "One of the boys went off for a hike about noon and hasn't returned. It would be helpful if you and the chopper could start a search. It's pretty cold up there."

The pilot yelled the message to Dick Franzell, the chopper pilot, who was halfway through his meal. Grabbing a coat and gloves, both men hurried across the runway to their planes. It was already late in the day, and the site was an hour away. Nearing the spot, the sun setting on ice glistened brilliantly. Don squinted, ignoring the beauty and scanning the sky for the helicopter. Once it was spotted he radioed. Each pilot selected an area, then moved off.

Don figured the boy went into the forest just below the camp. Since it was so dense—thick enough to obscure his view—he half expected to see smoke from a campfire. For many hours he waffled over the woods. At midnight the two planes rendezvoused on the beach to refuel. After talking over the situation, they agreed to move the search to higher ground.

Back in the air, Don radioed the tent. "It's almost morning, Scotty," he reported, "and still nothing."

The boy sounded concerned. He had come to like his partner, and it wasn't like him to just take off. Surely, he had had an accident.

"Look!" Don advised, "why don't you take the walkie-talkie

and follow his tracks as best you can. I'll fly near—maybe that way we can make some progress."

Scotty was quick to agree. He ran to grab a parka and boots; anything was better than the interminable waiting. Outside he heard the Super-Cub circling overhead. It was bitter cold. The ice provided an eerie glow which opened the path ahead as he turned on a flashlight and moved cautiously behind the light. Talking to the pilot with the hand-held radio was comforting while Scotty's eyes searched the sky; then locating the plane, he grinned.

The Cub droned on. After an hour, a deep frown surfaced because Don had lost contact with the walkie-talkie. The chopper responded to a call. Explaining that the small radios were notoriously weak, Don thought he would fly closer to the glacier in the direction of the last signal. The Cub's engine roared as the plane passed over a cliff where the ice mass slid into a deep ravine. On the sheer side were two still human forms. Don ragged at the speaker. "Dick! I got 'em—up here on the south side of the glacier. *MY GOD*, there are two bodies down there!" His tone was incredulous.

Evidencing shock, Dick answered quickly. "Fly to the beach where you can land. I'll take you back up in the chopper."

It was damp below. The ocean ebbed in the stillness. Once inside the cockpit while the men grabbed some coffee and a sandwich, Don outlined his plan. His pencil skidded across a hastily-drawn map. "There are high timbers on both sides of that ravine. It's not going to be easy. We'll need about 300 feet of rope, at least."

They had landed near a mining camp littered with small shacks. Combining rope from both craft, Don busied himself coiling and knotting, while Dick hurried through the camp banging on doors to get more rope. Eventually, they lifted off and rose over the trees.

The chopper slanted up shadowy ice walls, rising high over the summit. Just over the top it sunk close to the cliff's edge and hovered at three feet. Don struggled with the weight of the long coil, pushing it out and following after it. A gale from swirling blades throttled his body as he moved cautiously to the precipice.

Near the edge oily-looking weeds clumped down a slant which ended in a sheer drop. Pulling off the gloves, the pilot stooped to feel them—they were slick. Then, peering over and realizing where the bodies were, he mumbled, "They both made the same mistake. Scotty must have tracked Tim here. He saw the cliff, rushed up, slipped on this damned stuff and went careening into the chasm." Don swore. A few feet away there was a rock outcropping. The steady whir of rotor blades nearby comforted him as the pilot tugged on rope being secured to rock. Within minutes, it dropped below. Immediately, a loud curse rent the air. The rope was swinging in the breeze, eight feet short of the mark.

Quick decisions had always been the way of it. A cold wind tore at the lone figure standing above the steep chasm which had already claimed two victims. Dick Franzell saw the problem, circling just out from the scene. At least, help was available. Don went over the side, lowering slowly, tossing in the wind and concentrating until he neared the bottom. Without hesitation he leaped to the glacier below. Don's form seemed to bounce and slide, or so Dick said later. Don only knew it was cold and jolting. Excitement and the climb sucked away his breath, making him suddenly aware of exhaustion. A look of dismay arose as he saw his wet "Sunday shoes," now submerged in the recently-melted crust. His feet were already cold—he really regretted having forgotten his boots.

The bodies were quite a way below. With cautious but steady steps he made his way down the ice toward Scotty. Outstretched on the ice, the big form looked forlorn. A broken hip bone protruded from his pants. Congealed blood stained the ice, a reminder of the nature of the deed. He didn't seem to be breathing as Don felt for a pulse and touched warm fingers to the cold mouth. "Jesus, he's dead." Sober, sad eyes caressed the young man who had only hours before talked to the pilot on the walkie-talkie. "I'll try the other one," Don mumbled before sidestepping carefully down the slippery slope.

Long, cold hours had evaporated. The boy was at peace —not broken except for a large, dark bruise on the side of his head. Unzipping the jacket, Don pressed an ear to his heart, then lips to deathly skin, not wanting to believe the truth. For half a minute he tried to find life until in desperation he clasped the hand which was a frozen stump. Death was not unfamiliar—the pilot's world was full of it—but Tim was so young. Anger drew him quickly up the slope to the walkie-talkie laying nakedly beside Scotty's broken body. "It works!" Don yelled excitedly. "Dick, it's real bad. One of them is dead. I'm not certain about Scotty, but he's really hurt, and it's so damned cold down here."

"I already called the nearest station. The Coast Guard Medivac chopper is on the way. Hold tight buddy, it'll be a while."

For a long time Don stared at the bleak surroundings. "That chopper is two hours away," he grunted. "I'm damned cold—I could freeze to death here. Why the hell didn't I bring boots? Oh well, no use. . ." His words stopped as he quickly returned to Tim's body where he struggled for a long time trying to remove the dead man's boots. Once they were on his feet and body heat warmed him, a grin surfaced. At least, he would be warmer.

Hurrying back up the slope, Don knelt over Scotty and began to give mouth-to-mouth resuscitation. The lips seemed inordinately cold against his. He worked Scotty's arms and the one good leg, aiding circulation. After a while he realized the man was alive, and relief flooded the usually stoic face. Uttering a soothing sigh and going back for the dead man's coat to make a dry bed under Scotty kept Don warmer. The activity further tired the pilot, but he needed to keep moving for safety.

The hours passed slowly. At last, the musical sounds of two helicopters raised a hearty smile. Glancing up, Don saw the hoist already swinging a stretcher-basket overhead. Motioning them by arm, Don hoped they had arrived in time. Scotty would not be easy to load. He was over 200 pounds of dead weight. For a moment the vision of bears flashed through his mind. All those years of dragging heavy skins and meat were a blessing. He strained, rolling the man over into the basket; then strapping the stiff body tight, he watched it rise into the air. On the second drop, after securing the body, Don climbed on top of it, anxious for the warmth of the cockpit where he knew a hot cup of coffee would be waiting.

They deposited Don on the beach by the parked Super-Cub. He was bone-tired, there was no denying it, but Scotty was alive and on his way to good care in Juneau. He felt good.

Scotty's long recovery was painful. Eight torturous months passed before he walked, but he had life—a valuable commodity. And, when he was able, he called his two friends, Don Johnson and Dick Franzell, to offer his sincere thanks.

****

Advertising was beginning to pay off, and the fall of the year was preferable to most hunters who were interested in acquiring a Dall sheep. As far as Don was concerned, the Wrangells were definitely more acceptable, but locals preferred the Kenai Mountains near his home.

The map of Alaska sprawls over two pages in the Rand McNally *New International Atlas*. Seeing it will give the reader some scope of the distances covered by Don and his cover pilots. That picture is definitely worth 10,000 words.

The Wrangells, which run from the Canadian border to Chisto-china, contain some of the highest peaks in Alaska, are snow-covered year-round and are considered *the* place to hunt the prized Dall sheep. And, while wind up high is tearing, the weather can be as fierce as the arctic or as docile as southern California.

These beautiful specimens were in great abundance in the early 1900s. Sheep meat was a favorite among natives and miners alike. Market hunters supplied most of the meat for the territory, hauling it hundreds of miles on horses and dog sleds. The wholesale slaughter amounted to tons of meat, which was yarded to a cache by teams. Strychnine-laced sheep fat circled the bounty to prevent pilferage from fox, wolverine and the occasional wolf. It brought 50 cents a pound in Fairbanks, which then had a population of 15,000.

Of course, eventually, the animal numbers dropped to dangerous lows and, although market hunting ended in 1925, coyotes and wolf packs were increasing dramatically. These two canides furthered the reduction. Several years of deep snows on windblown ridges seriously damaged the sheep's food supply.

The herds were estimated to be around 10,000 in 1935, but by 1945 the count in the rich hunting grounds of McKinley Park range was a record low of 500. Previous to 1942, hunters were allowed two, even three, rams a year in various areas of the territory, but every year since, the limit has been one. Finally, in 1948, sheep season closed on the Kenai Peninsula and several other areas in Alaska. Fish and wildlife biologists have placed a figure of 12,000 sheep in the entire territory in 1949, when in 1941 the estimate had been around 40,000.

Nineteen-hundred-forty-nine saw the end of Dall hunting in the territory. It was later reopened, but carefully controlled.

Sheep hunting as a business began in the Wrangell Mountains in 1951. Sheep were plentiful at the time, and the guide had almost the entire southern side of the range to himself. Weather was reliable until the first week of September, when snowstorms regularly appeared at 4,000 feet.

In 1935, a miner named Oscar Anderson homesteaded near the town of McCarthy. By the time Don was seeking a camp, Oscar's dreams of striking it rich had faded, and McCarthy was a ghost town. The miner's hay field was ideal for landing the planes, and a comfortable cabin and outbuildings would service his hunters' needs. A large lake at the end of the homestead, flush with salmon during July and August, drew in grizzlies and black bears. Goats and moose were also available in the rugged terrain. Don decided the camp was in just the right spot.

The place served him well until Oscar's death in 1969. Since it was 10 years after statehood and a newly-appointed guide board was setting game areas on Alaskan outfitters, Don had a decision to make. He had already acquired Bear Lake and with it a large preserve. So, he asked for, and was granted, a small area in those mountains. It encompassed a 10-by-20-mile tract from McCarthy to the Lakenhased River, which was a tributary of the wide Copper River whose mouth was at Alaganik and fed in from Controller Bay in the Gulf of Alaska.

Anticipating change, Don had already built a small cabin there adjacent to Harding Glacier. At the end of the summer the pilot knew frequent blizzards would prohibit landings. The temperatures sometimes got down to 60-below in blistering winds blowing off permanent ice. For that reason the Wrangell camp is used only for two or three weeks in August each year.

Hunting with Super-Cubs seemed expedient to Don, whose clients might not be up to steep, rocky climbs. The sheep jaunts were only tolerable to the very hearty. Also the sheep, aware of being pursued and surefooted on shale, could move to higher, impassable terrain without effort. In a news article, one of Don's hunters claimed to be so exhausted he became ill; he was both sweating profusely and ice-cold after a long trek. He said he *thought* he had been in good shape.

Eventually, to avoid the problem, Don hired Steve Daniels, a parachutist, to work the ridges. After bailing out of the plane at about 300 feet above the ridge, he would fold his chute in 150- to 200-foot strips on a suitable mountain top. Then, positioning coded colored streamers, he signalled the pilot as to what supplies were needed to ream out a hasty landing strip. Later, the bush pilot would make an air drop after determining wind direction and velocity. By the time Don returned with the clients, it was ready.

Hairy flights to seemingly inaccessible places only enhanced the hunt. There is no doubt the scenery elicited high praise. Extraordinary pilots added to the hunt, flying precariously low in spire-rimmed passes, searching out their quarry.

One hunter's quote—that a succulent sheep roast on an open fire and a drink of warming whiskey after a climb in the beautiful Wrangells was ecstasy—seemed to say it all.

Chapter 6

Dangerous Hunt

F lying for O.N.I. consumed a good deal of time between hunts, but by late summer and early fall in 1955, Don scheduled trips into the Wrangell Mountains on the Alaska mainland, Kenai Peninsula and the Aleutian Chain. Not all the clients were non-Alaskans. Locals, accustomed to game meat subsistence, often had need of his services.

On one such hunt, he raced off the Kenai strip ferrying supplies for a group of Alaskans hunting Dall sheep in the Horseshoe Mountains. A base camp had been established at the 3,000-foot elevation alongside a picturesque lake in the Kenai Range.

Don relaxed, picturing his young son at the site helping the cook prepare mooseburgers. He was only eight at this juncture and had been excited when he was told he could go. Encouraging the boy to learn the business early seemed expedient.

Concern surfaced as an experienced eye surveyed black clouds forming to the west. Quickly, he reached for the microphone and requested current weather conditions.

Back at camp, Howard Wilson, the cook, hummed a catchy tune while slicing sharply at an onion with a long fish-knife.

Long years of cooking around Alaska produced quick, efficient motions. And while Howard loved to cook, camp cooking was infinitely more desirable than the stuffy, grease-smelling back rooms of banal local eateries.

Casting a sidelong glance out of the tent's flap, the Indian sniggered happily. A soughing wind rose in tall pines, rippling branches and loosening pine cones which plunked irregularly on canvas.

Sucking in brisk air full of aromatic pine and pungent with onions raised a slanted grin. The appeal was mirrored in glistening tarry retinas squinting through a curl of smoke rising from a cigarette dangling on one side of puckered lips. Suddenly a new sound distracted him. Howard looked beyond the flap. The wind was increasing; it drew him outside. The thick forest campsite barred any view of the sky. Hurrying to the lake bank and staring up, he was troubled by the leaden cover. He muttered, "Winter's sure in a damned big hurry."

Don's son, Warren, was fishing further down the bank.

The cook called loudly, instructing the boy to come back and get the gear stashed before the wind damaged it. Then seeing the boy nod, Howard hurried back to the stove where supper was burning. Sucking in the aroma, he said, "If it weren't for them damned bears, I'd love this life." Grimacing, he recalled two frightening experiences down Chain.

The first had occurred as he worked in Don's big cook tent. A powerful Brownie raked open the side of the canvas, renting the air with a terrifying growl as he entered. The Indian's eyes bulged at the thought of it. As Howard screamed out onto the tundra, the hunters raced out, driving off the bruin with rifle shots, but not before he had completely dismantled Howard's kitchen.

Another time, after a card game and before bed, the cook went to check on stores for an early breakfast. It was dark as he went toward the tent, slightly tipsy and humming. Two sows were just outside the tent when Howard happened onto them. He yelled so loud it frightened the pair away. It had taken half a bottle of Don's bourbon to calm his nerves. Now, glancing around nervously, Howard said out loud. "Yes, sir, I'll sure be glad when Don gets back."

Soon, he heard the plane. By the time Howard pulled the iron pan off the burner and hurried to the bank, the Super Cub's pontoons were rushing into rough water, mushing down and dovetailing a spray until the engine slowed. At the end of the lake, it turned and headed for shore.

"Dinner's almost ready," the cook called, smiling as the cockpit door popped open.

"Good, I'm starved. But I don't like the looks of that sky," the pilot yelled into the wind before handing supplies to waiting hands.

Shaggy clouds mushrooming overhead were getting darker steadily and were pushed by a cold, hard wind. The float plane bobbed irregularly, sloshing wet lake water against Howard Wilson's already-chilled body.

"There are two big trees down in the lagoon just ahead. What do you think?" he asked.

"Okay. Let's go take a look." Don climbed out, leaping to the shore. They both hurried up the bank to find a place to anchor the plane against the wind.

By now the lake was whitecapping. Two downed pines floated together, their thick bark lined black from seepage. Once in the water, the two men strained hard to push them apart. In a few minutes it was done. Bouncing and sliding on the churning water, the heavy wood forms slapped loudly. The Indian stuck an oar out lengthwise, preventing a collision as Don raced back to the float plane. The engine caught immediately; it was still warm. He taxied close to the spot while rising and falling in troubled water. Making certain he was close enough and moving into the path of the logs, Don cut the engine and jumped to the right float. Tricky tactics allowed him to jiggle the floats inside the timbers, sliding the plane along until it was safely sandwiched. They made it fast with two ropes. Grinning at each other from their accomplishment, then hopping onto the floats and pulling more rope over the struts, they made it secure. "Hell. That ought to hold it, Howard. Let's go eat." Don sympathized with the cook who stood shivering in the wind. They were both eager for the warmth of the tent and a good meal.

By now, the big trees swayed in the gusts, singing an eerie song. Inside, the men changed clothes and began to cook. A tantalizing aroma filled the tent. Warren scurried around setting their camp table as Don fixed himself a bourbon, neat. "It's getting worse," he said, taking a sip. "Might be a williwaw. Listen to that!"

The cook's concern mounted in a sweaty face—he was used to Alaskan storms, especially at Bear Lake (Birthplace of the Winds). The williwaw was reminiscent of winds down Chain which seem to grab a man, defy gravity and push him helplessly about. But his real fear was for the hunters up above, already trapped by the storm and facing a dangerous night.

"What's that, Dad?" the boy asked with apprehension.

"It's a kind of tornado. Winds get up to 70 knots." Don's eyes widened. "It'll come down Horseshoe Lake like a freight train, bringing snow squalls with it."

Fear grew in Warren's black eyes. Seeing it, Don tried to reassure him. "Hey, no need to worry, we'll be fine. Howard's just concerned about the hunters up on the mountain. They are in Siwash camps with little protection." Glancing over at the cook, Don continued. "We can't go get them now."

The wind sounded shrill, driving through the forest and pushing sheeting rain. Pine branches cracked loudly, and pieces of debris pummeled the tent, dumping cones in staccato succession on the canvas.

Dinner satisfied completely. They chatted, chewing contentedly, glad to be out of the fray and pausing occasionally at some unusual sound outside. They laughed often, trying to keep Warren's confidence from ebbing.

After mess chores, Don suggested they get some sleep. By the sound of the storm, it might be a long night. His concern for the hunters mounted as snow had already begun falling. Finally they slept, but around three a.m. the wind became erratic. The screaming force aroused everyone. "The tent's gonna go," Howard yelled, as they raced to anchor their weight at crucial spots. Warren dove under the camp table, amusing the men.

By six the sky began to show signs of light. The wind had not abated but howled even louder. Howard unzipped the flap; peering out toward the lake, he was frightened their lifeline was taking a beating. He yelled, and suddenly six anxious eyes stared out. The lake boiled. It looked more like an ocean as it crashed huge waves over their moored craft. Right before their eyes, the gale lifted the Super-Cub, trees and all, rising 50 feet like a red kite. One of the logs slipped, pulling the plane over. It was upside down as it crashed, partially severing one wing which hung nakedly away from the fuselage.

Warren gasped, saying in a tremulous voice, "What are we gonna do now, Dad?"

Don laughed. Shrugging nonchalantly while passing an exasperated look to the cook, he heaved a sigh. At least they were safe. The wind began to slow after the fury which flipped the plane as if nature wanted one last destructive belch. It was still shrill and after the snow, very cold.

"Where, exactly, did the hunting parties go?" Don asked the cook.

There was no way of knowing that two of the party, enamoured by crashing echoes of heavy-boned rams locked in mortal combat, had followed the sound out onto the glacier. These rams were big—perhaps nearing 200 pounds and creamy from age— a treasure to hang on a trophy-room wall. When they finally spotted them, far above the timber, the hunters were laced by tearing winds and trapped. The battle itself captivated them for a while. One of the rams was bleeding from the base of its horns, making angry grunts. After two attacks, they walked in opposite directions. Then, as if signalled, they reared on hind hooves before charging, head down, racing for the kill. The sound rose over the wind, making the hunters blink before they raised scopes and ended the battle.

The force had grown. It was harder, blistering down-covered forms, until one of them yelled loudly, "Let's leave them for later. Hell, this is fierce. Look at those clouds. We don't want to get caught out here in the open if snow comes."

Tracking with heads bent and scarves pulled taut over cold skin, leaving only goggled eyes exposed, they headed for timberline. Snow came all too quickly. It was blinding, leading them astray, but they were near the edge of the ice cliff, moving slowly and lost. A huge gust captured them, forcing one of the men over the edge. He flew down screaming. The bounce was hard, and even in the wind he heard the leg crack. Knowing he would die if left there, the other hunter raced away in search of gear. After finally locating it, he moved carefully to a thick crevice, and within two hours he had dragged the moaning man inside. At least they were out of the wind. There was liquor and coffee in their stores. It would be a long night, but with luck they would stay alive.

Howard squinted, remembering each party packing gear that morning. He had listened to the garbled, excited conversation as they sipped his camp coffee and munched on hot rations. They were Alaskans who knew the danger of hypothermia. Wanting to be protein-protected, they ate heartily.

"I think that man and his daughter went up Horseshoe Pass." The pair were locals who had been dropped off by another pilot, but who had visited in Don's camp. "Them two from Seward said they were headed for the glacier." Howard rattled the pot, issuing orders to Warren, trying to keep the boy busy. "I'll bet they split off at the summit. The sheep are high this year."

"Yeah," Don growled, feeling helpless. "It must have been bitter up there last night." Then, thinking they might have to search, Don advised the pair to eat well.

By 11 a.m. the storm had passed. The trees were snow-laden and blowing softly, drawing the group outside where they grinned at each other. Bright sunlight danced across the lake mirroring virgin peaks and pines puffed in fleece. Above them, a clear, crisp, cobalt sky; the whole scene poster-perfect. Howard's artistry was succulent in the morning air. They had survived the williwaw in one piece and were experiencing exhilaration while wondering if help would come and if the hunters were safe.

Don's accustomed ear heard it first. A sly grin arose. He

pointed high and yelled—clearing the opposite peak, a red-and-white speck was growing larger as it neared.

Dancing on the bank and howling happy, shrill cries, they watched the bush plane circle before dipping an acknowledging wing.

All the bush pilots flew with an eye to the ground. It was the way of life in an unrelenting land. They saved hundreds of lives a year, and after such a storm, the pilot knew there would be Alaskans in need. Shortly, he landed to pick up Don and headed for Anchorage where Don purchased a new Super-Cub. Three hours later, the red craft buzzed the camp. Alerting Howard and Warren, Don overflew them and headed for the peaks to begin the search. "At least," Don reasoned, "they don't know about the plane's destruction and have faith. Now let's hope everyone's alive."

Rising slowly, the float plane passed over a low mountain rise. Just past the pinnacle, he saw two men headed down a snaking trail toward base camp. Both had filled out. They were packing curled horns and capes of the Dalls on their backs. Don would learn later they had shot their sheep late in the day, found a cave and were sitting by a warm fire listening to the howling despot, thanking the fates for a haven. They would have been even more thankful if they had known the bear who usually denned there was being mounted in Seattle for some hunter's game room.

Pines, thick in the valley, carved a dense path up ravines before topping out on the summit. The density obliterated a view from the air, except for occasional clearings near a snow-covered trail.

Clear air enhanced the engine's whine. Don began circling, trying to alert the hunters. At last, he saw a figure racing toward the clearing, waving furiously. Lowering allowed a clear view as five men became visible. Some had filled out. Capes floated over heavy Army-surplus jackets, each face smiling broadly as they flailed their arms. "You earned them," Don muttered. "It must have been hell."

Twisting the wheel, he headed for the glacier. "Two more parties to go." Rising effortlessly, the red plane shadowed across the landscape in ever-widening circles. Up ahead the glacier-blinding pinnacle grew larger, its treachery subverted by a virgin mantle that hid deep caves and stiff ice which yearly took a good share of lives. He made two more passes. Don banked and wound up behind the peak, curving north and circling constantly. He didn't want to miss them.

When he spotted the pair, he swore. One of the party was down and obviously disabled. The binoculars confirmed his plight. From the look of it, the hunter had slid into a crevice, probably snow-blinded, and broke, at least, a leg. It was a long hike to that spot. With help they could lift him out. Dipping the wings to give them a signal before he floated toward the lake, he pushed the Super-Cub to its max.

Howard had already prepared hot soup and coffee in big thermoses, then he wrapped chunks of hot moose roast in containers. All the parties had been exposed. At least, if a search was imminent, he would be prepared.

Approaching the bank landing area, Don popped the door and yelled, "Got one down on the ice. Get a splint and bandages ready. I'll drop food and supplies first." A short time later he was back at the summit. Lowering, he swooped close to the crevice and dropped a canvas sack. The second hunter slipped eagerly across its face, anxious for the airborne help. Don watched it land, smiled, and turned south.

It was almost four when the party reached the glacier. Fortunately, the weather held. Warming rays melted new snow. Water dripped down constantly as they climbed the slushy trail, dragging a homemade sledge. They were efficient, raising the hunter in a sling on ropes strung over thick branches; then preparing for the arduous, slippery climb down. Don headed the rescue. This was his business, and it was never taken lightly. Every effort to maintain safe, satisfactory hunts was made. It would pay off in his long career and, ultimately, save a lot of lives.

It was only a 25-minute flight to Seward where a radio transmission would produce an ambulance waiting to take the injured hunter to the hospital. He had been lucky. The broken right femur would heal; hot food and rest would take care of the exposure, but another of the 11 had not been so lucky.

The group were all in camp by the time Don came in from the glacier with the exception of a father and his 11-year-old daughter who had been hunting on the mountain alone. Instructing some of the party to eat well and rest first, Don asked them to start a search. They left just after he was airborne and headed for Seward.

It was dark when he returned, landed and raced toward fires set on the bank's edges. Slowing, he saw Howard standing quietly, staring at the water. His smile faded. "What's wrong?" Don asked, jumping out of the Cub.

"The little girl is dead."

Thin eyelids closed; Don sighed over slumping shoulders. "How?"

"It was exposure. Her father is inside. I filled him full of booze; he's pretty bad off."

"Yeah—good." Lowering his head, the pilot walked dejectedly toward camp. He was tired. It had been an exhausting day. Warren ran out to greet his father who glanced lovingly at his son. Taking a deep breath and curling an arm around the boy, Don went inside to console the grieving parent.

Later, a silent group loaded the small, frozen form into the plane. It taxied slowly across the still water. This time there was no rush. The mortuary would wait.

Once the parties and gear were safely back in Kenai, Don prepared his salvage operation. It would not be easy. The engine and the floats on the plane were still good—even the wings were salvageable. A Super-Cub was valued at $5,400—it was definitely worth the effort.

Living in remote terrain, homesteading, flying the wilderness, hunting out of reach of help, taught the statehooders complete self-reliance. It wasn't just the money, although early on there was a little of it. Building camps; buying equipment; grading runways always battered by ice, wind, snow and mud; and buying and repairing airplanes consumed most of their funds. As a practical matter they learned ingenuity, and when there were no parts, they made them.

In this case Horseshoe Mountain Lake was inaccessible. There were no roads, and that was a problem. However, there was a dirt trail 15 miles from the lake. As Don pondered the problem, a friend came by, and during their conversation over coffee, he mentioned a new piece of equipment purchased by a wrecker Don knew. A small John Deere tractor—the first one ever to come to Alaska. "You ought to see that thing. It'll go right up on a flatbed truck and can pull like hell." Don's eyes widened. "Thanks, Charlie. That's just what I need."

For a price, it became available. They trucked it to Homer on a flatbed behind which was a small trailer and a ramp. The truck rocked over rough, half-frozen roads, lumbering to a spot adjacent to the lake.

Don was excited when they finally saw the lake in front of them. His plane was still moored upside down in the water, floating near the secured logs. It took some doing. The floats weren't damaged at all. Once the wings had been dismantled and the body righted, they slid the severed wings under the fuselage and towed the whole outfit across the lake using a long cable and the small tractor. It took a long time to pull the loaded trailer 15 miles through snow and forest to the waiting rig. Don was jubilant, bouncing over the ragged roads on the trip back.

Once the plane was back in the Kenai hangar, life became easier. The cost of repair was $1,800, but he had the Super-Cub intact. Owning two of them was practical and, although it hadn't occurred to him just yet, the Kenai Float Plane Service had just been hatched—a difficult birth, but a birth nevertheless.

He now owned three airplanes. They were getting calls from locals to fly emergency patients to the hospital in Anchorage. Of course, the cover pilots worked only when they were in camp—Don couldn't afford to keep them on full-time. But since there were no roads of any consequence leading to the mainland, and everyone on the peninsula had supply needs, it seemed expedient to put up a shack at the Kenai airport. His runway at

Don and friends prepare to haul the damaged plane out of the lake after the williwaw.

the homestead had no phone, and besides, it was too far out of town. Don mulled over the matter. He wouldn't be leaving for Point Hope for another month or two, and he had only a few flying jobs for O.N.I. He grinned at acceptance of the idea. Within three weeks, he and a few friends were busy constructing a building. By Thanksgiving, he took the family down to town to see the new structure and help put up the sign. It read, "Kenai Float Plane Service—Don Johnson, Proprietor."

By now Don and his wife had two sons. The future looked bright, and the family planned to fly to Iowa to spend a week with relatives after which Don would return to Point Hope. Neither of them was prepared for the fatal accident which would ensue and claim the life of the youngest boy. That sadness left a deep scar which, even 30 years later, he would refuse to talk about.

Shortly, the pilot returned to Alaska and packed for the winter's trek to the North Country.

Don with Snow Goat, next to Harding Glacier.

Guide Danny Lynch in Wrangell camp.

Howard Wilson, the Eskimo cook.

Chapter 7

Death Waiting in Black Water

U p until 1965, Don ran advertisements in U.S. sporting magazines and hunting journals for clients. They arrived during
the season, fully-equipped and eager to search for the ultimate
game.

Flights were arranged from Anchorage to Nome or Kotzebue,
where Don or one of his cover pilots would pick them up for
the trip north to Point Hope or other stations. Weather and sightings determined their destination and were always last-minute
decisions. And, since the hunting fraternity worldwide was so
tightly-knit, it wasn't long before he was able to discontinue advertising. Good outfitters were hard to find. Not only did he realize
their need to be comfortable, but he offered extraordinary flying
skills. The hunts were expensive. It was incumbent upon an outfitter to be efficient, although many of them weren't.

Don readily admitted that black water made him "damned
uncomfortable." Frostbite, consuming whiteouts, unpredictable
gales, thin ice, blizzards, man-tracking bears and an occasional
mishap, made ice-hunting a dangerous game. And still the hunters
came in increasing numbers.

Many mishaps were narrowly averted. Several times careless
hunters dropped shells down into the controls in the back of the
primitive Super-Cub. Once the pilot found the left aileron was
unusable while coming in for a dangerous landing during a

powerful gale. Don said, "It was like being on a tightrope and losing your balance. We were 10 feet from the ice and already committed. I used the rudder to compensate and gave him hell in no uncertain terms." Sometimes, hunters would get excited and jam a gunstock down in the rudder. Arctic flying was not without thrills.

Naturally, there were unexpected bonuses. Russian scientists, taking samples from beneath the ice, occasionally would be spotted. Don would always land and taxi to the party. For 15 to 20 minutes his hunters had the rare opportunity of communicating with foreigners by sign language. And, after a bit, trades of sunglasses, knives or trinkets would change hands for artifacts or coins. The hunters relished the stories and the experiences.

For a long time, Don Johnson and another outfitter were the only two guides hunting polar bear, but by the early '60s at least 12 others had joined the lucrative venture. Naturally, many of them were ill-equipped, and the danger of flying in that part of the world caused several fatal accidents. All together, 14 crashes were recorded. Unwary hunters responding to ads often found their way into untrained hands. That fact, and others like it, gave outfitters in Alaska a bad name. Don's future in the business came from careful tending.

The last hunt one season was a husband-and-wife team, Ken and Sally McConnel. Sally was a good shot, and since it was her turn for a bear, she was flying toward Russia with Don. Her husband was flying with Al in the cover plane.

The hunting party was unaware of the serious problems which awaited them as they flew over the soft ice. Don and Sally were climbing in the Super-Cub. Don went to 5,000 feet, desperately searching for a bridge. The ice pans were large and drifting far in high wind at record speeds. The party had gone out with a full load of gas and carrying as much extra fuel as the limited space allowed. If the weather remained good, there shouldn't have been any problems.

An excited smile played on Sally's greased lips as she scanned the ice. "Look, Don!" she exclaimed. "There's a ring-necked seal. What a prize! Let's go."

Reacting immediately, Don circled the area in search of a blow-hole. He frowned. The lead was miles away. That fact was inconsistent with seal habits, and the blowhole couldn't be located. Shrugging, he looked for a place to land while radioing the companion plane to stay out of the area.

A biting wind greeted the pair. They bent into it, consciously aware of the steady crunch beneath their boots while stalking. Eventually, the seal was located. It was a long shot. Motioning to his client, they huddled close to the ground to set up the shot. "We can't get any closer," he cautioned over the wind.

Nodding, Sally aimed and squinted into the scope of her new Weatherby. Pulling the butt tight against her padded shoulder, she aimed carefully and squeezed the trigger. The seal remained motionless.

"That's strange," Don said. "Shoot again."

Twice more the rifle spoke—but the game seem unperturbed. "I couldn't have missed him," Sally yelled over the wind. Amazed and perplexed, she stared open-mouthed at the guide. It was definitely unusual behavior. They got up and darted across the ice. Slowing near the game, Don grinned. "It's frozen stiff!" The damned thing's been dead a long time." They laughed good-naturedly and returned to the aircraft, leaving the frozen sentinel on the ice.

Within minutes they were airborne, cruising toward their cover plane which was up ahead scouting tracks.

Increasing winds pulsed long snow-trails across the frozen wasteland. Down below, it was bleak and unfriendly.

Sally leaned back contentedly. This hunt had been long-anticipated; it was thrilling. A low chortle escaped. The seal story was worth repeating, and up ahead was her long-awaited trophy. Glancing over at Don, she forced a smile. He was at home in this treacherous environment; that was definitely reassuring.

Al radioed a sighting, giving position and ground information in crisp tones. The Super-Cub droned on, its red fuselage the only color on top of the world.

Suddenly, Don banked while pointing below. Long prints, etched in drifting snow, disappeared into ridges. They would have to hurry before wind-driven fluff obliterated the trail. They landed and skied close to the spoor.

Sally felt resistance on the door. Heaving her shoulder hard against metal, she struggled out. The ruff around her face flipped away from delicate skin, and a sudden windburn raised a grimace. They bent into the force, following the tracks.

The bear's movement had been recent. Signs of the giant's presence were everywhere. Covering long distances gave bears insatiable appetites. And, if game wasn't available, man would suffice. Since staying upwind was imperative, the blowing snow gave them a visual advantage. Leading the way, clad in white, the guide tracked the bear's prints which disappeared into ice-carved towers. They searched for a long time following a writhing path, battered by the piercing winds which tormented their fur-encased bodies. Suddenly excited, adrenaline pulsed into Sally's cold limbs. At long last, they were near the prey. After a tiring track the bruin had stopped.

Don nudged his hunter, then motioned toward a low, crusted wall which concealed their presence. Once settled, the wind seemed louder, and the howling force consumed them. Across the ice, the huge mammal stood, pulling his regal body upright while a small head pivoted inquisitively. A carnivorous mouth opened as great growls filled the area—they were repeated, exposing awesome, jagged canine teeth.

Sally lifted the rifle, pressing hard, and scoped. One eye scrinched and she smiled, viewing him through cross-hairs while moving lower to get a lung shot as Don had instructed. Having discarded her outer pair of heavy gloves, she felt cold seep through the inner silk pair as she tightened her index finger on the trigger. Two volleys rose. A guttural death rattle pierced the wind followed by the huge frame toppling. Crashing to the ice, the ponderous animal forced a tear at the lead and slid into the sea.

After seeing the area, Don was prepared. He rushed out flinging a grappling hook 30 feet. Metal bit deep into fur while the guide jerked hard, restraining dead weight and skidding forward toward the break.

Excited and yelling, Sally rushed after him grabbing onto the escaping rope. By now they were sweating. Puffs of steam escaped from ruff past determined lips as they tugged hard. Nine-hundred pounds of bear, now wet, resisted their efforts. So intense was the struggle, they barely noticed rising beads of sweat, freezing instantly and chilling them.

The cover plane landed. Don's grin widened upon hearing its comforting whine. Ken McConnel reached them first. Al was just behind.

New strength grabbed the line just as Don's was ebbing. Heaving mightily, they jerked the bear partially up onto the ice. Don moved closer. He stretched as his gloved hand clenched the thick, wet mat and pulled. Suddenly, the milky sheet beneath his boots split, its deathly tear pulsing fear into the group and terror into the guide whose body slid heavily into black water. A blue blur flashed out of the parka's hood over plump lips, releasing smoke and a helpless cry. The agile frame seemed to leap, grasping hungrily for the rope and swimming onto the thin ice. In a minute, he would be dead or under the permanent sheet—lost forever.

What seemed an eternity was actually 15 seconds until Don's padded body wiggled onto harder ice. Tearing at wet clothes before they froze to warm, live skin, Don quickly undressed. A numbness surged into his extremities, slowing movement, while he yelled through chattering teeth to Al to pull off the boots and pants. Recovering from his momentary shock, Al stripped from his parka to wrap Don and then ran for the plane. The heaters worked only when they were airborne. Sally jerked at the boots as Don ripped away wet trousers.

Ken clung desperately to the bear, struggling to keep the beast from sliding back into the water. His mind was busy avoiding the niggling fear of dangerous ice just beneath his feet.

The engine roared to life and rose in a musical crescendo. The turmoil became organized. Sally held the coat around the guide while hurrying to the plane and then she pushed him inside. Just as the door slammed, Al gunned the craft forcing it out. They raced over the ice and into a leaden sky.

Pulling on new boots, Don forced the heat tubes into them with quivering, almost numb, fingers. The plane's lift elicited a soothing sigh. The warmth was ecstasy as blue, shaking lips grinned awkwardly and relief raised on his ruddy face.

Al glanced over concerned, muttering, "You okay?"

Nodding, Don groaned, "Yeah." The quaking was slowing. "That was too close for comfort." They cast a long benign look at each other. Their quick-wittedness had saved them many times, sharpening them, adding experience which kept them alive. It was all part of the game. They'd laugh about it later, but for now there was still a job to do, and it would be more difficult at this point.

After Al and Don were airborne, Sally hurried back to her husband, still struggling with the beast. Together they inched the matted frame to safer ice. She pushed and pulled, feeling exhaustion, but continuing until he was spread out beneath them, looking like the prize she had shot.

Ken encouraged her. "Get over there, Sally. I'll shoot some film." She grinned. Then glancing up into the sky, still concerned about Don, she poked out a glove. The plane was returning, and they both smiled with relief.

After landing, Al appeared with a shovel. He covered Don's clothes with snow and jumped up and down, pummeling powder against canvas and fur. Finally, the bulk of the water was extracted—it took only five minutes. It was a trick Don had learned from the Inuit.

Now they could get busy and skin the bear. The hide weighed 200 pounds. Wet, it was much heavier. Once it was skinned, Don dunked it up and down in the Chukchi Sea on the grappling hook, watching a vermilion trail seep into the black void, lessening with each flush until at last, the hide was pulled out on the ice and dragged to safety. Al shoveled snow onto the naturally water-shedding fur, and the drying process was repeated. They all got into the act. The sight of four bulky figures bouncing up and down on the bear hide was almost comic. At least the activity warmed them. It was 30-below zero, and they had been out on the ice an unusually long time.

The wind pressed harder, howling loudly, sucking away warmth, thoroughly chilling them and burning exposed skin. Sally pulled a wool wrapper tight over her face just under the goggles she'd worn during the entire hunt. Don's warning about snow-blindness was definitely heeded.

When the hide was almost dry, Don instructed them to drag it toward the plane. He pulled out a watertight bag, stuffed it inside and sealed it carefully.

The hunters were curious. "Listen!" Don said sharply. "if I put a wet hide in that airplane and turned on the heater, we'd soon have condensation and ice on the windshield." He grunted knowingly—remembering the first time that had happened raised an instant sneer. "Hell, I'd be scraping a hole with a penknife all the way back to Point Hope. We don't need any more problems in this place. Flying is tough enough."

Homeward-bound Ken McConnel thought of Francis Wile's words describing arctic waters. They were poetic but accurate. "The flowing water sealed." He savored their hunt; it had been exciting, and, thanks to quick thinking and experience, had not ended tragically.

The McConnels were the last hunters that season. It was time to head for home.

Fierce storms lashed the Chukchi and Point Hope that year, sometimes lasting two or three weeks. The arctic winter died hard. And, for the pilots, there was still the long flight to Kenai, inevitably through fog, whiteout, fierce winds, snow or maybe three of the four. Acceptance was part of it. They were uncomplaining and ultimately beat the elements at their own game.

Sally and Ken McConnel with Don and Eskimo child at the Point Hope Lodge.

Chapter 8

Near-Tragedy in Whiteout

On a January morning in 1956 smoke curled out a funneled tin chimney, misting as it mingled with arctic air. Drifting snow had almost submerged the 60-foot camp lodge nestled on a promontory near Point Hope, except at the long entrance corridor where its owner, Don Johnson, had shoveled an exit. Outside, two red ski planes startled the landscape. Don stepped into a caked mound leaving deep prints as he headed toward them. The fur-lined parka hood neatly surrounded his lean face from where breath smoked in the 20-below-zero weather. Wind feathered the fur as he leaned into it, hurrying toward the planes to ready them for the hunt.

Inside, Al Bontrigger watched the bacon sizzle in the cast-iron skillet. Sniffing generously, he cracked eggs into a deep bowl. 'That ought to bring them guys to the table,' he reasoned, knowing Don was always starved in the morning, and the aroma was wafting out the chimney. The hunter smelled it, too. His round face appeared in the doorway. "You knew that would roust me, didn't you, Al?"

The pilot-cook grunted knowingly and grinned. He used food regularly to move the hunters. Only drinkers, suffering from hangovers with queasy stomachs, ever refused his biscuits and gravy served on hot plates where he had first placed crisp, dark bacon beside plump scrambled eggs. Al laughed. He was an Alaskan, and breakfast wasn't real without eggs. This carton had been wrapped in woolen shirts and put onto the passenger seat in the plane on the last trip north. At least this batch didn't freeze. Real satisfaction surfaced on Al's face as he scooped the last of the eggs from the pan.

Flying cover for Don Johnson was his first love, but next to that he thought cooking a particularly rewarding occupation. When they weren't out on the tundra or skimming the ice, the kitchen enamoured him. The warmth in the room, succulent aromas, banging pans, and best of all, the compliments of hungry men, delighted him. Putting the food on the table, he yelled, "Come and get it!"

An hour later the threesome, bundled in arctic clothing, headed for the planes. Mounting excitement, obvious only in the hunter's eyes, registered slowly along his unshaven jaw, finally becoming an anxious smile.

Don recognized the look. Trophy hunting was a sport, an abject pleasure which usually manifested itself in playful cajoling or absolute silence. Buckling the seat belt, he glanced over before starting the engines and chuckled. The hunter was stoic.

Outside the windows the morning loomed dark as the planes raced out, lifting above the snow, climbing easily in cold air until they had cleared the mountains. For several hours the engines droned in an otherwise empty sky; down below the sea was a steel sheet.

After two hours they spotted the leads. Wind-shifted ice-packs crushed against anchor ice opening in large slits on whose edges hair seals collected. Swarms of krill surged into the leads attracting schools of fish which, while enjoying their delicate repast, then became breakfast for the seals. Their slick skins resembled tar patches on the ice.

Don scanned the barren wasteland from the cockpit window, his mouth pursed thoughtfully until recognition erupted there. The big bruins, although not yet visible, would not be far behind. Favorable westerly winds helped drive them some 175 miles east of the cape. The place looked just right.

The hunter leaned toward the glass. Down below a gray Alaskan day hovered over ice impressions, looking eerie in the half-glow. Hard-packs had been forced up into giant peaks, frozen in flight, as if created in cataclysmic shock. Except for the seals, there was no sign of life.

It looked peaceful enough; not the way he had imagined it, but awesome; a place where death occurred quickly. The wind would be bitter, but he had degreased his rifle to prevent the bolt from sticking, just as Don instructed, 'and the gear of fur and down with electric socks should provide enough warmth,' he thought. Then, glancing furtively at Don and knowing he had selected the right guide, he felt reassured. All of the planning seemed worth it.

Now, savoring the moment, he closed his eyes. Leaning his head against the glass for a second, he sighed. 'The trophy is out there,' he thought, 'Not in a book or my fantasy, but actually within reach.' Satisfaction pulsed through him.

For a moment he pictured the bear, a full mount, in his den with all of his other acquisitions. He wasn't interested in elephants or water buffalo—just one of the largest terrestrial carnivores. Saliva welled up in his mouth; he swallowed hard and remembered the book he had studied in spare moments. 'Pleistocene—was that it? Yes—the Ice Age bear—exquisite, powerful, hidden from the world in this almost impenetrable place.' Suddenly he realized his palms were moist with anticipation.

Something moved below. Don banked to the left, point down. A big male was lumbering away from the rift.

The hunter bolted forward, catching a glimpse as they passed above the bear. "Holy shit," he exclaimed. As if mesmerized, he stared at the raw speed; a thousand pounds of fat layers encompassed in thick ivory fur on snowshoe feet, galloping past deserted ice castles.

They made another pass, this time coming directly toward him. The bear stopped, peering at them with obsidian eyes above an expressionless mouth. Guard hairs glistened, creating an aura as he raised up to full height, exposing his jagged canine teeth and yawning a growl.

"There's your trophy," Don called in an even voice over the engine's whine.

The bear roared, pawing the air; then quite suddenly, his interest faded. The black-tipped snout culled seal scent, pulling him in the direction of the rift where a tasty meal awaited on that windy morning.

'The Inuit had aptly named him Pihogahig—the wanderer,' he thought.

At the water's edge the beast sank stealthily, disappearing beneath the ice where jointed paws moved in wide circular sweeps, pulling under pack-ice. Quickly, the giant body approached a gaping cut above which were shadowy forms. Sharp talons scratched the ice, their seductive sounds startling the seals. One baby flipped over into a carnivorous embrace.

A short while later in the eerie gray light, he ate the plump white-coat (baby seal), taking only skin and fat, chewing noisily until his hunger was satisfied. The remains were left scattered on the ice. They would not be there long. An ivory gull or one of the arctic foxes who followed the bear's wanderings would be along soon, knowing breakfast was certain. It would not go to waste.

Don's circling diminished as they re-sighted him. "He'll go at least 11, maybe more. That's a really good one," Don told the hunter.

"There he goes, Don," the hunter shouted excitedly.

They banked, flying over the bear in a straight line, passing the peaks behind which the sea had flattened before freezing. Then, while Al circled in the cover plane, they landed.

"He's heading right for you, Don," Al's husky voice advised over the radio.

Within seconds they were out on the ice, shocked by cold and biting wind.

Al watched while enlarging the cover plane's circle. He could see Don forcing a catalytic heater into the engine, then covering the nose cone before hurrying toward the ridge. The cover pilot had another job which was equally important. The bear might not be alone. They were usually loners, and this one had already eaten so he wouldn't be as alert. They were getting away from the leads; if there was a hungry animal asleep beneath a crusted wall who scented a man, it would be open season on hunter and hunted.

On foot the two men moved with care, protecting rifles, stepping delicately on chiseled mounds. The sound of the wind and the steady crunch seemed like music to the hunter. He knew he was upwind of the bear, directly in his path—close to a lifelong dream.

Once they reached the pinnacle, their prey could be sighted. Don reached the summit first. He glassed silently, a stoic face beneath the binoculars, until finally recognition grew. Nudging the hunter, he pointed ahead no less than 75 yards where fur rippled toward them. The hunter lifted his rifle, conscious of cold, blue steel in his hand which trembled slightly. For a split second a queasy surge erupted in his stomach, and adrenaline fused into his body until he heard the .338 Magnum explode. That reverberation against the glasslike walls filled the air, stopping the sound of the wind and his breath instantly.

"You got him!" Don screamed into the wind, as he lowered the rifle.

The hunter stiffened, gazing at his trophy. 'It's over,' he thought sadly, conscious of the years of dreaming and planning. The thought rippled away quickly. He turned, catching a glimpse of Al landing. It distracted him as the skis etched the ice heading toward the bear. Suddenly, the hunter felt the cold wind—his emotions ran the gamut: excited, satisfied, tense, and yet, cold.

They hurried down the peak until they reached the animal. As was prearranged, the hunter poised with the rifle aimed at the beast's head while Don kicked at him with a boot. "He's a goner," Don grinned at the man.

Al approached to photograph the kill. This was always a special moment, and Al had looked forward to it. Some guys didn't seem to show any enthusiasm, but this one was excited. He could always tell—the picture was almost as important as the skin. He clicked the shutter several times and rushed back to the plane. They still had to skin him, and the damned weather was getting bad.

Don rushed to get the gear. Shortly, they had rough-skinned the bruin, leaving head and paws intact, and wrapping the meat for the Eskimos. No one else wanted the meat, so it worked out fine. Once the huge chunks were bagged, Al helped Don carry them to his aircraft. Then, they returned for the hide which was carefully sealed inside an airtight container. It, too, was placed inside Don's plane. He had already instructed the hunter to get into the cover plane which was warmer at this juncture. The wind was increasing. Don yelled into it to Al. "Leave two flashlights on the ice. We need a beacon."

Two slices of yellow shone on the ice, burning like coals in the Alaskan darkness. The pilots hurried to the planes where they still had to start the fire-pots to warm the oil. By now each man was eager for the plane's warmth.

Finally, the engines roared into action and they took off in tandem, each watching the lights diminishing as they flew—they were reassured.

Searing head-winds pummeled the plane, complicating flight. Outside, a whiteout developed so rapidly the hunter was shocked. Alone, Don muttered under his breath. "It's like being in a damned milk bottle." He knew vertigo could defuse stability—it was dangerous. 'At least the early DEW line warning system is in effect,' he thought. From the flashlights the pilots could get a fix on radar. Their bearing was toward Cape Lisburne. They had enough fuel for about four hours, and by now they were probably paralleling the east-west coastline by two or three miles. "Al and the hunter should be right behind me in the cover plane," he murmured.

The sky was always a challenge. 'Like the sea,' he mused. Experience plus a natural ingenuity guided their homeward flight. With growing confidence he radioed the cover plane following. Being alert kept him alive; the plane, a necessary ingredient in his business, was a fixture in his life which he respected and used with care.

Now, floating in the suffocating fog, his thoughts drifted to Kenai Peninsula and his homestead on Cook's Inlet. He pictured the log cabin he had just built to prove up on his claim according to government regulations. There was peace there, especially in the not-too-distant mountains which were snow-covered most of the year—hovering above gray waters, contrasted by clumping fauna near the house where moose roamed with their young. Later, he told himself, he would build a hangar; all part of the latent dream, all possible now that the war was behind him.

The war—the word nagged, creeping out of his subconscious like a cancer he thought had been cured. Picturing the fray brought an instant sneer as he remembered with bitterness the North Atlantic ships, in raw, fierce winds, ice clinging to their hulls like white parasites as they searched for Nazi U-boats. For a moment the white, frozen decks pierced his mind—railings coated with slick ice as the ship heaved, crashing over swells, and where his comrades died beside him, smothered in flames, cursing the gunfire sucking away life.

The sound of the wind brought him back. He reached for the mike on the dashboard for contact with another human voice. "We're nearing the coast, Al," he instructed. Al's answering transmission was comforting.

Don's thoughts returned to the satisfaction of his life. The hunter in the cover plane was from New York, a buddy of a former hunter last season. Don knew he was happy; hunters always were after being successful on the ice. Knowing what they wanted was part of it; he had a feel for the frozen North and raw determination which hunters sensed, lending power to his position.

'I'll get out of this soup,' he muttered soberly, watching the wing tips with sharpness, his eyes ricocheting from side to side. Suddenly, seeing a flash back on the wing, he jerked back on the stick, simultaneously yelling into the mike, "Al, go straight up—straight up to 3500!" The engine roared in the howling wind, pulling the plane to new heights away from the frozen peak. An instinct told him he was free of it; outside, the murky pale continued. Clicking the mike button, his voice reflected relief. He called, "Hey, that was a close one—you okay?"

There was a deathly silence. Don's thumb ragged at the button, while repeating the transmission over and over. The silence grew larger. He took a fix on their position. "Damn fog!" he yelled angrily.

Banking deeply, he lowered to 2,600 feet deciding he was at Mount Hamlet. Anxious fingers groped at the radio dials until he clicked onto HF at 5544. 'Got to reach Fairbanks,' he told himself. It was 900 miles to the distant voice which consoled him. "Get me pinpointed on radar," he instructed. "My cover plane is down."

Fairbanks heard the words—they were not that infrequent. The weather had claimed a lot of lives, but one of those men in the plane was his old friend and he had to find them.

For many hours, as yet unlived, he would remember the transmission—"You are 11 miles east of Cape Lisburne."

'We had only one target,' he thought. 'Al knew we were headed for Point Hope and were coming into Mount Hamlet. Al disappeared over that.' Opening the line he said, "I'll keep circling until you get a good reading on me." Static crackled out of the speaker, finally clearing. The anxious look tightened, responding to the faceless voice. "Sorry, you can't land at Cape Lisburne—zero visibility—go 40 miles northeast to Cape Beaufort." "Okay," Don shouted. "Tell them to get on the vehicle lights and start the oil-drum fires. I'm about out of gas."

The gauge looked ominous in the cockpit. "Ah, hell—there's a strong tailwind—I'll make it," was mumbled.

The plane droned on, suspended in a web of clutching fog which pressed against the windshield. Don examined mental pictures of the geography—mapping it across his mind—searching blindly for the airport. Finally he saw the bulldozer's ghostly glare mingled with oil-drum fires below and the runway opening as he neared, racing into welcoming light and the comfort of skis crunching ice.

Sweaty palms released the wheel; he glanced out; the men

in the airport rushed toward the plane. They were partners against the weather, protecting each other daily, knowing their lives depended on it. They knew Al and liked him.

While they refueled the Piper Super-Cub, Don downed a few cups of hot coffee. The warmth soothed while he considered his plan. Shortly, he climbed back into the plane for a continuing search. The temperature outside was 40-below-zero with a hefty windchill factor. If they survived the crash, it was damned cold. But, they had Wood's Four Star sleeping bags, which were good in 70-below weather, and coffee and food.

Don pictured the man in the cover plane, his old friend Al, as he cooked in the lodge, sniffing the food with a relish that had always amused. They flew together, depending on one another for their livelihood. He looked up into the swirling fog—Al was out there, somewhere. The dials flicked as he turned them, trying to relocate Fairbanks. This time they'd watch him on radar. For three hours he lifted wings over dense air, calling out repeatedly, hoping for a sign of life, but to no avail. Exhaustion began to take its toll. Banking slowly he headed toward Cape Beaufort. The fog was separating as he made his approach.

After he ate, the mechanics gave him a bed in the crew shack where he slept for two hours before hurrying back to the airplane for another try. It was almost daybreak in the bleak, ice-covered Alaskan world. The mountains' irregular walls, although frozen solid, mounded on top with new snow that had swirled like meringue into spires. Miles of the lifeless range passed under the wings until, nearing the area where they had lost contact, he saw it. Don's eyes widened; he yelled excitedly while he stared out at the red fuselage marring snow in a saddle near the summit. Al's plane was intact. The Super-Cub swooped down, banking slightly for a clear view. The 180 had slid into a snow mound, mushing, but not breaking up. They had skidded 200 feet by the looks of it. 'The gear's gone, but there are sleeping bags on top of the snow'—"Hot dog!" he yelled, banking deep before searching for a place to land.

The hunter stiffened in the bag. 'A noise,' his brain repeated.

'An engine!' Laughter choked in his throat, startling him as he desperately tried to sit up. Caught in the arctic bag in blackness, his fingers clutched at cloth where he felt for the cold, metal zipper.

Al listened to his garbled voice as he tried to extricate himself. A small grin widened on the pilot's mouth. "It's Don!" he yelled. Unzipping the bag, he scampered up where he could see the red wings lowering above him. "I knew he'd be back!" he hollered, dancing in the snow still clutching the heavy bag around him.

The hunter's face masked the fear lurking in his eyes.

"I told you he'd find us—didn't I?" Al said, waving anxiously.

Bile rose in the hunter's throat as awareness swept through his being. It had been the longest night of his life, full of howling wind and frightening dreams where wolves crept hungrily toward him. In the dream the rifle wouldn't fire, and the cold seeped into his weary body. Exhaustion had finally brought sleep, but not before he relived the terrifying moment of the crash. He stood shaking his head trying to remember his nightmares. "The bear," he muttered.

"What did you say?" Al questioned.

"Nothing—no, nothing," he answered in an uncertain voice. It occurred to him: the adventure was exciting, he had his bear—a magnificent trophy—and what a story to tell.

Tilting the plane away from the precipice and lowering slowly allowed Don to jump the downed plane and slide in behind it to land. Tricky flying, but always a thrill when it was accomplished. Each experience made the next time easier; he grinned, pulling open the door and yelling out to them.

"You guys okay?"

"Boy, am I glad to see you, Johnson," the hunter's still-panicked voice called as he headed toward the plane.

Don laughed. "Yeah, I kind of figured you would be glad to see me about now."

Al pulled the bag over his shoulders, approaching slowly. "What the hell kept you?" he growled, grinning at his friend.

Their eyes cemented. Al's appreciation passed silently to Don.

IN MEMORIAM

Al Bontrigger, cover pilot, killed in a plane crash. Wasilla, Alaska, 1964

Snorting, Don's voice deepened. "Hell, I knew I wouldn't get no breakfast unless I came back for you. How bad is she?"

"Not bad. Gear's damaged, but we can pick up parts at Point Hope." Al paused, scratching his head as he thought about it. "Yeah, we can do it right here—she'll be as good as new."

"Okay!" Don growled. "Let's go and get some food. I'm starved."

Slim Gale hovers over a whale jawbone on shores of the Bering Sea.

Trapper Tim Okonek.

Left to right, cover pilot Harold McCready, Don and parachutist Steve Daniels.

Chapter 9

Russian Cub

Repairing the crash-landed plane on top of a mountaintop took a bit more time than was expected. Wind laced the spire which had refrozen, trapping the craft's skis. It had taken a long time rocking the ship loose, after which Al flattened a path for takeoff. Once the gear was stable, they put the fire-pots under the oil sump to ready the engine. Don got in and flipped the ignition—the sound of its purring raised broad grins. That having been accomplished, it was time to head for Point Hope.

Toward the end of that season, two engineers from Anchorage who had drawn polar bear permits arrived in camp. Each of them owned a plane and flew the trip tandem. After landing near the lodge, they were invited inside for food and coffee. Don liked them. Over lunch they made it clear they were greenhorns and would appreciate the guide's counsel.

"Look," Don offered pleasantly, "it's almost the end of the season. We've only got one more hunter due. Feel free to use my camp as a base."

For several evenings, while the weather was bad, they discussed the hunt. Don explained that they should wait for a good, clear day, fly toward Russia where there was more game, and look for larger leads. He knew they lacked experience on the ice and their going at all was chancy, but they seemed determined.

The following day Don and his cover pilot took off with the

new hunter. At five p.m. they returned to find the pair missing and both planes gone. Around six they heard an incoming P.A.-18 roaring over the camp. When it landed they realized it was the two engineers, a bit shaken and obviously glad to be back in camp. Don yelled, "Dinner's almost ready—come on in and let's hear this story."

"We're never going out over the ice again," one of them said. "We lost the other plane."

Expecting them to ask if he would help recover it, Don prepared to fly. "Where were you?" he asked.

"Somewhere near the Siberian coast. We were searching when the engine quit. Joe landed and I followed." The man's face paled and his gray eyes grew distant. "It was so damned cold. I figured the crankshaft was broken." A quick glance at his buddy confirmed the appraisal. They both shook disbelieving heads, not mentioning that the ice was groaning badly—tearing—and the wind screaming beyond description. "We got out of there fast." A crack in the voice indicated real fear.

"Come on. We'll get some parts and go back," Don offered.

"NO!" It was emphatic. "I'm never going out there again!" the owner of the lost plane shouted. Then, after a long, thoughtful pause, he added, "Don, if you find it, you can keep it." The hunter was white, still frightened by the experience.

After a good dinner, Don thought they might reconsider, but they were both adamant. "Look, I've only got one hunter here," Don told them. "At least let me take you for a good bear." They had killed one small bruin and had it in the plane. They seemed pleased at the prospect and accepted.

For two days the weather came down. Everyone stayed in the lodge, playing cards and resting by a warm stove. On the third day Don took them out for a successful hunt, and by the week's end the party departed for Anchorage.

Early the following day, Dick Gunlogson, Don's cover pilot, an Inuit named Gus Kawana and Don, flew out toward Siberia. The men reasoned Cape Lisburne radar might offer some advice.

Surely the pilots had made radio contact with someone during the emergency, and perhaps they had been observed on radar. It was worth a try.

Fortunately, the weather near Russia was clear. They searched for 60 minutes, burning up precious fuel, to no avail. Gus, who was with Don in the lead plane, suddenly yelled, "Don, turn right." Unquestioning, Don banked sharply and flew back some three miles. The hummocks were unending—continuous crusted gray walls of ice, and one open, flat area, where a lone airplane sat shivering in the wind. Loud shouts could be heard on the radios as both planes swooped low to land.

Outside it was bitter. As expected, the ship was icebound. It was late—there wasn't time to heat the oil, and the ice was too rough to tow the plane. "Let's get a good bearing on her," Don instructed. "We'd better head for Point Hope."

For the next few days they were weathered in. Meanwhile, Don and Dick pulled the engine from one of the Super-Cubs and put it in the back of the 180. When it was time, Gus and Dick crammed inside behind Don. The cockpit seemed overflowing with tools, tents, food, fire-pots and the engine, but at least the sky was clear.

Don skimmed ice all the way to Siberia, heading straight for the abandoned Piper; this time it was easy to locate. Moving rapidly, a tent was thrown over the cowling and fire-pots hissed into action as six hands busied themselves with the engine. Gus went to the Cessna, rummaging for a long time. Don called to him. "Hey, Gus, bring the fitting that goes from the carburetor to the sediment bulb." The Inuit came back empty-handed. Don swore. "All right. We better go back for it." The two men wanted to stay with the Piper. Seeing their faces, he argued. "Something might go wrong. It's too chancy. Hell, the weather could sour, or I might have a mechanical. Damn it, I'm not leavin' you two here on the ice."

Dick scrinched an eye. "The 180 is fast, and without all of the weight, you'll make it fast. We've got plenty to keep us busy— get goin'." He laughed.

Gus nodded stoically. Reluctantly, Don left, but the flight was filled with anxiety. After landing, he instructed the Inuits to work fast. Knowing his friends were helpless out there increased the tension. The Piper's engine was removed from his plane while others rushed to fill extra gas cans for the cover plane. Don hurried inside to locate the missing part; within 20 minutes he was airborne, roaring back to the "other side of the world." Certainly there was a good bearing on the plane, but the ice was breaking up and it was damned risky.

Hours later, approaching the coast, the pilot groaned after seeing how badly the ice had shriveled and mushed. Everything in the area looked different. He began to fly a grid pattern, straining hard over marbled sea, keeping a wary eye on his gas gauge.

After finishing their repair job, the pair had climbed into the cockpit, trying to stay warm in the wind-battered craft. Of course, there was no heat. Occasionally they would climb out and hop around on snow to get their blood flowing again. They were beginning to worry when they heard the sound of the engine. It was hard to hear along with the petrifying sounds of tearing ice reverberating across the Chukchi.

The ELT emergency beacon began its eerie cry—a ray of hope. The two men on the ice had heard his engine. They knew help was on its way, but Don was flying away from them. Dick was a good pilot and knew Don would figure out what he was doing. They had been together a long time. Every time the plane moved in the wrong direction, he would turn the beacon back on.

Turning and banking, the pilot searched lower, finally spotting the two figures eagerly dancing and waving below.

Within 10 minutes after landing, the motor roared to life mingled with cheers raised raucously in that desolate place. As Don raced out in the lead plane, he saw their smiles. The warmth from the new engine was filling the cabin, thawing numb fingers and toes.

Later, back at camp, Don took the old engine apart. It had swallowed a valve. By this time they had nicknamed the ship the "Russian Cub."

In June of that year, Don went to Anchorage and contacted the engineer to tell him the story. The grateful hunter signed the plane over to the guide; it was worth $12,000. Today Piper Super-Cubs are valued at $40,000. Flying the bush wasn't, and isn't, cheap.

Mishaps were often complicated. Many of the guides were good pilots, but the situations required special skills. In one case a pilot broke a ski on takeoff over the ice. His companion plane observed it and radioed that it was dangling. The hunters spent a long time hanging out of the plane trying to shoot it off before landing in Kotzebue. Finally, a hunter in the plane accomplished the task. The crash-landing on one ski was dangerous, but thankfully not fatal.

Planes were falling through the ice regularly, and sometimes disappeared altogether. Three fatal accidents were in blinding whiteout. To these incidents Don commented, "Some guys can see better in fog than others."

Gary Swanson, one of America's leading wildlife artists—himself a hunter and former taxidermist—said the following about Don: "Up until 1972 when polar bear hunting was ended, Don Johnson was undoubtedly 'King of the Ice.' "

Don felt confident as he landed in Kenai and taxied for the first time to a tie-down next to his own business. The sign was proof; sight of it drew a satisfied grin. He owned three airplanes and with the Russian Cub there would be four.

The Point Hope bear season had been lucrative. He began to speculate on the business of flying passengers. The ambulance flying wasn't working out. Most of the people were satisfied, even grateful, at the time of the emergency, but when it was over and they were faced with a hospital bill, they rarely remembered owing the pilot who flew them there.

He still worked intermittently for the oil companies and O.N.I., and there were numerous requests to fly engineers all over Alaska. The money was too good to turn down, and Don was enjoying a notoriety of sorts because of his flying skills. And since he was so good, the requests were now made with tact and with deference to his other interests. But doing both was becoming a problem.

While taking a well-earned rest and visiting with his family, he read and re-read the pile of letters from hunters. Word spread rapidly throughout the hunting fraternity, and Bear Lake was becoming a famous spot. Of course, there was also a rented sheep camp at McCarthy in the Wrangell Mountains. Most of the hunters eventually wanted the famous Dall sheep. Airplanes made all the difference, but the weather in the Wrangells near Harding Glacier turned bad as early as October, and Don kept those hunts short.

A snug two-room cabin now rested beside the Bear River. It was tight against the fierce Aleutian winds and could sleep six comfortably. They had also raised a flushing shed and an outhouse, and with any luck, that year he would build two more one-room huts behind the lodge facing the river.

Down Chain he was fast becoming a mentor to the Aleuts, as he had with the Inuit. There were always requests for flights around the fishing villages and supplies to be brought to his friends from the mainland. The sight of his airplane at the start of the fishing season elicited excited waves as he soared over remote fishing shacks along the coast. A quick radio message confirmed his greeting as he circled low and dropped anxiously-awaited parts or clothing.

Fishermen, as well as hunters, were requesting reservations. With more housing he could accommodate many more clients. That fact and the sporadic hunting would keep the lodge busy at least until he went north to Point Hope.

The hunters who were coming in were getting much more sophisticated, and Don could see the need for better housing, food and, of course, more interesting hunts.

Chapter 10

Trip to Burning Hell

While still at Point Hope that year, Don received a notice from O.N.I. announcing the start of operations at Homer. He was tired and looking forward to a well-earned vacation with his family at the homestead. The children—his son Warren and daughters Lori and Audry—were growing up. He would enjoy spending time with them and sitting down to the tasty regular meals which his wife was planning. Kenai was growing. For a week after his return the family entertained friends and neighbors who always looked forward to the stories which had resulted during the hunts in the arctic.

Don's desk was piled with letters from hunters answering the ads, but they could wait. The money made from flying supplies and for emergencies would be sufficient to build a small lodge at Bear Lake. Don had been planning it all winter as he flew over the ice.

Since 1951, when the government built the White Alice DEW Line Site at Port Moller, Reeve Aleutian Airlines was making regular runs to that port. It was a real boon to Bear Lake. Hunters could fly into Anchorage and grab a commuter down to Port Moller, just a 25-minute flight from the lodge. In fact, it was so convenient that business was increasing tremendously. Don could easily control the dates. But now, there was a real need for a building to house his clients who expected a little more than tents.

After a much-needed rest, he packed and drove to the end of the peninsula where O.N.I. housed the armada of pilots in a Quonset-hut dormitory. The pilot was happy; life was moving along very well, and the flying he did for O.N.I. was always diverse and interesting.

Shortly after his arrival at Homer, the ocean-bound volcano at St. Augustine erupted after being dormant for 30 years.

A camp had been established just below the cone at 700 feet. There were two men on it whose lives were now in great jeopardy

Rushing to the Super-Cub, Don took off, knowing Burt Johnson, one of O.N.I.'s helicopter pilots, wouldn't be far behind. It was 70 miles out to the spot and fortunately, the weather was good enough to see the volcano displaying its fireworks in the sky.

The company's radio issued regular information to the plane. "It's spewing lava and rocks down to ravines dangerously close to the camp. One man is seriously hurt. Better try to take him out first, Don," the operator said. "We'll have an ambulance ready."

Nearing the spot, Don banked toward the giant cone whose fury was being unleashed, sending smoke and debris up 12,000 feet. At close range it was a frightening sight. The lava oozing over the crater in two sections created a "Y" on the side just above and below the camp. Hot lava rocks, the size of automobiles, blasted free, rising unprecedented heights before crashing to earth. A series of tents in camp were already burning.

"It must be hotter than hell down there," Don muttered, as hot air buffeted the Cub. Lowering slowly, he landed about 200 feet from the tent on a 30-degree grade. It seemed an eternity, although it was only minutes, as he helped the radio operator carry the wounded man to the Cub. Don saw his fear and pitied the man who would have to wait for the G-2 to arrive. "He's on his way," he yelled. "I'll be right back. Hang on."

Racing the Cub to a turn, he took off downhill, sweating from heat and coughing as the acrid sulphur fumes engulfed the plane. Incredible noise from rapid explosions deafened him, reminding

Don of the cannon on the battleship in the North Atlantic and at Attu.

The man in the tail section was badly burned—his moans increased during what seemed an interminable flight. Back at Homer, ambulance attendants quickly removed the victim. Don leaped from the Cub and raced to the float plane for the return run. 'At least,' he reasoned, 'Burt could lift the operator with the chopper and return them to a safe spot on the beach. The way it is going, landing on the slope would be next to impossible.'

Burt's voice blared out of the speaker as the two men firmed the plan.

Up ahead the scenery was overwhelming. The men at the station had been setting fixed beams for navigation when the volcano errupted; they had saved a lot of lives. With any luck, this man's would also be saved.

Banking deep, Don landed in the ocean now churning from heat and debris being dropped from enormous heights. He taxied to shore and stopped just beneath the helicopter as they had planned. It was efficient. Outside the air was a blast-furnace as the Bell rose 700 feet to the camp. The noise mounted, causing the pilots to cringe with each explosion. It looked as if the whole mountain was coming down.

Burt lowered the chopper as Don edged out, clutching the struts and putting a foot on the skids ready to spring to the ground.

There was no visibility, only a pale veil of gray cluttered with ash. Outside the tents were burning. In the center of the compound stood the radio operator whose eyes were fixed glass. The look had gone beyond fear; sheer terror possessed him—a pillar of hot flesh waiting to die.

Don raced toward him.

Suddenly, Burt forced the chopper straight up as the mountain exploded with such force that the sides blew out. That absurd happening pulsed hot fear through both men, who were rooted and watching their last chance at life lift to the sky.

They were being asphyxiated from fumes in a putrid sulphurized atmosphere where the heat was indescribably intense.

Quickly, Don brushed past the man and ran into the main tent where he grabbed the Shoran electronics. It took two trips before he had all the equipment.

Back outside he could see Burt lowering just above his head. The operator stood frigid. "GET IN, DAMN IT!" screamed Don over the fray. It was as though he had not heard, but was in limbo far away. Just as the skids seemed within reach, Don pushed the helpless man into the cockpit, then effortlessly threw the equipment in behind. Climbing onto the skids, he clung in desperation, praying Burt would make it out of the burning torment. A rush of rancid air brushed his nostrils, but he grinned knowing they had a chance. The chopper tilted. Speed drew them out and away as deafening explosions reverberated, shaking the world and the sky.

Don flinched, gasping for air. Eventually, he sucked a breath which was cleaner, away from the immediate vicinity. It was sweet and life-giving—he gulped and coughed repeatedly.

In only a few minutes the skids bounced on the beach. Don dropped off, gazing with disbelief up at the spot where they had been picked up. Almost immediately, his eyes searched for the seaplane bobbing helplessly and moving further out to sea.

"Use the prop wash, Burt," he yelled, wading out into the hot surf.

"Yeah, I'll force her...," Burt answered, unheard.

The chopper blades whirred a roar, floating over the waves until it was above and beyond the light aircraft pushing it directly into Don's path. His sweat-covered body barely felt the water which was the same temperature, but exhilaration pulsed adrenaline into his limbs, and he swam toward the floats. Ash, debris and dregs of earth floated around; it was like swimming in a pumice bog. Climbing on board, Don laughed nervously. In seconds he flipped the ignition, swiping liquid on filthy cloth and swearing repeatedly—it had been unreal. The engine's purr was musical, bringing pure joy, as he felt the rush of floats bumping over the sea and carving a neat path through the waves. Finally, he rose over the ocean.

Now, for the first time, he could view the scene objectively. The cone had sheared away. A magnificent river of bright orange lava flowed straight down, disgorging St. Augustine's bowels. Gray air, where hot ash floated in giant billows, lifted thousands of feet.

The stench from sulphur still burned in his nostrils; he was hungry for a sea breeze. But there was one final act to complete. Turning, he flew back as close as he dared to the campsite. It was gone. "CHRIST!" he said aloud, as ever-widening eyes viewed lava oozing over the small plateau where the camp had been. Had it all really happened? It was a nightmare. He sighed, it was over; they were all safe and homeward-bound.

Newsmen were all over the field at Homer, waiting for the story of daring which had taken place out in the ocean. Don grinned broadly at Burt as they were questioned. They had been to hell and made it back, but Don was much more interested in another matter. Rushing to his room, he collected some of the camera equipment he usually kept in the plane. Then dashing out, he hurried to the 180. This was too good to miss. Back at the burning cone, his camera whirred. Later, when Don would show the film, people questioned its validity, saying no one could get that close. He laughed; he always did when he cheated death. He had thought for a long time that some unseen force protected him, and that thought would grow stronger in the years to come.

****

Winter came early in 1957. Don left for Point Hope with Dick Gunlogson after loading supplies in both planes. The first hunter was due in Nome within a week, and he wanted the camp ready and a plane waiting to pick him up. 'Besides,' he mused, 'I'm anxious to see my Eskimo friends—I have a lot to tell them.'

Don and hunter on the Chukchi Sea off Russia.

Chapter 11

Polar Bear Bonanza

All records were broken during the winter of 1958 in the North Country. A fury unleashed from the arctic brought 50-knot gales and whirlwind snow for weeks on end. Don left Kotzebue with two hunters headed for the Siberian coast. Since there would be only two hours of daylight, flying was carefully calculated.

Hours later, flying in the Alaskan darkness, the Super-Cub suddenly banked deep lowering close to the frigid sea. Headlights bounced too many shadows and could not be used. They were close to Uelen.

Al radioed, "Hey, Don, look at all those tracks. I've never seen so many."

Don's laughter sounded raspy mingled with static. "Yeah, hell, must be a polar bear convention up ahead. Let's pick out a good track and follow it."

They were eight miles off the Russian coast, and the spoor trailed inland veering west. After crossing the international dateline near Little Diomede Island, it was certain they were almost to land. Uelen Bay's 10-mile expanse, surrounded by lowland, had a narrow mouth. It was impossible from the air to tell where the snow-blanketed earth began and the icebound sea ended. The tracks were thick. Don whistled, telling his hunter, "There's a bonanza ahead. You'll get your pick of the litter."

85

Bolting upright, the hunter became excited. He had never been on the ice before. The trip from Nome, where the Anchorage flight terminated and where he switched to a bush plane for a four-hour flight, absolutely astounded him. There was no real preparation for the eternal darkness or the sterile earth below. The scene created new respect for the man at the controls and the Inuit who serviced the aircraft. He wanted a bear enough to tough out the climate and the frigid world it lived in. It was the end of the earth, he thought, a seemingly abandoned universe except for the white beasts who lived there comfortably. Listening attentively the previous evenings to Don's accounts of former hunts only whetted his appetite. Even as searing winds howled outside the comfortable camp living room, he had not been daunted. And now, almost in Siberia, his innards tightened at the prospect.

"We are inland about 10 miles," Don offered.

The hunter appeared mesmerized, only distracted when Don yelled, "Will you look at that!"

In the glare a great beached whale spread across the ice surrounded by white giants happily feasting. The plane roared in a circle. "I counted 18 polar bears," he yelled into the mike. Al circled to count again.

"Holy Toledo, Don, it's a real crapshoot."

"Let's go," the pilot answered, eagerly grinning over at the client and twisting the wheel. A powerful ascent pulled them up and away from the predators, being careful not to disturb what promised to be an unusual hunt. It would be a 15- to 20-minute hike before they finally approached the unique sight.

Leaving the plane's warmth shocked the hunter. It felt unreal. Hiking in cumbersome clothes kept them warmer. The guide finally called in a low voice, "Okay, pick your game."

There were two hunters. Eventually, selection was made; they set up the shots and fired. Two bears fell as the lung shots absorbed lead per Don's advice. Repeated volleys echoed across the bay.

The noise startled the bruins who set up a unified roar. Suddenly spooked and in turmoil, they lumbered away into hummocks and disappeared—their guttural cries melting into darkness until, at last, it was quiet.

Nature had provided a break. The ice in the bay was fairly smooth. Don waved, advising them to hurry back to the planes. They would taxi to their quarry then take pictures of the whale and their trophies. The added bonus was apparent in their faces in each photograph.

After the skinning, the foursome headed for Kotzebue. The wind was bad in an otherwise clear sky, and the homeward flight thankfully uneventful.

Four days later they embarked with another hunter, heading for the fertile bay where they knew selection was available. It wasn't usually that easy. Don was smug, feeling confident his hunter would go home satisfied with a good bear after having the rare opportunity of selecting it from a group.

The tracks were still visible soaring toward Uelen. Over-flying the entrance to the bay, lights pulsing ice, they picked up dog-sled tracks heading toward the whale. At the site, frozen blood indicated yet another kill. Don estimated it to be at least a day old.

They landed. Humping across irregular hardness before cutting the engines, he instructed the hunter to stay warm while he set up the catalytic heaters and covered the cowling. The wind was fierce; they bent into it, trudging along as fast as they dared, only slowing when they approached the whale.

The mammals were busy gouging its great, torn carcass. The hunter actually gaped. In his life he never hoped to see anything like it. He was in Russia privy to the enormity of an Atlantean mammal whose blubber was being ravaged by 20 giants. Bulging eyes absorbed the scene wanting to remember every detail. What a great story to tell his hunting club.

The guide nudged him impatiently. "Did you pick one out yet?"

"Huh? Oh, no. Just." He seemed embarrassed. "I'll get to it," he choked out, raising his Weatherby quickly, then slowing for accuracy.

The delay was understandable. Don couldn't deny it. He

guessed the guy just didn't understand how bad the weather could get in 10 minutes or how dangerous the long flight home could be.

Seconds later a huge male fell. Leaping up, the hunter actually danced as a horde of bruins hurried off growling in unison toward cover. Al skinned the bear while Don and the hunter raised rifles, straining to see in the darkness. They were in jeopardy. The bruins weren't far away, and the enemy had been scented. A lookout would be maintained all the way to the planes. The skin was heavy and trailing blood as they dragged it across the ice.

Once they were aloft the hunter leaned over curiously. "What's beyond the bay, Don?"

"A little Russian village, not much." Staring over, the pilot recognized his client's eagerness.

"You want to see it?"

"I sure do."

They banked low over the village making two passes. It looked peaceful enough—just six tarpaper shacks emitting smoke from tin chimneys and not a sign of life.

Snapping pictures and calling over, the hunter thanked him in excited tones.

Hours later, they landed beside the Kotzebue camp. An Eskimo flusher came out with two friends to tie down the aircraft and take the skin to be salted.

Al was hungry and anxious to get inside the warm cabin for a hot meal. They always ate hearty. Tramping in the cold used up energy fast.

Four days later, just before the last hunter was preparing to leave, they heard a plane come in. Minutes later, two stoic-looking men entered the lodge and asked for Don Johnson.

"That's me," Don answered, looking a bit restrained.

"Were you hunting in Uelen a few days ago?" one of them asked officiously.

"Who are you?" It sounded curt.

The taller of the two flashed a badge—"State Department." The statement sobered the group.

Forcing a smile, Don asked, "You want some coffee?" A wary

eye sneaked a glance at the badge which he had no doubt was official.

They nodded and sat down while Don brushed past Al clearing dishes. He poured two mugsful. Al smirked, waiting for more conversation and banging a few pots noisily.

It was suddenly silent except for a newspaper being rattled out of a parka. "Did you happen to see this?" the agent asked, extending it.

Examining an article circled in red, Don saw, "U.S. polar bear hunters take game from Russia" in bold print. Calmly, he put on his glasses to complete the article, then he looked up over slightly-lowered frames. "So?" It was soft and matter-of-fact.

The official's voice rose dramatically, "3903-Zulu—that's your number, isn't it?"

"Yeah."

"Russia has a 17-mile limit. Don't tell me you don't know that."

The atmosphere grew tense. Al banged a pot loudly on the cast-iron stove, causing the men to stiffen.

"Oh! Right," Don spat out, "and it's three miles over here. That's just great—you guys make the rules, RIGHT?"

The agent's eyes narrowed into slits, creasing at the corners. "If you get into trouble over there and get caught, don't expect us to bail you out."

Standing, Don banged the cup down. "If I get into trouble, you guys would be the last people I'd call for help."

It was silent while they glared at each other for a few tense seconds. Then the men stood silently, buttoned their parkas and left, leaving Don and Al smirking at each other.

The guide shrugged mischievously, "Well, hell, Al, I never actually admitted it was us—now, did I? Besides," he cracked, "those bastards wouldn't help us anyway."

They laughed hard and prepared to pack up the camp. It was time to head back to Point Hope.

The season ended successfully. Don was anxious to return to the homestead after receiving a letter from home saying he had mail from the State Department. It piqued his curiosity—for all the world he couldn't imagine what they would want—except he thought he must be in some kind of trouble. As it turned out, the letter was a request for a hunt involving a VIP.

Chapter 12

The King of Nepal

J ust prior to statehood a monarch visiting Washington, D.C.,
requested to see the grandeur of the territory of Alaska. His
visit was immediately arranged.

Naturally, guests of the State Department receive red-carpet
treatment, and the sight of the King of Nepal deplaning with much
pomp and an elaborate entourage, created quite a stir in the then
still-primitive town of Anchorage. Extraordinary news coverage
followed, much to the chagrin of those who would later deal with
him. And since the King wanted to be taken on a hunt and Don
Johnson was the guide who was selected, the matter became an
embarrassment. The news articles called the trip an expensive
boondoggle.

Their initial meeting took place in a hotel. Don reacted with
his usual nonchalance but was polite. When he was told the King
wanted a goat, sheep, caribou, moose and bear, he grinned, confidently knowing that would be no problem. An interpreter
explained the King's enthusiasm had been heightened by the sight
of Don's trophies in glass cases in the Anchorage air terminal.
By now Don wanted the man to have a good hunt.

Nepal lies on the southern slope of the great Himalayan Range
between Tibet and India. The range includes part of the world-
famous Mount Everest, the rest of the peak being in Tibet. It
is a constitutional monarchy ruled from an exotic palace in the

capital city of Kathmandu.

The country is narrow and small by any standards—a little over 54,000 square miles, some 530-miles long and 150-miles wide at its extreme. However, this cylinder of enormous mountains is home to over 10,000,000 people of whom 500,000 live in the capital. Former rulers isolated their subjects who are mainly Hindus and Buddhists.

It was understandable how impressed the King was with Alaska's almost uninhabited vastness. When he was informed by a State Department aide of the 586,000 square miles which contains 20,000-foot Mount McKinley, the King smiled and said he knew, and then added, "Please do not forget the Yukon River which is 1,400-miles long." Later, Don learned the King knew of all the game and where they were located.

Once the man had donned his hunting clothes, he looked just like any other client with the exception of a swarthy complexion and sloe eyes whose retinas sparkled like black opals. Don rather enjoyed watching enthusiasm rising out of those eyes as they soared over the Wrangell Mountains where the King saw his first Dall sheep balanced on a rocky crag.

After his client shot a goat and a sheep, the party headed for Bear Lake.

The King turned out to be quite capable with a gun. That fact, and that fact alone, impressed Don who spoke sparingly to the man. Don's language was his airplane with which he exposed the beauty of his land from 150 feet where his guest had a superb view.

After five days on the tundra, the King had acquired beautiful trophies which were being flushed and readied for the taxidermist in Seattle. The guide made it quite clear, through the interpreter who was constantly in attendance, that the animals would be treated with special care and finished with the same perfection as his own.

It was fall. Signs of an early winter were beginning to cover the Aleutians as a cold front brought deep snow and bitter wind.

Near the end of what had become a successful hunt, Don flew

north to Mother Goose Lake. The area is remote and raw, and game sighted there is often quite large. About 80 miles out of King Salmon, a cannery and fishing port, Don spotted two big caribou doing battle. He pointed below. Swooping and banking, he roared directly over the ungulates, now in mortal combat. His passengers were captivated. As the Super-Cub circled the area, Don searched for a place to land in rough terrain, now under several feet of new snow. Landing would be too dangerous. After explaining that fact to the interpreter, Don saw disappointment on the monarch's face. Eventually he left the scene, moving toward King Salmon's airport for fuel, after which they flew back to the site of the battle.

Returning, Don lowered and pointed to the scene. The animals, who were wounded and had become hopelessly horn-locked, lay dying in a ravine. Seeing the King's frustration, Don said to the interpreter. "Tell the King he will have those racks, I promise."

Several days later, as the party prepared for departure, the King murmured something in parting. The interpreter nodded effusively, then approached Don. "His majesty wishes to remind you of your promise."

Don cocked his head and smiled broadly, saying, "Tell the King I will keep that promise." The pair then shook hands as a look of gratitude passed between them.

Later when Don was asked what he called the monarch, he answered simply and with a smile. "I called him King; that was his name."

Spring came early. Don flew into Bear Lake to ready the camp for the first hunts. He had not forgotten his promise. Taking a hunter to Mother Goose Lake was actually out of the way, but after recounting the story the hunter was anxious to go.

Finding the animals who died together was easier said than done. Early rains and melting snow had changed the terrain tremendously. Don frowned, circling for a long time, then enlarging the pattern. Eventually, he spotted the bones which had been ravaged by wolves. Later, after finding a landing area close to the racks, they hiked to the spot and claimed the antlers.

Don was excited. He could only imagine how pleased the ruler would be to have double racks, hopelessly locked, hanging in his palace game room. Of course, they were the topic of conversation that evening at dinner as Don told his hunters the story.

It was over a week before Don could get to a phone. A fierce storm pelted the Aleutians, and the phone at the cannery was out. Finally, he made the call. He asked for the man in the Foreign Service Office at the State Department who had been to Bear Lake with the King of Nepal. As the guide explained the situation, he expected the men on the other end to show some enthusiasm. Instead, there was a long pause and finally he said. "I'm sorry, Don, the King of Nepal died a short time ago."

Don felt real remorse. Only a true hunter would understand.

The double caribou antlers are still at Bear Lake, a memento to one of their famous guests.

Chapter 13

A European's Hunt for a Guide

For Baron Eltz a hunting trip into the Alaskan wilds would be the culmination of a lifelong dream. Several years before Alaska achieved statehood, he had begun his inquiries. The deduction that civilization would ultimately spoil an untamed preserve seemed reasonable and, being a thoughtful man, he made a systematic effort to peruse the outfitters who regularly advertised in sports magazines. The process of elimination finally reduced the field to one—Don Johnson of Kenai.

Alex Eltz lived in Salzberg, not too far from the game preserves which he had learned to hunt as a boy. Being a professional hunter, he had great respect for the formality of those hunts, but was longing to become acquainted with the place called Alaska and the people for whom he held great curiosity.

The plan included a three-week stint. It seemed sensible to allow a week's hunt for each of three animals. The first of these was the Dall found in the Wrangell Mountains; the second would be moose on the Kenai Peninsula; and the third, the brown bear which he would hunt on the Aleutian Chain. But, before any of this would occur, the Austrian decided to interrupt a business trip to Japan and spend a weekend flying with the guide. Given the weather of Alaska and the remoteness of the terrain, his plan was to make certain he was in capable hands.

At this juncture, Don had been contracted to ferry engineers all over Alaska. He had been flying for over 20 years, and his skills were apparent to the European after just three, long days in the bush plane. They would start flying at four a.m. and remain aloft past 10 p.m. The man emerged from the experience totally satisfied after filming moose, sheep, bear, volcanic craters, whales, Indian villages and the tidal flats, where the float plane almost became stuck as the tide went out.

In one village, fishermen bragged that they had killed six brown bears the day before from the deck of their trawler.

The maiden trip was the first of many visits to that part of the world. Alex and his wife, Bubby, returned seven times to Bear Lake and Kenai, and in the course of those years an ever-lasting friendship developed with Don. Later, they would send their son to the Aleutians during the summers completely under Don's tutelage.

On September 27, Don landed at Naknek uneasy about his floats. Alex noticed Don's attention to them after each takeoff—he was trying to see if spray was escaping once they were airborne. After the next landing, they used a tree trunk to lift one float out of the water. Two compartments were completely flooded. The long gash was hammered straight with a rock, then once the metal dried, it was sealed with aluminum cement. Aluminum really can't be welded, and water still seeped in, so a pump was carried at all times.

The mishap turned out to be a bonus. On the second evening at Naknek, they overheard a conversation between three Indians in the bar. Don leaned toward the natives, winking at the Baron as he listened. "They've seen a big bull near Big Creek," he murmured.

"Would it be fair to use that information, Don?" the gentleman asked.

Grinning before he spoke, "They care only about the meat. They don't even think about trophies."

Nodding thoughtfully, the European listened more attentively.

"See, they wouldn't hunt an old bull—the meat's too tough. Besides, if they say he's big, after all the moose they've seen, you can bet it's a *big* one."

The client brightened. "Well, in that case, let's go first thing tomorrow."

Don pursed his lips, concentrating and wrinkling a frown. "Yeah, there's just one problem. Big Creek is not the best place to set a float plane down—but. . ." The deep voice trailed off, and Alex could see acceptance rising in the guide's look.

In the morning Don riveted a patch on the damaged float, using the U.S. Fish and Wildlife Service crane to lift the plane. It was a beautiful morning, but later in the day the usual storm clouds rolled in over the valley where the creek flowed its torturous route. The one bonus they needed was evident—the water level was high enough in spots for the float plane to land.

For a while they spotted game trails and several medium-sized bulls. As they flew further north, the wind was in their favor coming southeasterly, allowing for slow flight 100 feet above the ground. They were 40 miles upriver before the sighting occurred.

Two bulls faced each other across the river. They were both good-sized. The Baron laughed excitedly. In fact, he couldn't decide which one he liked better. Don flew off, not wanting to disturb them. And although the choice was difficult, they decided the one on the right bank was easier to get to. The European glassed him. "He's got an abnormal point about a foot long under his left palm, Don," he exclaimed loudly. "I'd recognize that rack again anywhere in the world."

It was evident the European was excited and more than pleased at the size of the game. Wanting him to have a good hunt, Don roared upriver searching for a place to land, and when they found one, it wasn't deep enough. They skimmed along for 100 feet grimacing at the sickening sounds of gravel scraping the floats. The engine raced until they hit deeper water and ultimately, an eddy, where they tied up to some alder roots and a paddle sunk deep into the mud. The Baron was quoted as later saying, "Other pilots would have become hopelessly stuck in the mud, but Don raced the engine forcing the plane upstream."

Once on foot, the two men climbed a low ridge which ran

parallel to the riverbed until they came to a promontory high enough to spot the animal. A cow, browsing close to the group, started toward them. Stiff, cold winds clutched the earth, pushing the hunter down into the valley. He knew from experience that moose weren't too smart, and if he was able to approach quickly—and get a shot off—he would likely prevent them from moving off before he had his quarry. In open country he would have stalked; it was preferable.

After the animals moved into the alder and willow thicket, their view was badly obscured. A limping cow sauntered closer. They could only hope the bull would follow. About 100 feet away, she picked up their scent, turned, and trotted downriver. The bull was alerted; he listened cautiously, then followed along. Not masking his disappointment, the Baron said, "I only saw those unusual antlers for a moment, and then the champion disappeared."

Don hurried away. Anxious to get to the bush plane, he motioned for the hunter to follow.

Within an hour they were aloft and had spotted their prey.

The animals were crossing a loop, moving downriver all the while and covering a lot of ground.

The Super-Cub droned on for a long way downstream while Don was calculating the animals' speed. This time, he explained to Alex, they would hike a ridge, moving back toward the game and directly into their path. For an hour-and-a-half they searched without a glimpse of the big bull or its limping companion. Finally, at a point where the river was close and beneath a bluff, they spotted the antlers. Hunching down, the two men remained motionless for a long time. The moose seemed to be watching them in typical fashion, not realizing his rack stood high above his cover. Suddenly, a black form moved to the left. The Baron raised his rifle, staring into the scope to fire, when he realized he was viewing its face. At 100 yards the enormity of the beast started him; he actually gaped.

Within seconds the moose emerged. Two rapid shots followed, hitting him broadside. The hollow pops they heard indicated a hit, but the giant trotted away. "Hit him again, now" Don yelled. The hunter fired, missing the target at 200 yards. They both glassed from their vantage point, following him through the willows until he disappeared and then, swam the river.

Dejected, the hunter sobered, watching his trophy climb the opposite bank. For an instant the moose reared up and, as if in slow motion, dramatically fell backward into the river. A huge geyser erupted as 2,200 pounds hit the water.

The Baron sucked a deep breath, captivated and feeling frustration.

"You shot off one of his antlers," Don said dryly, flinging out the remark as they raced toward the river. Puffing hard and tearing toward the spot where the moose had fallen, they saw nothing. Alex quickly pulled up the binoculars tracing the path where the animal must have gone. It was floating with one rack showing.

"You shot off one of his antlers," Don repeated.

For a moment the hunter believed him. Without hesitation, he raced along the bluff trying to keep up with the hulk floating in the torrent. It was useless.

"Wait!" Don yelled. "We'll go get the plane."

A long time later, soaring downstream, Don convinced Alex that the current was running too fast for them to land. They could see the game wedged against a sandbar in the middle with both antlers standing straight up.

Heaving a sign, while casting a suspicious glance at his guide, Alex grunted.

Don laughed out loud.

The incident would be better in the retelling and had cemented what promised to be a wonderful friendship.

Don had spotted a boat miles upstream. He suggested they go get it.

They were both excited; flying low over the craft they saw an outboard attached to the stern. Alex only hoped there was gas in it. As they landed, they saw a tent on the nearby bank and a young man emerging.

After explaining the problem, Don asked to borrow the skiff.

They could see the young man was sympathetic before he spoke. He told them there were two blades missing from the outboard motor, but otherwise they were welcome to it.

The young man's partner returned shortly to find an endless discussion in progress regarding the salvage operation.

The Baron watched, amused. He had come to know his Alaskan guide; well-aware that he never gave up, he was waiting for Don's ingenuity to surface.

"Loan me the boat and you can keep the meat," Don said.

The boat was used to act as a drag on the floats of the seaplane, slowing them enough to allow pontoons to float them to the kill. Once they attached it to the boat, the men turned on the vibrating engine—one blade working—and dragged the moose ashore.

They had tied ropes to the animal's legs. Then, prying it loose from the sandbar and drifting to a shallow spot, they brought it in. It took all four men, pulling to their limit, to move it. Once that was accomplished, satisfied grins arose.

For the Austrian the feat was tantalizing. This trophy had a 78%-inch spread with 220 points. The world's record for 14 years was 250 points.

The campers fixed coffee, and as they drank it a deal was struck. It was agreed that the campers would deliver the rack and cape to King Salmon on their return trip. Don would have already arranged for its shipment to Europe for taxidermy. In return for the favor, Don would buy blades for their outboard motor, which he would fly back that day and drop into the camp.

Within hours the pilot fulfilled his part of the bargain. The sound of the engine alerted the campers who raced out onto the bank and waved. The promised blades had been packed into a cardboard carton with long, cotton streamers tied to it. The Baron opened the side window on the second pass, prepared to make the drop. Air pressure forced it out of his hand—it thudded against the tail section and dropped into the river. Fortunately, the water was shallow. Don stretched out of his window to inspect the fuselage, scrunching a grimace and finally, breathing a sigh of relief. There was no damage. A broad grin passed between the guide and hunter as they flew out.

On their second trip, the Eltzes became enamoured of Don's camp cook, Howard Wilson, who possessed an unusual sense of humor.

Alex hated other people's sandwiches. "They are never the way I want them," he said emphatically as he delved into the luxury of Hungarian salami, several dozen small cans of pate-de-foie-gras, as well as many boxes of triangular Swiss Tiger cheese.

The cook accepted this fact good-naturedly. He and the Baron had been acquainted since a previous hunt. The Baron decided that Howard's claims of having a chosen name of Howard Wilson were as false as his Scottish ancestry. The truth, in fact, was that his mother was Eskimo and his father a half-Russian by the name of Miskihov, which reminded Alex that Alaska's history included Russian dominance.

One of Howard's greatest attributes was his cleanliness. The food he prepared was quite good, and it was reassuring to the clients to see his constant polishing and cleaning efforts.

During the war, Howard served in the Aleutians on Attu. It was there he learned to fear bears. He also was an alcoholic and was wont to disappear for four- to six-week binges after which he would severely chastise anyone who even drank a beer. Altogether, Howard was a character who radiated charm and amused the guests.

His personal life was rather unusual also. He ran away with his best friend's wife and married her, although she was never divorced from the first husband. Admittedly, he had a son in Paris but said he had him annulled. At one point the Baron asked if he had been married in the Russian church to which Howard replied, "NO. It was the Salvation Army."

The "little lodge" as it came to be called, had only two rooms. Everyone slept comfortably in one room. During one hunt, Don awoke to hear a strange voice saying, "You son-of-a-bitch, I told you not to die there." Don sat up abruptly. Howard was having a nightmare and kept repeating the phrase. Later, out of reach of the cook's hearing, he explained to the clients what was happening.

It seemed that during Howard's bouts with John Barleycorn he was almost always arrested and put in jail, after which the Alaskan jailers would put him to work burying bodies. Indigents, who came to an ultimely end in that part of the world, had to be put into a frozen potter's field. Suffering painful hangovers, Howard would be put out on rigid earth to dig the graves. Standing alongside the crude boxes, Howard passed the time of day telling the departed what he thought, and when he slept the memory of that experience had a way of surfacing.

The trips to Alaska were full of hardship, but the Baron and his wife lived each hunt with enthusiasm, Cold, deprivation, fear of storms and lack of creature comforts never daunted, but rather enhanced, the adventures. They learned to savor each visit. Their faith in Don was untiring, both in the air and on the ground. In an edited diary presented to the guide by his friends in Austria, the Baron depicts the many situations endured with complete tact and the expected Austrian affability—an interesting analogy of reactions from someone who had obviously lived such a sophisticated life.

The Baron's extraordinary knowledge of the geography of Alaska was in itself impressive. His advance studies of the country, its game, its people and economics, allowed for a profound exposure to the new surroundings.

Photography was an avocation even more pronounced as he acquired close-ups of bears digging for ground squirrels and taking a chance of exposure without fear. Later, in the comfort of his Austrian fireside, he would relive those trips, completely categorized and captured on film, with tapes explaining the moments he and Bubby had shared.

He wrote: "Limiting gear became a constant problem; the bush plane's size prohibited much equipment. It was helpful that a cover plane assisted—two pilots, two machines—in case of difficulties which arose constantly." It was obvious that bush pilots of Don's caliber knew instinctively how to use ingenuity during emergencies. "Skis and floats were often damaged during takeoff and landing. We were often arriving in camps where few people had been for long periods of time. All this and more was endured without complaint.

"A good-sized roll of adhesive tape was a staple after the first hunt. Shell boxes, even wet, don't fall to pieces when wrapped in such tape. A small piece of tape over the muzzle of your rifle is very useful in the rain. You never take it off. Don't worry, you shoot it off. Raincoats get rips. Here again adhesive tape will do the trick. My sleeping bag developed rips, and feathers were all over the place in the morning. Good outfitters will provide sleeping bags—good—put yours inside the offered one. On a cold night two covers are welcome."

Alex Eltz was a true sportsman. He felt airplanes detracted from the hunt, but given the distances to preserves, he knew they were a necessity.

The Baron arrived on one trip with a special gun, which he had used on a hunt in Africa, Since it had belonged to Theodore Roosevelt, it was treated with respect. Don examined the stock, rubbing his fingers thoughtfully over the dead President's initials inlaid in the wood. Meditating for the moment, he thought what stories it might tell if that were possible. It intrigued the guide that it was to be used to get a bear in his camp.

The next day they took the boat to the end of the lake. In a valley just beyond and after a good morning's stalk, they spotted a bruin moving slowly up the ravine just below them. Don nudged his client. The Baron had seen the animal; they moved to an alder clump and crouched. Eventually, the British-made .450 exploded. He had used 500-grain softpoint shells, and Don was waiting for the animal to fall. "I missed," the Baron groused.

"Shoot!" Don yelled, puzzled that he hadn't fired again.

The startled animal reversed and fled down the cut in the mountain, disappearing into thick brush below.

"Why didn't you fire?" Don asked sharply.

"If I miss at that distance the bear deserves to live," the Austrian cracked and turned away. His voice had a ring of finality. They took the boat back to camp. On the way the client made several derogatory remarks about the gun—to which Don laughed.

Back at camp, the guide began to razz his friend, claiming the gun was accurate. "It's the hunter," Don repeated. And for a while, it seemed amusing to keep up the goading.

Finally, the Austrian balked. Getting up, he moved outside onto the tundra. He was carrying the weapon. When they were just beyond the buildings, Baron Eltz took off his custom-made Jaghut and threw it out onto the bog. Cocking an eye, he handed the rifle to his host, who was trailing along curiously. "I challenge you."

"Are you sure you want me to do that?" Don asked with a slanted grin.

"I'm certain," was the firm response.

Don scoped the green felt and fired, hitting it dead center.

Turning, he heard a grunt and watched the hunter turn and stride defiantly back inside. The Baron never used the gun again.

Moose

Of the three species of North American moose, the Alaskan *(Alces gigas)* is the largest. Kenai Peninsula holds records for bulls weighing up to 1,800 pounds, standing sometimes 10 or 12 feet in length and with his head up as high as 12 feet.

Escaping extermination by man, they migrated north just ahead of woodsmen denuding their habitats. A century ago there were no moose in Alaska.

Not exactly the beauty of the animal kingdom, nevertheless he is almost a must for any game-room collection, is displayed prominently and is always mounted eyes front.

His Roman overhang nose can strip bark and pull down limbs to nibble. A ropelike hide drooping from a big neck acts as a drain for water after an aquatic feed. They have been verified as diving as deep as 12 feet to reach succulent vegetation. Beady, red-rimmed eyes seem inadequate, but he is blessed with extraordinary hearing and a keen snout.

Antlers start in April, reaching full growth by July when racks begin to harden. Imagine developing 50 to 90 pounds of bone in less than 14 weeks! The rack is his crown, used to establish breeding dominance rather than a defense system. It takes 10 years to establish maximum-size racks, after which regression takes place and odd conformations often grow. They have been known to live up to 17 years under ideal conditions, but that is rare.

Splayed feet on bog make them fairly easy to track as ungulates lumber through swamp or boggy muskeg.

In late September he can be heard giving off a cacophony of seductive grunts. And, if one is calling with a birchbark horn or some new electronic gadget, be prepared. Even wolves fear the rack. In the rut he isn't particularly pretty, having urinated in his scrapes and being covered with mud, but you won't mistake the odor.

Moose meat is barely affected by the rut, as is most other game. It is tender, tasty and has considerably lower caloric content than similar cuts of beef. In fact, comparable servings will vary as many as 400 calories and, if properly prepared, will taste the same. Since Don insists no running animals be shot for food, tough meat is never served at the lodge. It is his opinion that adrenaline flowing in the animal toughens the flesh.

After the war, a group of steers were left on a remote island in the Aleutians for testing in that climate. They had gone wild and were eating just what other game does. They now tasted like moose and were hunted just like wild game. Several times a year Don flies to the island, selects a couple of steers, shoots and skins them, thus adding another taste to Bear Lake's already adequate menu.

Since hunters rarely take moose meat home with them, Bear Lake regularly grinds up several thousand pounds of it. Local residents receive whatever is not used in camp.

Butchering this particular animal is done in a special way. Don cautions hunters to cut it clean. "Do not cut it up with a band-saw as you would beef. Take muscles apart; they run in different directions. Then, cut it across the grain. I don't like moose roasts and would rather cut meat into steaks. The rest is made into mooseburger and sausage."

To cook the steaks he first fries diced onions in bacon grease or beef tallow. They keep beef tallow on hand at all times because game is so lean. The steaks are then fried in a very hot pan and seasoned to taste—Don uses salt, pepper and Accent.® Hamburgers are fixed much the same way.

Ribs are washed and put into a pressure cooker, which is heated to about 15 pounds for a 10-minute period. Take them out and put them in a large shallow pan, cover with barbeque sauce and bake at 375 degrees for 45 minutes.

Goulash is always tasty on a cold day. Dice up moose steaks and a half-pound of bacon. Fry them both in a hot pan until tender. Drain off grease. Cover meat with tomato juice and add a can of whole, peeled tomatoes and one can of mushrooms. Add diced parsley and onions, then boil for five minutes. Add one package of spaghetti or macaroni and salt and pepper to taste. Cook slowly until pasta is tender and flavor has been absorbed.

Alaska boasts herds of upwards to 150,000 moose, and these are the largest members of the species. They do well at survival and are usually not hard to approach unless harassed. Of course, on the Chain where food is plentiful and vast tundra prairies available, they reproduce well and often. Their reproduction capability is impressive. For instance, on the island of Newfoundland off Eastern Canada two pair of New Brunswick animals were introduced in 1904. Today the herd numbers some 35,000 animals.

Moose consume 50 to 75 pounds of food per day, depending on their size. They forage mostly on water plants and browse, rather than graze. Considering their size, they are exceptional swimmers and have been known to go over 12 miles.

They need a low annual temperature and truly belong in the North. Long legs make them quite mobile in deep snow where deer become yarded-up, which prevents feeding.

The ungulates are so tough they do well even against wolf packs. However, the predators seem to know when the time is

Don with his own trophy, 1968.

ripe and have been known to do well against big, old bulls, calves or yearlings.

Only the extinct Irish elk ever equalled the Alaska-Yukon moose, and then only in antler size which spread to 12 feet.

Don says that about September 15 they go into rut. "You can usually call them right to you from as far away as one to one-and-a-half miles. I've done it many times. It really helps instead of packing them. The most important thing is to call only once or twice, then be very patient and wait until they get close. Then I rub some dry sticks on a bush once or twice. You might have to wait an hour or more. Patience is the name of the game. Again, go for a lung shot.

"The biggest moose I ever guided was the one I helped Baron Eltz get. It is in a museum now and was a beauty. It measured out at 79½ across."

Prince Louie in Wrangell camp with his trophies, 1963.

Baron Eltz with record moose.

Chapter 14

Bear Hunt with Prince Louie and Mrs. Eltz

In the early days at Bear Lake accommodations were sparse. They had finally built a two-room lodge which contained double bunks and minimal cooking facilities. It certainly surpassed the former tent arrangements, being adequately heated with a space heater which was comforting against the Aleutian winds.

Sophisticated European hunters never had a problem with deprivation. To these people, hunting was a profession which they took seriously. The game, a once-in-a-lifetime proposition, had to be studied carefully before acquisition. If it took more than one hunt to find the right animal, so be it. The planning produced excitement, stalking even a larger thrill, and the decision to shoot always involved much finality followed by a somber ritual.

On a fall hunt in the middle '50s, Baron Eltz returned to Bear Lake with his wife, Bubby, and a cousin, Prince Louie of Liechtenstein. The Prince, an enormous man whose stature seemed greater under green woolen attire suitable for the Alps or the Austrian preserves, was excited about the Alaskan hunt. During his European hunts he was always driven in a motor car to the private gaming area after which the hunters were taken to a great hall for the celebrated game feast. He had, however, spent long evenings with his cousins in Austria during which they discussed at length the rugged Alaskan hunts and the man they called Don. However unlikely their clothing, each man respected the prowess of the other and was eager to begin their search.

The day was unusually pleasant as they stowed their gear in Don's river boat which was docked in the Bear River adjacent to the lake. When the winds were down, they maneuvered the eight miles easily, heaving toward a white glacier sandwiched between black volcanic mountatins. On the sloping foothills in the center were clumps of tangled alders in which the bears found cover. The Alaskans named it Bear Patch.

Prince Louie rested comfortably against the gunnels in the bow, chatting to his cousin's wife in explicit German.

"He thinks it is beautiful here," she told Don.

"It is, isn't it?" he answered smugly, knowing full well that there was no other place on earth to surpass it. In fact, as Don steered the outboard toward the south lakeshore, he was enjoying an immense pleasure. Up ahead, and on nearby islands, lived the greatest carnivores in North America challenged only by exceptional specimens of polar bear. His hunter would revel at their size. It was much more satisfying to guide a professional to his trophy, and although they could communicate only through an interpreter, the look on his face would suffice. The Prince would have a good hunt.

'It is as they described it,' Louie thought. 'A place unlike any other—vast and rugged where animals roam free.'

Excitement mounted as they neared the shore and felt the bow run aground.

Don's frown troubled Bubby. "What's wrong?" she called over the outboard engine.

"Those clouds forming over the glacier don't look friendly."

She glanced around, looking up at an ominous sky. Wincing, she turned back, staring anxiously at Don's serious face. She nodded and asked, "Is it a problem?"

"No, it'll be fine," he grinned. Jumping out of the boat he dragged it onto the beach and anchored it.

They walked up the riverbed to a place where the creek

widened to about 50 yards. The mountain rose behind them, its sloping edge dropping to the thicket nearby. Then they moved off, crouching quietly for about an hour as Don glassed.

Finally, he saw him—a big male lumbering along the shallows looking for salmon.

They were upwind of the bruin. Don backed up, raising his rifle as he nodded to the Prince to shoot the 10-foot bruin.

It was cooler now; a stiff wind had risen around them. The alders flailed; their rustling sang with the wind and the steady splash of the animal's feet.

For the Prince, the moment had come. His experienced fingers caressed his custom-made 8mm German rifle with a Mauser action. He fired an angling shot which penetrated the heart and lungs, breaking the opposite shoulder. As the beast fell, he dropped into the creek with a thud. Suddenly, it was silent except for the increasing sound of the wind as they waited patiently for the game to move before approaching cautiously.

Bubby grinned broadly, watching Louie's expression, knowing his joy while listening to the flawless German outcries.

When they approached the beast Don knew there would be a ceremony. While his eyes scanned the horizon, the Prince picked a twig from near the animal's mouth and placed it inside. Then, stopping again, he took a leaf, dipping it into the wound; he stood at attention before saying, "Veis Man Heil." Bubby moved closer. Reaching for the bloodied leaf and waiting for the Prince to bend down, she placed it in the twisted silk cords of his felt fedora. Then, Don and Bubby offered congratulations. There was honor in tradition, and this particular one added spice to the hunt. Don was, however, glad it was over. The animal had to be skinned which would take at least 20 minutes, and the lake was fast becoming unnavigable.

Louie was all smiles. As he turned toward Don, his thanks coming in alien sounds, he suddenly paled and began to grunt from quivering lips—"Ungh! Ungh!"

Don and Bubby were preparing to skin the bear. "Ungh— ungh." the Prince repeated, looking directly behind them. The pair reeled in the direction of his fear. There were six bears in assorted sizes fairly surrounding them. Louie's grunts increased.

Bubby, who had been here before, reacted immediately, flailing her hands, while laughing lightly at first at the big man's guttural sounds. Don's amusement filtered out until they were both dancing in the creek, laughing loudly and shooing the bears away. Their splashing frightened the bears who fled one by one, leaving an astonished Louie, embarrassed, in the creek.

Finally, they rough-skinned the bear for a full mount, which Louie was already picturing in his game room. Eventually Don folded the huge paws inside, rolling up the hide and motioning to Louie to help him lift it down the creek bed to the boat. Bubby collected the remainder of the gear, following behind them still snickering over the comic scene. 'Louie,' she thought, 'will enjoy this story as much as anyone—at a later date.'

The wind consoled her as she entered the boat, thinking about how much she enjoyed the place and the people. She was a good shot and, after many trips to Alaska, fairly used to the rugged camp. 'The Baron' (her husband, who was resting at the cabin), 'will love hearing it,' she thought. Don caught her smile as she conveyed the gaiety they had just felt.

Experience taught Don the lake could be treacherous. It was boiling by the time they shoved off. The Prince's size deleted poise; he was clumsy in the small boat. Once they shoved off and were being tossed by the huge swells, Louie stood up.

Don's voice became edgy as he yelled, "Tell Louie to sit down."

Bubby sobered, calling instructions to the Prince who was obviously very uncomfortable still teetering in the bow.

The outboard roared noisily, pushing them out along the edge of the lake. Even with the enormous weight in the boat, it tossed perilously. Mrs. Eltz clutched the gunnels from a perch in the bottom of the boat while Don's experienced hands guided the outboard along the beach as close to shore as he dared. The wind was lacing the boat, forcing it against the waves where cold spray poured over their bodies. It took all of Don's strength to hold onto the boat.

Suddenly Louie stood up, just as they hit a big swell. The boat rose; turning sideways it began to flip over. Louie hit the water first, followed closely by the bear skin and the gear. Don and Bubby leaped away from the wooden hull as it crashed into the lake. The water wasn't very deep, and within a few minutes the party dragged itself out of the water tugging the bear skin and rifles behind them. Now soaking wet, they shivered under the raw wind.

"This thing weighs a ton," Don yelled as he helped Louie drag the skin onto the pebbled beach to spread it out. When they stood up, they saw Bubby clutching her arms around her, shivering noticeably. Don hurried into a nearby alder patch carrying a five-gallon gas can which he squirted into the wet branches. After a few minutes and several attempts with his lighter, the wood caught, flaming into a light burn which eventually grew.

"You'd better strip down and try to dry some of your clothes, Bubby. Tell the Prince to do the same," Don instructed.

Within an hour they were fairly dry and considerably warmer, except for Louie whose thick woolens had matted and become heavier. His knickers clung wet to flesh where cold, damp wind whipped against them.

While the threesome were drying out, Don gave serious thought to their plight. 'The motor is wet and cannot be used, at least for now. The storm has increased and from the look of it isn't about to let up; we're a long way from the lodge, so, I'll let them decide.' Staring at them for a moment, he began to speak.

"Well, we've got three choices: we can stay in here for the night; or walk to a cabin I have about three-and-a-half miles from here; or we can try to make it to the lodge." The question hung in the air. Finally Bubby discussed the matter in German with the Prince.

He could see agreement. "The Prince and I want to try to get to the cabin, okay?" she asked politely.

"Yeah, good idea," Don answered. 'At least, there will be food and blankets there for them,' he thought, 'so it'll be all right.'

Wind chill rose above the alders, outside of which there was no protection and where pelting rain would delay their movement. They were miserable for the time being, but at least warmth and food was an eventuality. That thought drove them up the foothills against bone-chilling Aleutian winds. It took four hours of grueling climb; they were soaking wet, tired and hungry, especially Louie, whose woolen hunting gear had absorbed double its original weight.

Night had already descended when they reached the spike camp. Don went in first, reaching around in the darkness for familiar objects, but to no avail. Nothing was where it should be, he thought, and suddenly he realized that he could hear the lake spattering outside as though it was right beside him. "Strange," he muttered. Finally he located a lamp without a globe which he quickly lit.

As the light filtered around them Bubby's startled voice yelled, "Oh, God!" Two of the walls were completely gone. The stove had been battered beyond description, the canned goods were all bitten in half, and the furniture was broken, slung against walls into splinters. Another wall just alongside of them was ripped open where the bears had exited.

"It looks as though they were just here," she exclaimed, staring, shocked, at the rubble.

Don wanted to laugh, it was so absurd, but he didn't dare. It could have just happened, he didn't really know, but it also could have happened weeks ago. 'But hell, it's spooky,' he thought.

Bubby was angry. Turning toward Don, her wet face flickering in the lamp light, she snapped, "You knew it, didn't you?"

His blue eyes widened, becoming glassy, hiding the hint of embarrassment lurking in their corners. "No! I swear I didn't know it."

"I'll bet." The pique rose around them in the disheveled room while she explained to the Prince in an alien tongue.

Don listened to the ire, feeling remorse about the long night ahead. Louie couldn't complain, at least, not to him. He watched intently, waiting for her wrath.

"I want to leave," Bubby demanded. "It's not safe here."

"Okay, we'll go right now," Don said firmly, and started out. The walk to the lodge was a rough one. They would have to go inland, skirting the Rock of Gibralter, which jutted far out into the lake. It was a dangerous trail, past miles of alders where the animals were bedded down. He knew the bears were accustomed to nocturnal strolls, but there was one advantage—they were too big to be quiet. Don was tired, but particularly alert.

Halfway back, Louie began to grunt again. A hefty sweat rose in his face as he plodded along, carrying the weight of his huge body burdened under sopping woolens.

As Don led the way, he heard an animal just ahead of them. "Louie, quit that gruntin'," he said aloud.

Bubby was just behind Don. "What's the matter?" she called.

"Get Louie to quit sayin' that—he's callin' a damned moose!"

Bubby moved up closer to Don. "What are you talking about?" she asked in exasperated tones.

"Well, listen to that."

"Oh, my God," she said, half-frightened, "there are two Louies!"

"Two Louies, my butt," Don bellowed. "That's a moose!"

Louie was 20 steps behind them, dragging along, sweating and grunting loudly—"UNGH! UNGH! UNGH!"—louder with each step.

The last grunt was all it took as the huge moose crashed through the alders wide-open and not 15 feet away.

Anticipating the charge, Don already had his rifle tight against his shoulder. There was barely time for two shots.

"I don't want to kill you," he mumbled, "but I sure want you to change direction," as he squeezed the trigger, putting a bullet right over the moose's horn, followed immediately by a second shot which exploded in the wind right in front of them. The crashing sounded like an elephant crushing wood until the bullets skidded his rack, turning him instantly. It lasted only a few minutes but took their breath away and frightened Louie out of his wits.

Suddenly, it was quiet. The wind rose above them until their

Prince Louie of Liechtenstein at Bear Lake, 1963.

fatigue, coupled with tension, brought about nervous laughter as they continued through the brush. In a little while they opened onto the beach where they could see the lemon slices of light coming from the windows of the lodge.

Later, the Baron got out of bed and fixed them a brandy while they gave their account of the adventure. They jumped into bed, sans the wet clothing, happy and tired and still snickering. Prince Louie had bagged his bear and had an adventure which would be told and retold in Austria.

Chapter 15

Fish and Game

Before spring hunts it was customary for Don to fly in and ready the camp for the hunters. Bear Lake was still in its primitive stage. The two-room cabin which had been built seemed diminutive against the enormity of the surrounding scenery. The cabin, two one-room huts and flushing shed were the only buildings within 50 miles except for a small Fish and Game shed a mile upriver. The Department of Fish and Game determined escapement policies for Alaskan fishermen from the fike net count taken at that spot.

Ferrying groceries and liquor in preparation for the bear hunt, Don turned inland from the sea and followed the path of the now-swollen river which led to the lake. Lowering to 150 feet on the normal route, his eye caught five brightly-painted planes moored at his tie-downs adjacent to the cabin. Then he saw movement around the Fish and Game cabin.

"Those bastards," he uttered angrily, just as the floats hit the water sweeping past the red bunalow and racing upriver. Almost immediately after shutting down the engine, he leaped out onto the bank and tied up the float plane. Then, running inside, he snatched up a long fish knife and hurried out to the runway. The act was swift as the knife sliced the tow lines. He smirked. The orange airplanes floated into the tearing wind moving upriver. Standing very still, Don listened to the shouting taking place upstream as someone noticed the airplanes being tossed about .

Don went inside and fixed a pot of coffee—and waited. It took all of 10 minutes before four of what turned out to be nine employees raced down to the door of Don's lodge and began their demonstration.

As they reached his doorstep, they were goading for a fight. Listening for a moment, the pilot slowly opened the door and stood rigid in the doorway. The voices were simultaneous fury. One of them yelled, "Who do you think you are? You can't do that!"

"I just did it," Don snarled. "Tie them up there again, and I'll do it again."

In a split second, the agent reached for the gun in his holster, hesitating before he drew it.

One blue eye squinted before Don said in a hard voice, "If you pull that thing, you'd better kill me good, 'cause if you don't I'll go in that cabin and get a 30-ought-six and put a hole in your gut right now."

The man blanched. He backed down, walking away as the others continued to argue vehemently.

With that, Don raised both palms in the air, quieting them. "Now, get your asses off my land and don't ever let me catch you tying down here again." Turning on his heels he went inside and slammed the door.

Much later, he noticed the bright orange fuselages on their aircraft tied to alder bushes far up the tundra. He had spent an hour considering the matter and getting angrier all the while. Statehood had brought many rules, and some were pretty hard to swallow. He had scratched his lodge from the earth with his bare hands and his airplane, and nobody was going to ruin what he had built. His anger drew him to the float plane in rapid strides. When he was airborne, he could see the group moving across a bog, spilling white flour in a straight line to make a landing spot on what they considered to be their land.

It was a short flight to the cannery over a mountain where he landed on an airstrip paralleling the Bering Sea. Rushing into the office, he hurried toward the phone, ignoring the employees who were calling greetings. Within seconds, he had placed a call to the governor in Juneau.

Fortunately, it was an hour later in the capital. Governor Egan was just enjoying his morning coffee and asked who was calling. Upon hearing his friend's name he smiled, completely unaware of the rancor waiting on the line.

The governor stiffened as he listened, but was patient waiting for a chance to interrupt. "Now, Don," he said sternly, "wait just a minute. If you'll give me a chance I'll take care of it, but promise me you won't take any action for at least four hours."

Reluctantly, Don capitulated. "All right," he answered in a terse voice, "but four hours and no more." By then he was calmer and mumbled a "Thank you."

'After all,' he reasoned, 'here were nine freeloaders on $26 per day per diem, flying airplanes on tax money, who took off and landed all day long to go scavenging on the beach. Then, they had the audacity to feel they were entitled to encroach on his game preserve.' He remembered telling Governor Egan, "Those goddamned orange planes in and out all day will frighten my game away."

"WELL, OKAY!" he said out loud as he climbed into the truck to go back out to the runway. I'll wait four hours and no more."

Hours later, Don's ears picked up the sound of big engines overhead. Rushing outside, he spotted a Goose lumbering toward the lake where it splashed down and raced toward the west end. It was moving too fast. The pilot was obviously not used to the plane and definitely unfamiliar with the lake. Sarcastic laughter erupted as Don's accustomed ear listened to the racing engine trying to disgorge itself from the mud. "He'll burn the damn thing up if he keeps that up," he offered to a companion.

There were five men in the plane. Glassing the group, Don saw that they were officials from Anchorage, who at this point had an eight-mile hike up the lake to the lodge. He went inside and put on another pot of coffee.

The party finally arrived. They were asked inside and offered a chair and a hot mug of coffee. Two were ranking officials: the head of the Federal Bureau of Land Management and the director of the Alaskan State Police. Once they were seated, Don listened attentively. It was obvious the governor had kept his word. They were polite if not condescending. At one point in the conversation, the director said, "Listen, Don, we can't have this sort of thing. You've got to be cooperative."

Don stood, reached for the cups in front of them and swooped them from the table. The glare returned to his eyes. "Get your ass out of my lodge," he shouted. The official recoiled. He stood. "Look! We came here to make a deal." It was rhetorical.

"No deal," Don growled. "Except to get that bunch of monkeys off my land."

"But, we have no other place to send them," the man answered half-pleading. 'After all,' the director thought, 'the governor wanted this—it was political.' Suddenly, he smiled, awaiting an answer.

"That's your problem," Don told him.

"Well, is there another place in this area?" he asked, almost too politely.

"Yeah—Hoodo Lake."

"Does it have a good airstrip?"

"I land on it every day," Don grinned, knowing only an experienced bush pilot could make that landing. He wasn't going to make life any easier for these people, and he definitely wanted them out of the area. It was obvious they meant to take liberties with his preserve.

The official's eyes cemented. "Fine." One of them said, "Then, we'll have them go over there." They all seemed happier. The solution was really very simple; cooler heads had prevailed.

After they left, Don's ire was receding. He groused at the incident, thinking how much it had cost the taxpayers. The Goose had burned out an engine, so they radioed Anchorage for two bush planes to take the officials back the next day. The five airplanes had flown, collectively, 20 times that day, and those bureaucrats were all being paid. He fixed a bourbon. Things were changing, and he didn't like it. The life they had was just right. He had fought all the battles alone, and he would probably go on fighting.

A knock on the door distracted him, and he went to open it. Outside stood the head of the Bureau of Land Management.

"What do you want?" Don growled.

The official's face softened before he spoke. "Listen, Don." It sounded apologetic. "I've heard both sides of this story, and I'm on your side."

Taken aback and submerging some of his hostility, Don stared suspiciously while the man continued.

"I feel the same way as you do." He paused, glancing out toward the lake, lowered his voice and asked, "Do you think I could stay here tonight?"

Laughter curled out. "Sure. Come on in."

They talked amicably, had dinner and a few drinks and went to bed.

In the morning a plane flew in. It was bright orange, unmistakably an Alaskan Fish and Game plane. Hiking up his pants, Don walked out to the runway to intercept the pilot.

The agent who had threatened Don the day before stepped out. He seemed reluctant to speak and kept staring at the back of the lodge where a visitor had parked a helicopter.

"What do you want?" Don demanded.

The man shuffled, staring down at his boots before he spoke. "We've had one of our planes crash on the damned little runway at Hoodo Lake. We need that chopper." He paused and took a deep breath. "I mean, it's the only way," his voice trailed off.

"The hell you do," the pilot answered firmly.

"Look, Johnson, we really need it."

"I don't give a damn—you're not gonna get it."

Turning, he climbed aboard the plane and without further argument, flew out.

Later that day, the charters arrived to ferry the officials to Anchorage. It had been a difficult three days. Everyone, including Don, was glad it was over. Feelings of disgust, remorse and

Hoodoo Lake on the Aleutian Chain.

humiliation ran rampant in just about everyone, except the lodge owner who had convinced the federal agent that he needed permission for mile-runways that crisscrossed. It was a far-sighted request.

Later, Federal Aviation requirements would allow two-mile access for approaches to mile runways. Now Don had two-mile protection around his hunting camp on two sides. The rest of it was river, lake and mountains. His hunting lodge sits alone and protected to this day. The entire fiasco had paid off. There was one rub—he had become the target for future harassment. The battle would last for some 20 years, and even today its mention raises a cold, hard glare from Don.

Being tough had been necessary to survive, but a way of life was beginning to erode. It would come in the form of government interference. There would be the Mammal Act, which would stop polar bear hunting; the sheep preserve would be taken away; statehood had already arrived and with it would come more legislation and restraints; and finally, free men would allow laws against firearms.

Chapter 16

Gillpin

Not long after the 1963 episode, a game warden named Gillpin arrived at Bear Lake—cocky, strolling into the old lodge wearing an Australian bush hat pushed jauntily to one side over a bearded face. Two plump thumbs poked into an oversized hand-tooled gun belt which contained a small pearl-handled revolver.

Don was entertaining two of his favorite European hunters—Baron Eltz and his wife, Bubby. The Eltzes were regular clients now, having been to Alaska many times. And while they were Austrian royalty, their appreciation and prowess in the outdoors and their friendship made them exceedingly welcome.

Gillpin's air irritated the guide, who listened attentively as Gillpin asked officiously to see licenses and tags. Producing the necessary paperwork, Don's jaw tightened over clenched teeth while cold eyes hardened into a glare settling on the man.

The game warden snatched up the papers, chewing diligently on a wad of tobacco and slowing at each glance. Finally stopping, he spat on the floor.

A fury rose. Don grabbed Gillpin by the scruff of the neck and the seat of the pants, dragging the startled man out to the lake where he threw him in head-first.

The Eltzes rushed out, alarmed at first, then breaking into gales of laughter at the comic scene.

The game warden rose out of the glacier water like the Loch

Ness monster. Flailing, soaked, humiliated and enraged, he raced toward the orange Fish and Game plane and flew out.

Of course, the incident grew larger in the game warden's officious mind with the passage of time. There had been other incidents. This statehooder had to be dealt a severe lesson.

Long after the Austrians' departure from Bear Lake, Gillpin became a frequent visitor to the lodge. The increasing trips were to make certain Johnson's hunters were not in violation. Don was careful, only further evoking Gillpin's ire, but the warden was patient and consistent.

Getting used to the rules had been hard enough, and Don had been at it for a long time. The state was so rigid about tags and licenses, etc. It all seemed so foolish in this remote place, yet he knew they had targeted him.

In the fall of 1964, Don had completed a successful bear hunt for a southern gentleman from Tennessee who was delighted with his hide. The flusher was salting it in a small shack behind the old lodge while inside Don prepared a bourbon as a toast to a good hunt. Laughter echoed out of the lone building as the hunters relaxed, sipping at their drinks, smelling a moose roast baking on the cook stove and considering their good fortune. Don's clever stories, embellished and witty, strengthened their growing camaraderie.

No one heard the Fish and Game plane land. They were surprised when Gillpin pushed open the door, breaking up the party, and started shouting an accusation.

"There's no tag on the bear skin in the flushing shack." His face glowed with triumph.

Don's blue eyes grew steely as he listened; a rosy glaze appeared under his ruddy skin.

The gentleman from Tennessee apologized profusely, jumping to his feet and exiting to his room. He was flustered as he returned, offering a camera case which protected the promised bear tag.

"Here, Mr. Gillpin. Ah'm sorry, suh," he said in an exaggerated, repentant southern drawl. "Ah'm afraid Ah thought Ah'd lose it. You surely understand?"

Gillpin snatched it, glaring.

Don's deep voice rose evenly, "Give the man back his tag."

The game warden launched into a long dissertation on the law, commanding everyone's attention except Don's. Moving quickly to the wall, Don took down a .30-06 which he cocked and laid on the table.

"Do it!" Don demanded.

"No!" the warden replied emphatically.

"Give the man back his tag." Don's voice was gravelly, unrelenting as his hand drifted toward the gun.

Gillpin eyed the guide, blanching. "All right. Then I'll have to take that hide for evidence."

It became deathly still. Suddenly Don shouted, "Listen, Gillpin! You take that hide to Cold Bay, freeze it and send it to Jonas Brothers in Seattle." The deep resonance grew harder.

"If anything happens to that man's trophy, I'll have your ass. You got it?"

As Gillpin departed, carrying the evidence from the flusher and headed for the plane, Don stood spreadlegged on the runway, rifle in hand, glaring. Gillpin's steps quickened.

A week later Don was called to Cold Bay. A summons had been filed.

There was a storm raging over the stark community. Blustery Aleutian winds battered the metal Quonset-hut as they entered the hearing room. The hearing officer was a plump female magistrate whose current amour was the game warden named Gillpin. The Australian bush hat was unusually positioned as the game warden leaned toward his lady love. A slight, satisfied sneer melted between the beard and teeth, watching Don's entrance. Supported by two of his hunters and a pilot, the foursome approached the bench. One of the hunters was a lawyer who, concealing that fact, promised aid but cautioned Don to remain cool at all costs.

"Are you Johnson?" the magistrate asked with rancor.

"Yeah," he answered curtly.

It was cold and still in the large metal room. Hostility heightened as the judge banged her gavel. It echoed, causing them to stiffen, startled.

"You three are excused," she said, eyeing Don's friends and waving one hand. The men reluctantly moved out, glancing back at the lone figure before the bench. Outside, they left the door ajar and bent close to hear the proceedings.

"Mr. Johnson, you are guilty as charged," the judge said in a loud voice. "Bond is set at the usual $2,500." As she concluded she squinted one eye, continuing with a slanted smirk. "You know I could make it $5,000."

'Battle ax!' Don thought, pursing his lips and remembering the lawyer's caution. Biting the inside of one cheek and feeling a slight exhilaration, he said evenly, "I want a change of venue."

Determination flooded the fat face. "No." Her sharp eyes flashed to the game warden.

The door flew open, and Don's lawyer raced up, yelling, "You cannot refuse this man a change of venue."

It took the judge by surprise. Her gaze widened, questioning his apparent knowledge and confidence and causing consternation.

"I am a lawyer, your honor, and Mr. Johnson's friend. He is not only entitled to a change of venue, but you cannot exceed the $2,500 limit on bond, which you have already stated is customary."

A slow acceptance filtered through the judge's eyes. She was nonplussed, acquiescing reluctantly, silently, and removing the smirk from Gillpin's arrogant face.

For a long moment there was only the sound of the wind against the metal building.

"Can I give you a check?" Don asked politely, looking dour, but impish.

The judge's shoulders rose as smugness became apparent. "We only take cash."

Four heads converged while nimble fingers groped for wallets. A comic scene ensued as they emptied the leather, counting and recounting. When that was accomplished, satisfied grins were passed and the blood money placed on the bench. Most people would not have been able to come up with the sizable fine, but they were hunters used to greasing palms in order to move coveted trophies out of countries. Don resisted a smile as he placed the money on the bench. A cold glare drifted to the game warden who looked a bit chagrined.

Months later, Don appeared in Superior Court in Anchorage flanked by his lawyer.

Gillpin, wearing his usual costume, strutted to the stand after the jury was empaneled and took the oath.

Following preliminaries, Don's lawyer questioned the official.

"Mr. Gillpin, did you tag the evidence you took from Mr. Johnson's camp before you sent it to Seattle for taxidermy?"

Gillpin squirmed in the chair, resisting Don's gaze and answered, "Yes."

"Well, Mr. Gillpin, isn't it Alaskan law that no hide can be shipped out of this state without a tag?"

The judge cocked an eyebrow before turning toward the game warden who was momentarily mute and whose color suddenly had faded. Finally, in a faltering voice he answered, "Yes."

The lawyer continued. "I have here the reputed tag which you say you used." He flashed it in Gillpin's ashen face.

"Your honor, I'd like to enter this into evidence. It has never been used."

The judge banged his gavel and said, "Case dismissed."

A murmur rose. Gillpin stood and fled down the aisle.

Don rushed up to the bench. "Your honor, where can I get my $2,500 back?"

"Down the hall, Mr. Johnson, the first door on the left." He smiled softly and nodded.

Gillpin was fired and left Alaska. At last report, he had joined the ministry and was practicing martial arts in the Orient.

****

When Don returned from Anchorage, he found a letter from Alex Eltz saying his son Peter was on his way to Kenai. Don had to leave for camp but left word for Peter to wait at the homestead.

Two weeks later, Don picked up the young man at the airport.

Peter had been well-schooled in what to expect from the Alaskan by his parents. He was, however, a trifle shocked when Don's first words were, "Get in the plane." After loading more supplies and seeing Peter's questioning glance, Don added, "You can sit on the lettuce crates in the back."

During the first week, Peter was sent to Nelson Lagoon to aid a schoolteacher who had obtained a fishing permit and was residing in a shack on the beach. The lady was being harassed by a marauding bear. Fortunately, Peter was a hunter—he had been well-trained by his father on the Austrian preserve.

On his first night in the small shack, the bear pummeled the door of the house and entered, renting ferocious growls. The young Austrian jumped up from the cot where he had been sleeping, grabbed the gun and finished off the Brownie with one close-range shot. The somewhat-shocked schoolteacher collapsed in tears and promised eternal gratefulness.

On the following day, she encouraged Peter to join her on the skiff to pick salmon from the nets anchored on the beach up the Nelson River. Peter was agog. He only had been in Alaska for three days, and things seemed to be happening awfully fast.

It was a blustery day, and the tossing boat rapidly rocked him into seasickness. Peter also was finding the salmon slippery as he hurried to pull them out of the nets. It appeared the speed with which his work was accomplished was being carefully monitored. The schoolteacher, who had obviously forgotten his heroism of the previous evening, began to taunt the foreigner for his clumsiness.

Turning slightly green from nausea and becoming increasingly agitated, Peter's fingers slid off the salmon which popped up and back into the sea. The schoolteacher's voice raised over the water as she yelled, "You are no help at all!"

Just then, the Fish and Game plane landed on the beach, and the warden hurried toward them. Peter was too preoccupied to notice; besides, he had no idea what it was all about.

Eventually it became evident that the game warden was quite upset and was talking about him. He wrote out a ticket and handed it to the schoolteacher, saying, "You know the penalty for fishing without a license."

Peter was in shock. He only had been in the state less than a week. He was dealing with a man who never smiled, who put him into a shack to sleep with a woman he didn't know and where he had shot a bear out of season. He was seasick, homesick, and now he had been arrested.

Minutes later, when the news of the Fish and Game plane reached Bear Lake, Don was airborne. Circling, he yelled to Peter to walk up the beach where he would pick him up.

Peter struggled through the next week while he was waiting to be arraigned. Don's comments at meals included, "I wonder how you'll like Alaskan jails?" and, "I thought at least you could stay out of trouble for a week."

The young man was beginning to think Don was the worst man he had ever met. His experience prior to this time had been limited to private schools in Austria and summers on his grandmother's New York estate.

The Baron wanted his son to become a man, and Don was going to accomplish it for him. However, the schooling seemed to be a crash course.

Don and Peter flew to Cold Bay a week later. Peter was sweating even though the weather belied that fact. The magistrate was Don's old friend, Gillpin's lady. They stood before her looking very restrained at which time the officer used everything in her legal bag of tricks. At the termination of the lengthy dissertation, Don pulled out his wallet and forked over $500. A gavel signaled the end of the unpleasant discussion.

They were silent going back to the plane as Don glanced over at his young helper and said in a dour way, "Hell, Peter, why didn't you show the game warden your driver's license and speak

German?"

They both started to laugh. Peter's slow sniggering grew into raucous belly laughts. It was the start of a lifelong friendship which exists to this day. Peter was well on his way to becoming a man.

The Austrian was extremely intelligent—just inexperienced. It didn't take him long to learn Don's ways and reciprocate. He had a good sense of humor and, like his father and mother, was very pleasant.

Don was strict about people working. He told both his son, Warren, and Peter to get a boat and start fishing. They had to pay their way in camp.

Warren directed them up the bay to where Don had an old skiff anchored. It was leaking badly, and it seemed to Peter they spent more time bailing water than fishing. After two days the boys were exhausted but had caught very few fish, and they knew Don soon would be asking questions. Everyone else was coming into the cannery daily with huge catches. Payment would be made at the end of the month, and the boys were ashamed as they unloaded their fish on the dock.

On the following day, a storm pelted the Bering Sea. Peter and Warren were out in the leaky boat which was listing badly. Battering waves washed over them, they were soaked to the skin, in danger of sinking and had lost all of their catch. Warren started to swear. Yelling over the wind, he shouted, "Let's get the hell out of here, I'm finished with this."

Getting back to shore was another matter. They almost lost the boat and were sopping wet when they crawled into the deserted army barracks in the cove. Warren built a fire, and they dried their clothes. Suddenly, Warren's face lit up. "Say, Peter, I know what we can do."

Of course, Peter was game for almost anything at this point. He listened attentively as Warren explained the Fish and Game had fike nets on the Bear River. Every morning, as the wardens slept, the fike nets filled with salmon.

Warren had been flying for only a year, but he had been taught by the best pilot in the Aleutians; besides, he was his father's son. The whole idea smacked of treachery, and Warren wasn't feeling too benevolent toward the officials anyway. A pact was made.

At 3:30 a.m. the boys crept out of their cottage and slipped down the Bear River on foot. The night before, in darkness, they had rolled two oil-drums down the pebbled beach and stashed them in the reeds, out of sight. It was becoming light, but they knew no one would be up. They were quiet as they approached the Fish and Game cabin. Within half an hour, they had filled both barrels and were confidently rolling them out of view of the red-and-white cabin.

After breakfast at six a.m., they headed for their fishing site in the plane, making one stop farther down the beach where they filled the tail section with fresh fish, which they later dumped into the skiff.

By the end of the month, Don was really impressed with the amount of money they had made. But there was hell to pay when he overheard a radio transmission from the Fish and Game cabin complaining about the lack of fish in the fike net every morning. Don put two and two together, had a good laugh and then called the boys to the table in the dining room for a good dressing down. His last words were, "No money—no food—suit yourself."

Warren and Peter had a month to go before the season ended and Peter was to return to Austria. They had made quite a bit of money, but were practical and didn't want to spend it. Peter was determined to go home with a big bank account. He had been sent to Alaska with just his plane fare, and it was now a matter of honor to go home with a fat wallet.

Flying the next day, Peter observed the seal rookeries below. "Say, Warren," he said in a rather offhand way, "seal skins are bringing a good price in Anchorage; I heard Don say so." Warren cocked his head and grunted—then the idea took root, and Warren dove on the volcanic rocks below. There were hundreds of them. "I can't land close to where they are," he yelled over the engine.

Later that night they formulated a plan. Warren would fly low and Peter would hang out of the doorless Super-Cub with a baseball bat. Of course, it would take some doing. They had no luck on the first few tries, but after a bit it worked. The seal skins brought $150 per pelt. By the end of the season they were several thousand dollars richer. Don just shook his head when he learned they hadn't been fishing at all. It was too late to chastise the pair and frankly, he thought, the idea showed real ingenuity.

Unfortunately, the young pilot was unaware of the tides in that area. Don said later, "The tides race back in there with a fury—he could have lost the plane and drowned—I'm glad I didn't know it."

Times were different in those days, and seal skins were in much demand. The method of killing the animals had been used for centuries. Warren had been on the Chain since he was a small boy and learned to accept the survival skills he had observed. All the while, he was sharpening his flying skills and would later become a successful bush pilot.

Chapter 17

Airplanes

Much of the intrigue surrounding the hunts was due to the use of Super-Cubs which were flown low and could land in unlikely places.

During Don's long career, there have been some 45 planes in the fleet. At least 12 were totaled—prey to winds sometimes of hurricane velocity. Sudden storms would catch pilots unaware and send the ships cartwheeling across the tundra. A few were lost in the river. One slid into the glacier river nose-down through splitting ice and froze there. Don tore down a nearby outhouse and used the planks to pry it loose, thus salvaging the ski plane.

Whatever had to be done to survive and protect the lifeline, was, as Don came to know the planes in a special way. And what appears to be a devil-may-care attitude is actually constant diligence beneath a stoic exterior, while years of skill make the feat appear incredibly easy. Strife toughens this quiet, tenuous man, but his ingenuity ultimately saved hundreds of thousands of dollars of valuable equipment and many lives.

Some say Don wears the airplane.

Once in early summer while flying a client to Cold Bay to catch a flight for Anchorage, Don landed at Nelson Lagoon, a fishing village 45 minutes from the lodge. There were two men waiting. The passengers turned out to be fishermen returning home at the end of the salmon season. Midway through the flight, the elder of the two tapped Don on the shoulder and asked, "Say, are you Don Johnson?"

The pilot grunted, "Yeah, why?"

"Hey, that's great!" he answered with a broad smile.

Don repeated, "Why?"

"Well, there have been three really famous bush pilots in Alaska. Flying with you today caps it. Now I can say I rode with each of you—hot dog!"

The other two, Bob Reeves and Don Sheldon, had died, leaving Don Johnson as Alaska's greatest living bush pilot.

The trapper-guides who work at Bear Lake, Tim Okonek and Slim Gale, once revealed, "Eighteen seconds from the lodge kitchen to the air with a full cup of coffee on the dash is Don's record."

No one who flies with him is without comment.

Mishaps, sometimes caused by carelessness, make the pilot really angry.

While bringing a hunter in from a mountain spike camp, Don spotted a fox on the runway. He pointed it out. The client couldn't wait to land and was out of the airplane in a flash. In the excitement he fired his rifle without proper aim, and the bullet exploded into the Super-Cub's wing.

Don's eyes widened as he exclaimed in harsh tones, "Goddamn it, you shot my airplane!"

His 45-year love affair with airplanes often prevented him from selling them, even when it would have been expedient. At this writing he owns 20, which include: Cessna 180s, 185s, Super-Cubs, Aztecs, a Widgeon, a Navajo and a little Pitts which he uses for skywriting.

The Grumman Widgeon has sat in the Kenai hangar since it was salvaged from Nash Harbor on Nunivak Island, where it had crashed and sunk in a remote marshy lake. During a routine flight in 1960, Don spotted it and made plans to raise the fuselage and repair it.

Don set up a repair team which included Peter Eltz, the Baron's son, who was 18 at the time; Warren, Don's son who was 16 at the time; and mechanic Dick Rinc. Their seaplane was stuffed full of tools, supplies and camping gear. They landed and taxied to an abandoned Aleut schoolhouse where they could get in out of the weather.

Lifting the fuselage, which was completely submerged, wasn't going to be easy. Don and Dick gave the matter much consideration before deciding what materials they would need. Whatever they came up with had to be collected in total and ferried a long way. It was at least 350 miles from the camp to the island. There was no way to call a store or drive to a nearby junkyard for a part. They decided to use huge innertubes which would inflate to six- or seven-feet high. A gasoline generator was available along with a compressor with a long hose whose clamp could be released from the innertube's stem fairly easily.

At the site, they went into the water and attached the deflated rubber tubes to the Widgeon's vitals. Once that was accomplished, inflating the tubes was easy as the generator's steady thumping hummed in the wind.

Eventually, the Grumman floated to the surface as silently as the Phoenix emerged from the ashes. Its crew cheered as they watched the silver fuselage oozing water while flashing and bobbing.

The gear was miraculously undamaged; however, one pontoon bore a deep gash and its tanks were full of murky water. Dashing into the lake, the men strained to pull it up onto the beach. The boys had already prepared tie-downs and were quick to anchor the plane with long ropes. No one wanted to repeat the process.

They were all eager to climb inside where stripping the interior would begin immediately. It took several days to gut the walls, seats and carpets, which were laid out in the wind to dry.

The engine was another matter. Fortunately, the mechanic had been this route before. Don made a cursory check of necessities and flew out.

While the interior was drying and the mechanic began work on the engines, the boys used the time to hunt and scavenge Aleut graves. Each evening they came back excited while proudly exhibiting their finds. Artifacts were plentiful—mostly handcarved bone knives, spearheads, shovels and bowls. In one grave, deep in a volcanic cave which pocked the black mountains, there was a gun rusted beyond use and a leather pouch filled with silver coins. They surmised the soul was going to buy his way into heaven and, if that failed, he'd fight.

Meanwhile, the mechanic was making real progress. He hummed a catchy tune realizing that the next day they could probably start the Pratt & Whitney engines. Fortunately, the weather had held. The wind blew constantly but rain escaped them, allowing the Widgeon's interior parts to dry sufficiently for the men to replace them bit by bit.

The following morning loomed gray and blustery. Dick was anxious as they flipped the ignition. Soon, the prop rolled around and caught as the sound filled the air, cutting the shrill wind as both of them purred, then roared. There was real enthusiasm from the crew.

Dick felt good. Glancing at his watch, he grinned. Don was due in soon, and the party could head home.

Peter Eltz helped Warren prepare breakfast and pack the gear. No one had mentioned the navigation problem which lay ahead. Peter said later, "We knew Don had already decided what to do."

The lagoon was wide but short and at its end, facing the sea, were two closely-placed high bluffs. If the Widgeon couldn't get enough altitude it wouldn't clear the summits, and its wings certainly couldn't fit between them.

Everyone was quiet as Don started the engines. Their pulsing power vibrated and raised a din as the plane taxied to the end of the marshy lake and turned. Raw power widened a huge wake, dovetailing a spray as the pilot roared downstream. The lift was slow—a sluggish refusal which caused the occupants to catch a breath and tense up. Just as they reached the bluffs, Don flipped the plane sideways, one wing almost in the water as they passed precariously close to the volcanic slag heap barring their exit. They roared out to sea.

A cheer raised in the cabin as everyone breathed a sigh of relief.

Don just chuckled. He had the Widgeon—a real prize—for his collection.

Later, when he was questioned as to the wisdom of the retreat, he laughed and said, "Aw, hell, I wasn't even close to the water."

Peter's mother, Bubby Eltz, has her own stories of hair-raising flights.

During one hunt, Don and a friend flew two moose racks out of Mother Goose Lake to be shipped to Anchorage and on to Europe.

The pilot had not returned in three days, and the entire time a terrible storm pelted the camp. The occupants were concerned about the cover plane which was being throttled by winds as it bobbed in the lake. Somehow it survived the winds.

In the meantime, Don had tied up at a boat dock in King Salmon just prior to the big blow. A boat broke its mooring and jammed the floats; the seaplane sank in 40 feet of water. Except for one wing tip poking out of the bay, it was totally submerged.

The military were in the area. Ten soldiers, Don and his friend spent the entire night raising the plane in a fierce storm. Getting it to the surface meant first totally submerging it and sending divers down before the craft could be lifted slowly. It took another day to dry it out—engines and all. Then, they flew it back to Mother Goose Lake where anxious clients waited. The ship had one slightly crumpled wing.

That particular hunt included a stint at Bear Lake. One day the weather started to act up. Wind gusts up to 70 mph were recorded on the dining room windometer.

During the storm, a Cessna 180 appeared over the lake and tried to land several times. Watching helplessly, the people in the cabins were apprehensive about the pilot and passengers who eventually gave up and flew away. Don took off on a search as soon as possible, but was never able to locate the mystery plane.

Black columns continued to move in from the Bering Sea. If anything, the storms were increasing. After one of them passed, Don suggested they leave. Bubby Eltz related the story with a shiver:

"We flew straight into a boiling, black sky. Hail riddled the plane, which was being tossed about like a toy. Don banked deep to the left, then down to the right. Looking down we could see the ground, but ahead, absolutely nothing. I was convinced we were heading straight for a mountain. Once again we turned directly into the heart of the black, swirling void. Don turned to me and said, 'It's kind of like a trip to heaven, isn't it?'

"We headed for the coast, thinking our companion plane had turned back. They were nowhere in sight, and Don was definitely not going back into the soup. The black columns surfaced again. Lowering, Don hoped we might land on the beach. The tides were so high, it was hopeless.

"By now we were experiencing real fear. The torturous funnels contained 70-mph winds, and the wings iced up immediately. On and on we flew, darting around the columns whenever possible."

Bubby thought it was horrible and turned to watch Don. He was flipping a coin. "I quickly spurted out, 'Don Johnson! What are you doing?'

"He laughed. 'Well, as long as you caught me at it, you decide. Which way do we try to avoid that thing? To the right, flying inland more, or to the left out over that stormy sea?'

"There was no hesitation in my voice. Flying out over that raging sea without pontoons was not my idea of fun. So, to the right we went. We were flying so slowly I thought landing in the muskeg, if necessary, wouldn't be too bad—maybe. There was fog and icing over land which Don didn't like too much.

"Finally, we reached Port Heiden and landed crossways on the runway. We struggled out of the cockpit, pushing our way against the wind into the building where eight or 10 men were sitting. One of them yelled, 'Don, don't you know better than to fly in weather like this?' We just gasped out a sigh and stared at each other."

The next year, during a caribou hunt, Don and the Baron landed on an empty riverbed. They rumbled down the wash comfortably until a huge rock tossed the plane over onto its nose. Getting out, Don made an exasperated gesture before pulling out a pocket knife. With a steady hand he made small slits in the linen fuselage on both sides. The two men pulled the plane back and righted her. Grabbing a roll of tape from inside, the pilot patched his craft. A cursory inspection of the prop followed. Don grunted and waved the Baron inside the ship, and shortly they were aloft.

Peter Eltz was only 14 when he first arrived at Bear Lake. For the following five summers he returned to the Aleutians and worked in camp and on the sea. Since his parents were regular clients, he had little fear of flying with the bush pilot.

During an interview in Salzberg, he related the following:

"It was the fall of the year, and the weather had been exceptionally bad. We were enroute from Kenai heading for Bear Lake to ready the camp for bear hunters due in the following day.

"Leaving King Salmon, where we'd stopped for fuel, we encountered a terrible rainstorm. The water gushing off the windshield defied description. Don lowered over the coast following a torturous route, explaining if he could see whitecaps he knew he was close to the shoreline and could use it as a road map to the Port Moller runway."

True, he had been flying it for over 20 years, but it was pitch-black outside and raging.

During the fall, darkness comes early. Warren and Peter became apprehensive flying a few feet off a pounding surf where huge waves lifted white foam high in the air in front of the plane. A sheeting rain, driven with brute force, buffeted the ship and rendered the windshield wipers useless. Peter was 16 at the time. And, although he had complete trust in the stern man at the controls, fear began to grow.

Peter continued. "Outside an unbelievable storm tormented the ship. The sound of the wind grew as the ship was swallowed in a black void.

"Don lowered dangerously close to the waves. Experience really counted. He knew exactly how many miles it was to the deserted cannery runway after having flown it hundreds of times.

"Nearing the airport, the rain increased, gushing rivers of water over glass, blinding the pilot who yelled, 'Warren, open that door. Hold Peter by the legs outside. Peter, lean down and when I'm three feet off the runway, raise an arm. I can't see.'

"The door opened. A rush of rain washed over us. Warren forced himself into position, bracing a back against metal and grabbing a death grip on my legs as I lowered beneath the fuselage. As soon as my eyes adjusted to being pelted by rain, I saw the ground and screamed into the wind, 'NOW!' "

Warren dragged Peter inside just as the 180 bounced roughly onto tar. Peter's eyes were popping. The frozen look drifted toward Warren, also wide-eyed.

When the plane finally stopped and stood shuddering in the wind, Don turned and said, "See, I told you something protects me."

Sally and Ken McConnel flew in for a sheep hunt years after their adventure at Point Hope. They remembered Don with affection and were as anxious to see the guide again as they were to hunt.

Don flew them toward Mount Blackburn's 16,000-foot summit, and circling the glacier allowed Steve Daniels to parachute out at 300 feet. The hunters were excited watching the unusual event. Don continued over-flying the area searching for a good trophy. The weather was holding in a place where scenery caused cameras to whirr constantly. Don enjoyed the comments of hunters who appreciated the land he loved and in which there was immense pride.

Eventually, they landed and began a long track. The ram was moving higher. It was cold, and stiff winds buffeted the foursome, causing much huddling into down and fur. Up ahead, Don glassed a statuesque creature poised on an ice ledge 175 yards away. A wave of an arm moved the party on.

Finally, he stopped. His voice lowered to a whisper as he said, "Sally, shoot broadside. Go up the front legs and when you get to the fuselage about halfway up the body, go six or eight inches to the stern of that." The Weatherby recoiled twice, its sound loud against the wind.

Her bullets hit their mark and, as if in slow motion, the Dall toppled over and disappeared. Everyone raced to the spot. The big ram had careened 250 feet into an ice crevasse.

Don's sentiments echoed over the glacier. After sucking in a deep breath and grimacing, he said, "You three stay here. Move around to keep warm, but don't leave this spot. I'll fly to the nearest town for enough rope. I'll be back soon."

Hurrying off, the pilot ran to the plane and took off. He had already decided McCarthy was too far away and would fly to a camp town on the Copper River called Chitina.

Later at the trading post, Don purchased 300 feet of ⅜-inch rope, remembering the problem at Yakutat years earlier when he had dropped on the glacier and the line was too short.

Miners and locals in the store were keeping up a running conversation. Visitors were always a treat, especially bush pilots who were privy to news from around the territory. Don became impatient with their questions. Finally, he explained his plight and hurried off.

Sally and Ken were obeying the guide's instructions, stomping around in circles and feeling the cold as the day waned. Steve advised them to rest periodically.

Fortunately, he knew the area and just how long the flight should take. If there was a problem with the plane or sudden weather, the party could hike down the mountain to a protected spot and build a fire. At least Don's hunters were rarely novices, and difficult situations were usually tolerated without complaint. But since it was late in the day, he would watch the time carefully. Staying on the ice after dark and surviving would be risky for the clients.

The sound of an engine raised instant smiles. Within half-an-hour, the men were watching Don go over the ledge and down into an icy abyss while Sally filmed the act.

Once the animal was secured, Don yelled. Cold seeped into his body, but he grinned as he watched it rise to the ledge.

He was tired and not looking forward to the long climb back up. Shrugging and grunting, Don's hands clasped the rope now

Wind claims another sea plane.   *Widgeon saved from a watery grave.*

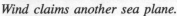

Ready for take-off at Bear Lake.

dangling just over his head and where up above sure hands were reaching to pull him out.

By nightfall the party was rested, enjoying a drink to celebrate and sniffing the tangy aroma of sheep ribs roasting over a crackling fire.

Sally had her precious trophy and yet another good story to tell.

Chapter 18

Flying the Frozen Bush

A ir mileage between Kenai, Fairbanks (where they refueled), and the ice-bound hunting areas, encompassed great distances over rough mountainous terrain. Bush pilots considered the aggravation run-of-the-mill, but kept a careful watch on weather and fuel, all the while flying tandem to protect each other.

In the early '60s, Harold McGrady and Don left the homestead runway headed for Kotzebue on a cloudy afternoon. By the time they reached Galena, the sky was becoming more threatening. They were both flying high, trying to stay above the fog in a wind that had risen to 60 knots. Don flipped on the radio. "Harold, we've got to go into the soup. It's too windy now."

They were in the Purcell Mountains near the headwaters of the Selawick River, and both were low on gas. Once the area was frozen and snow-blanketed, skimming rivers between mountains was the only way to navigate. "I'll search for a spot to set down," Don radioed. "Stay close."

Eventually, they spotted a frozen swamp just in range. Visibility in the blowing snow was zero. As he shut down the engine, Don noticed Harold's plane was almost obscured and yet, he knew, they were wing-tip to wing-tip. Climbing around in the seat, both pilots dragged out extra gas cans and went up on the wings to refill the tanks. Just as Don finished pouring the last of his fuel, he saw Harold coming alongside the door. "Harold," he demanded, "get in the plane quick. Your face is frostbitten." The sickening white skin frightened the hunter who knew what dire consequences could follow.

Engines sputtered and roared as the two red craft rushed off frozen mounds into a snow-riddled sky. Harold radioed as Don veered to the left, "Got you, Don." But, within seconds during the next transmission, he heard, "I've lost you."

"All right," Don answered. "Go downriver. I'll keep trying to find you." The voice on the radio grew dimmer by the mile. Deciding Harold must be going in the opposite direction, Don banked and headed upriver. Harold made the same decision.

Outside flurries thickened, blowing hard against the ship. It seemed hopeless for a while, and gas was the deciding factor. Checking the compass, Don turned and went north to Koyukuk. As he neared the settlement, the storm slackened, giving him easy access to the strip and fuel.

In the meantime, Harold dropped low. The plane's gauge gave him real concern until, suddenly, he saw a trapper's camp on the riverbank and heaved a sigh of relief.

Eskimo trapper shacks were saviors. At all times they were left stocked with dry wood, matches, water, food and animal skins. A fire was laid, ready for a match at any needed moment. The preparations were necessary in the relentless cold; they had saved many lives and in this particular case, would save Harold's.

He lit the stove with shaking fingers impatient for enough heat to thaw the frozen kettle which rested on the iron top. After first wrapping his down-covered body with caribou hides, he knelt in front of the stove. The room's chill defied description, but the sound of crackling wood was soothing. While Harold blew hot breath on his fingers, he rose to collect a mug and tea from a tin on a crude shelf. A glow from the newly-lit oil lamp softened the room suddenly pungent with wood smoke. While waiting, he found some gas cans and decided to borrow one for the plane. Except for fate, that act might have been his last. If Don could not locate the cover plane, Harold would be forced to land again without the good fortune of locating a spike camp. Death came quickly in that land.

After refueling, Don turned back, searching the route and ragging at the mike in the plane. Hours had passed since there had been any communication; he was really worried. The radio crackled, then cleared, making Don smile as Harold's voice boomed out of the speaker. "Don, the storm is better. I'll try to get airborne and find the river."

It occurred to the guide that they must be back at the headwaters of the Selawick. A quick call confirmed Harold's opinion that they were. "I'm on a river—wait a minute. Hey!" It was decidedly cheerful. "I can see you. You're right above me."

By the time Don landed, Harold's cover plane was frozen up solid. The wind racing across the ice jammed its force against Don's plane—almost preventing its landing. Outside, the temperature had dropped to 20-below-zero. Pulsing against the fray, the Cessna carved a path across the river, stopping next to the cover plane. In it were extra gas cans for his partner's plane. They put a fire-pot in the engine to thaw the oil and refueled. Within 30 minutes, they were ready, grinning at each other as they listened to purring engines. Later that night they arrived in Kotzebue, bone-tired and ready for a hot meal.

All the pilots became close friends. Staying alive meant complete cooperation and quick-wittedness. Before it was over, Don would have survived five of them.

Lesser problems, sometimes ludicrous ones, also plagued the pilots.

Each year, hunting aircraft were outfitted with new engines before it was time to head up toward the Arctic.

Al Bontrigger was a good aircraft-engine mechanic. He worked daily, readying the Super-Cubs for the hunts. While he worked on the cover plane, Don's engine laid on the hangar floor for three or four months—with the exhaust open. Finally, both planes were ready. All that was left to do was pack their gear.

After a smooth takeoff into an oppressive sky, they headed for Fairbanks. Before landing at their first stop, Don noticed the oil was heating up and the pressure dropping severely. Deciding it was just a quirk in the new engine, the two pilots had dinner before spending the night. By morning they flew out on their way north, eager to get to camp before incoming hunters arrived. Four miles off the strip, Don's oil was heating badly, and the oil pressure dropped to zero. The turn was sharp. Radioing the cover plane, he raced back to Phillips Field, calling an emergency landing to the tower. Al landed just behind him turning right to the hangar. On foot, Al raced toward the plane and went immediately to the oil screen. It was cracked and completely clogged. Shaking a wiry head, Al stared blankly at Don. "What the hell is this? I've never seen anything like it before!" The two men hurried inside the hangar to the tubs and flushed the debris on a screen. It was obviously hair and bits of pulp and rag. Going back to the aircraft, Al removed the oil case. They found seven mice skulls in it. They gave each other an incredulous look, then laughed really hard. Al said, "Well, there is a first time for everything."

That season ended in April. The storms had been exceptionally bad. A blizzard was in progress when they pulled out of Point Hope. The whiteout developed rapidly—so rapidly, they lost each other almost immediately. Don kept up radio contact, but failed to get a response. Punching the mike button repeatedly, he finally heard his cover pilot's brief message saying he was turning back. Instead of following him, Al flew over to Kotzebue, landing safely and, in the excitement, forgetting to cancel their flight plan.

Don's plane filtered out of the murk at Selawick where two Indians came out to tie him down and refuel the Cessna. They had been working on a new schoolhouse.

A teacher, upon hearing the plane, rushed out and called to Don to hurry inside. Grinning and beckoning for him to follow immediately, she led him down a passageway and through a bathroom door. Before entering, she pushed a finger against her lips for silence. The pilot was puzzled but obediently followed. There were four small Eskimo boys sitting on the floor around a gleaming white toilet, completely captivated by the water rushing in a circular motion and disappearing, while one of them proudly pulled the handle for the others.

The whiteout lasted for three days. Don was given shelter and hot meals. On the way out, he stopped at McGrath for fuel, only to learn he was presumed lost, and an air search throughout the interior was in progress.

Between hunts in the months to follow, Don would be flying for the Rand Corporation and Systems Development to radar sites. Starting at Barter Island, the flights would usually terminate at Point Barrow.

He was also flying the DEW line when he wasn't ferrying supplies to the arctic researchers at Point Barrow. The base at Barrow was being used by the Navy, the DEW line people, and scientists checking ice floes.

The sea-level station on permafrost soil had no drainage. All of the waste was flushed with fuel oil which went out to sea. No one smoked in the Quonset huts where food and libation was plentiful. For a tired bush pilot, a few days at the facility was a pleasant sojourn, especially when operations were on cost-plus contracts. Everyone ate like kings. At dinner each man received his own loaf of bread, gallon of milk, pound of butter, plate of steaks (suitably marked: well, medium and rare), and assorted pies—one of each. After dinner, whatever was left was swooped into a trash can. To a pilot-guide who was used to hauling supplies thousands of miles in a bush plane to remote camps where there was a shortage of everything, the waste was appalling.

On the Arctic Circle's outer edge sits a little-known frozen island—Ostrov Vrangel'a. The Russian spot is, as the crow flies, directly in line with the top of the world and adjacent to Anadyrskoje Ploskpgorje on the tip-end of Russia's land mass. The island, 250 miles due west of Point Barrow, is 375 hard air-miles from the Point Hope camp.

Scientists, studying ice movement in the Arctic Circle, were being flown from Barrow out to the desolate area. For Don it was a routine flight, and he passed the time spotting polar bears. After several trips with men and equipment, Don decided there was no doubt Ostrov Vrangel'a was *the* place to hunt the bruins.

His biggest polar bear, weighing 1,600 pounds and measuring out at 11 feet-10 inches, was displayed in the Anchorage airport until the record earthquake of 1964.

On that day, while terrified Anchorage residents fled into the streets, a whole city block in the middle of the city dropped two stories beneath the street. Several miles away, the airport terminal rumbled off its foundations, sending the roof crashing down and crushing a row of glass cases exhibiting all of that state's game animals.

Since that day, Don had been scouting the Chukchi hoping to find another trophy to replace the one lost in the tragedy.

Just before landing on the ice at Ostrov Vrangel'a, he spotted a spectacular specimen.

It was a long way to camp, and the bruin had the capacity to travel great distances. The guide was unprepared for a hunt, but cocking his brow, he thought, 'I'll be back—that one's too good to pass up.' Anyway, he reasoned, the scientists would need a lift back, and the schedule was within a week.

When the time came, Don left early after overloading the Super-Cub with gear and supplies. His cover plane was returning two hunters to Nome for the flight back to the states. He would go alone.

Fortunately, the weather was decent. There probably should have been concern considering the place and time of year, but the pilot was preoccupied with thoughts of a record trophy.

The hunt for the bruin took longer than he expected, burning up precious fuel. Almost reaching the point of no return, Don spotted a bear which looked familiar. At least, he was exceptionally big. But after circling, he found it difficult to locate a spot on which to land. When one did open, it was rough. Don was quick, grabbing a rifle from the tail section and pulling on gloves and a hat.

A hefty wind accompanied the lone figure twisting through the hummocks trying to stay downwind while constantly searching a track. Once he thought he heard a growl, but the wind distorted sound, and shrugging, Don plowed on. Eventually,

Don's polar bear in Anchorage International Airport as referred to in letter on next page.

reason took over—the search was futile, he had been out on the ice long enough and was getting too far away from the plane. Instinctively, he turned. The bear had been tracking him—a giant on snowshoed feet just 50 yards away and moving fast. Startled and moving quickly, he drew the rifle and got off two lung shots and, suddenly, it was silent except for the untiring wind.

Later at camp, his cover pilot whistled as they flushed the skin; this one was almost as big as the one which was destroyed and for Don, there was satisfaction. All the best outfitters competed to have record mounts in the airport—hunting was their business.

Harry N. Dodds, manager of the Anchorage International Airport, wrote Don the following letter:

STATE OF ALASKA

WILLIAM A. EGAN, GOVERNOR

DEPARTMENT OF PUBLIC WORKS

DIVISION OF AVIATION / BOX 6-204 — ANCHORAGE 99502
ANCHORAGE INTERNATIONAL AIRPORT

October 25, 1966

Don Johnson
Kenai Float Plane Service
Kenai, Alaska

Dear Mr. Johnson:

We would like permission to place the Polar Bear, that you so kindly donated to the Anchorage International Airport, in the new international reception building.

We think that he (the Polar Bear) would be a great attraction to the foreign travelers. Naturally we do not wish to relocate the display of the Polar Bear without your permission. Incidently this Polar Bear is probably one of the most photographed Polar Bears in all Alaska and I wish to thank you for allowing us to display this trophy bear.

Very truly yours,

Harry N. Dodds, Manager
Anchorage International Airport

HND:eb

NORTH TO THE FUTURE IN 1967!

Chapter 19

Predators

D uring long Alaskan winters, frozen tundra sleeps beneath a recurring snow blanket. Bear Lake becomes a steel sheet while rigid ice wedges its banks, lumping snow mounds cover the buildings; the scene from the air is peaceful except for the piercing Aleutian wind trailing snow-fingers across the landscape.

And while many of the animals den-up in catacombed worlds away from tormenting cold, wolves roam in packs hungrily searching for meat.

Since wolves prey mainly on moose and caribou in the Alaskan wilds, hunters consider them a prize. Often packs will run in relays trying to tire their quarry. If they can drive the animal into a lake or out onto the ice, they can prevent it from eating. Once the animal is weak, the kill becomes simple.

It is a widespread belief that wolves hamstring big game; that is, sever the Achilles tendon to bring them down. However, this action would make them too vulnerable to the animal's dangerous hoofs. A bull moose or a caribou can pack a wallop as hard and as accurate as a mule. Instead, wolves ham-slash deep bites on the flanks, attempting evisceration. When that has been accomplished and the blood flow is mortal, the pack gorges itself and goes off to rest. Scavenger birds will move in immediately to peck out the eyes and tear away bits of flesh for a meal. The pack will return to the carrion later for a second meal and, before long, only a skeleton remains.

Recently, books and movies about wolves have become popular. They depict their unquestioned beauty and mating habits and have been interesting, even touching, but wolves are not pets and are extremely destructive. Don readily admitted they play an important part in the balance of nature by culling out sick, injured, aged and immature animals. "But," he said with stoic sincerity, "make no mistake about the myth."

He grimaced, remembering the sight of a healthy bull moose swinging its rack and impaling the wolves one at a time on the tines. Then, with a sweep, the mammal would fling the bleeding fur into the air. It would land in a heap and die. In one measured jump, the moose had actually leaped 27 feet in an effort to evade the pack. Wolves are highly intelligent opportunists. They are well aware of the hazards of rib-crushing hoofs or clubbing or shearing in the heat of mortal combat.

Don's comment was, "In the wilderness there are no favorites; they live wild and they die hard."

In late winter months, Don enjoyed a respite from guiding. And, when he wasn't off to the corners of the world hunting, he used the time to fly over the frozen wasteland in search of wolf packs. The sport is only for the hearty. Outside the plane, temperatures drop to 50-below-zero, and frostbite is a genuine concern. Spiraling the Super-Cub from 500 feet gave him a clear view of the group. The shewolf, always the largest in the pack, was the target. Weighing upwards of 150 pounds, she would lead the predators along snow drifts following the scent. Occasionally, she would stop, lift her head and emit a lugubrious howl. That sound, eerie in the night, tenders fear in man and animals alike.

One January, while cruising over frozen mountains, he spotted a big pack. Usually, the variegated animals moved in groups of four or five; in this case there were 17. The wolves were attacking a 2,000-pound moose. Moving with unprecedented speed, they chased the animal into a ravine filled with trees, making it impossible for Don to land. Don forced the Cub down, buzzing the pack, trying to frighten them away from the helpless moose. They ignored him. The foliage prevented the pilot from getting off a shot.

The animal was trudging through three feet of snow, covering about 50 feet before they would charge again at his hind quarters, tearing into plump flesh from which red ran onto the snow. The bloody trail curled down the hill, trickling lighter each time. After each rip, he would painfully pull his huge body up and race away.

Losing the view in the trees, Don gained altitude hoping for an opening where he might get a shot at them. Peering out, he saw it was too late. The moose had been ravaged, and the wolves were grinding through its leg bones.

Later that winter while flying over the Wrangell Mountains, he saw a large pack attacking a huge Dall sheep. By the time he circled lower, they had killed the animal. Within 45 minutes the sheep was devoured. He circled, watching them until they left the scene, going single-file down the mountain.

On another hunt Don's brother, Quentin, climbed into the plane before he took off.

The skis etched a deep groove in virgin snow on the runway as the plane roared out. Lifting quickly, they cleared Cook's Inlet near the Kenai homestead and banked toward the mountains. They flew for almost an hour. Quentin's voice rose evenly above the engine. "There, Don, coming over the rise." His excitement grew as they moved nearer to the pack. "Look! A whole bunch of them," he shouted.

"Okay," Don answered, "we're goin' down."

Quentin already had his weapon out of the window. The Cub circled, turning for a head-on approach as Quentin's weapon discharged. Don's arm steadied his 12-gauge on a wire taped to the struts. He was using No. 2 buckshot as he aimed and fired, while handling the plane with one hand. The wolves were silver-tipped with a few gray mixed in. "Bang, bang," the volley rose above the engine in clear, crisp, freezing air. Each pass diminished the pack. Don counted 13 on the original approach, and after a long time 12 lay dead. One big gray had been wounded. Powerful legs sprinted him up over a bank and into the trees. They made two more passes—each time the trees blocked the shot. "We'd better land," his brother instructed.

"Yeah, can't leave him out there wounded."

They circled sharply, looking for an opening where the snow looked fairly flat. After the landing, Don skied in as close to the kill as possible. Quentin got out to stalk the wolf.

Once Don was airborne again, he searched for the wounded killer. Spotting the prey he stiffened. The wolf was dangerously close to Quentin, charging from behind the bank. Even wounded, the wolf's instincts brought it back to its enemy.

Quentin moved carefully through the snow, watching with an experienced eye for the furious animal. He heard the growling cry and swung around in the direction of the charge, firing his weapon simultaneously.

Suddenly, it was silent in that vast, white world except for the sound of the plane returning to pick him up.

There were 13 pelts hanging on the overhang by the log cabin the next day.

Two of Don's guides remain at Bear Lake during winters to trap and caretake the lodge. Tim Okonek and Slim Gale have 10- or 15-mile trap-lines dotted by a few, small line-shacks. Trapping was good business in the early days, but Don no longer does it. Naturally, fur is always a bounty for rugs, coats and boots. The two young guides, altruistic by nature, took the winter's entire catch to make a fox coat for Slim's mother. The unsuspecting lady must have been really happy that Christmas.

The Eskimos cure the hides with urine or by chewing to soften them. The fur-lined leg and feet covers are soft and warm. Caribou hairs are hollow, and their hides are much warmer than other fur, but wolverine hide will not collect frost and is in much demand for the ruff in coats and parkas.

Don explained there are five or six species of fox. The fox on the Aleutian Chain have coarser pelts and are not as soft as the interior fox. Inland Alaska is colder, and the coat grows longer and thicker. Down the Chain they are rife with silver. The interior cross-fox are red, silver, almost black, and chocolate with a big white-tipped tail which brings higher prices. Arctic foxes are pure white.

The little Alaskan fox is a loner except during mating season.

When the wolf has good hunting for game, the fox may have a good feed on the remains. He also is not above stealthily slinking in while the larger predators, after eating their fill, are off resting. It is not uncommon for him to sniff out a choice morsel which the wolves have cached in their wanderings.

Unfortunately, the marmot, ground squirrels and other rodents, which are his favorite diet, hibernate in winter. If the population of the snowshoe hare is at a low ebb, hunting may be difficult. And in that case, the fox himself may become the prey.

As far as courage is concerned, this little fellow has few equals and has even been filmed taking on a grizzly which came too close to the den. Because of speed and cunning, the fox actually drove the bear off.

The fox sleeps with its nose and all four pads tucked into the comforting warmth of its thick, luxurious tail. Sucking in sub-zero air through the fur warms it before it enters the lungs.

Naturally, Don hunted Kodiak Island—reputed to be great fox country. Now it is part of the Kodiak National Wildlife Refuge.

While the Aleutians turn white and bitter winds scour the snow, the pilot would often see the small, lone vigilante pulsing across the tundra in search of a meal.

One matter Don suggested hunters look for is damaged pelts. He said, "If spring arrives early, foxes lay outside their dens. Their body heat will melt the snow. If it starts to quickly refreeze, a sudden move will pull the hair out and ruin the hide."

Tim recalled several mishaps while hunting foxes and wolverines:

Once his snowmobile broke through the lake's ice. He was up to his armpits in freezing water. After draining the water out of the gas tank, the snowmobile floated. He dragged it up to safer ice and returned to the lodge in a frozen snowsuit, teeth chattering all the way.

Tim talked about the wolverines which are the bane of the

*Cover pilot
Dick Gunlogson
exhibits skin
from she-wolf
which attacked
Don's plane
between Point
Hope and
Kotzebue.*

trapper. Contantly on the move, this fierce predator can make 25 or 30 miles a night. The Eskimos call him "little bear" or "Gulo Gulo" (which means glutton). That title is appropriate. At tops, he might weigh 45 pounds and usually has an accomplice in tow. They kill just to kill and will take on almost anything. They are feared by all sizes of man and beast.

Tim recounted approaching one caught in his trap which he thought was dead. As he stepped over it, the sly animal struck. With razor-sharp teeth, the animal took a bite out of Tim's boot. After a few choice words from the angry trapper, he finished off Gulo Gulo, which then became a skin for Tim's collection.

On one occasion late in winter, Tim and Mike were hiking back from Bear Patch with their skins. A storm approached which was so sudden and fierce they decided it would be perilous in the boat. While standing at the shore discussing the matter, they were surprised by a bear. They were used to quick decisions. Tim shot it. The pair then gutted the animal and crawled inside for a warm night's sleep. At daybreak Don began to search for them in the Super-Cub. Seeing the bear lying on the beach, he swooped down for a closer look, mouthing, "What the hell?" and shaking his experienced head. The sound of the plane awakened the trappers who shocked Don by climbing out of the bear and waving excitedly.

Chapter 20

Life Down Chain

Bear Lake had all the clients it could handle by 1965, and Don discontinued advertising. Word spread rapidly throughout the hunting fraternity, and the lodge was becoming a famous spot—so famous that Don found it expedient to begin building spike camps on the 100-mile preserve which surrounded the lake.

Alaska was now a state. Having been grandfathered in his realm to the chagrin of officious Fish and Game wardens, the pilot had to maintain buildings on many of the sites. Often curious, wandering and hungry bears would actually make splinters out of the small shacks. Because of the preserve's terms, they had to be immediately rebuilt.

Super-Cubs had improved the hunting tremendously. Pilots who flew for Don became extremely skilled; that is, when he could find men who could handle the weather. After a while, they could land and take off on beaches, tundra, islands, mountain tops and washes—using skis and floats on gullies, lakes and rivers. There were few places these durable planes couldn't go with the right man at the throttle.

Don's bush airline, Kenai Float Plane Service, no longer in its infancy, was the prime mover on the Aleutian Chain. The canneries made regular requests for medical emergencies during fishing season. Of course, he flew the fleet for them and also hauled fishermen to different ports.

The radio at the lodge blared constantly with calls from Aleut residents at Nelson Lagoon, a fishing village 40 minutes away from Bear Lake Lodge. Their needs were numerous and their dependency growing as they called for boat parts, medicine and clothing. On the long, barren beach of the Bering Sea where a lone fisherman lived, it was not unusual to see the red plane spiral down and drop a much-needed package into a boat sitting idly in the yard. Within seconds, a grateful recipient would be out in the wind, waving a thank-you. While the figure waited for an acknowledging dip of a wing, Don would already be rooting in the tail section for the next drop.

Naturally, there were sea disasters. Many a dark, stormy night, long after everyone else was sleeping, the pilot was called from a warm bed to take off and rescue fishermen who were adrift in treacherous seas or had been beached in some God-forsaken spot. He never refused, and the demands became a heavy burden.

Flying Tiger had established a base at Cold Bay, and Reeve Aleutian Airlines was flying regular runs from Anchorage to that spot and others down the long coast. It was now customary for Don, or his pilots, to pick up their clients at that station to be flown to Bear Lake.

Kenai Float Plane Service had bid and received the contract to fly the mail on the Aleutians. The matter was largely efficient since they were already running regular flights to King Salmon, Port Moller, Port Heiden, Sand Point, Cold Bay, Bear Lake, Naknek, Nelson Lagoon and Kodiak Island. The airline also had service to and from Anchorage, Kenai Peninsula and Seward, which was handled from the homestead hangar.

One day during the late '60s, after collecting a mail sack in the Quonset-hut airport post office at Cold Bay, 120 miles from the lodge, he found a letter addressed to a Russian priest. The place was the Bear River village, Carpa and Yolman's home. After inquiring in other villages, he came to the conclusion that there had not been a priest at the site for a good many years. The letter was postmarked Paris, France.

Weeks later, he opened the letter and read it. Strangely enough, it was from an old woman who had been born there. She was dying and sought solace from her Russian Orthodox clergyman. Don put 50 dollars in an envelope along with a note, which he sent back to France.

Unfortunately, the mail did not always go through. Fierce storms sometimes prevented delivery for weeks on end.

The postmistress was an old Aleut woman whose smile warmed even an Aleutian Island winter day. Don always joked with her, and it was obvious the friendship was mutual. She was, however, her own lady. When an officious Federal Postal Inspector arrived by plane to inspect the facility, he was met with considerable hostility. It seems he objected to her somewhat unorthodox methods of storing funds and stamps. After a brief discussion, she told him where he could put the cigar box, and for a brief period there was no postmistress at Cold Bay.

For a while, Don became the postmaster and although he was efficient, there was no denying his methods didn't quite come up to federal standards. His actions and comments were similar to the Aleut lady's, and after several years Kenai Float Plane Service stopped flying the mail.

All aircraft were serviced in Kenai under the capable hands of mechanic Dick Rinc and other seasonal help. Naturally, hunters who came into Anchorage at the same time were picked up there, housed at the homestead and later ferried to Bear Lake on returning aircraft.

During crab season, the huge boats would often overload their decks with iron crab-traps which made them top-heavy. In turbulent seas, the ships would list badly and sometimes overturn. Quick calls brought out the Super-Cub to over-fly the area in search of survivors. If they made it to the beach, he would land, often in 50-knot winds, and pick them up. But many times his low-flying craft was used to notify rescue vessels if and where there were survivors.

Life in the North Country was not tame, and it always had humorous highlights.

During spring and summer, between fishing or hunting clients,

Don would become engrossed in numerous projects—all unusual and all ultimately lucrative. While flying the beaches with passengers, hunting for dead walrus became a steady pastime because ivory was valuable. Their custom was to fly low where keen, experienced eyes could spot treasures instantly. Don and his pilots never flew the coast without searching along the way, and there was a fierce race to get to it first. They took both tusks and oosiks (walrus penis) from the rank, black carcasses. Many of the guests would buy a set for game room collections, and the price would reach as high as $8,000.

On one such trip, Don left early in the morning. His son, Warren, was 15 at the time and a new pilot. The two had developed a strong competition for good finds. When Don returned, his son asked which way he had flown. Don answered, "North." 'Surely, the north was stripped,' the young aviator thought as he decided to fly south.

Don was back in the air ferrying fuel to the lodge when he heard his son on the radio. "I found a bomb!" the boy exclaimed, feeling certain that his remark would elicit a positive, if not startled, response. After all, that was a unique item.

"A what?" Don asked, deciding he had heard wrong.

"A bomb." It was repeated with pride.

"Well, leave the damn thing alone," came back in terse tones.

"I can't. I've already got it in the plane."

The pilot was shocked. "Well, bring it in, but be careful."

The red Super-Cub returned, looking lopsided and rather primitive, with a long canister attached to its struts; almost a rerun of Lafayette Escadrille.

Watching with apprehension as he landed, Don heaved a sigh as the plane taxied over the rough strip and stopped near the lodge.

"How about that?" he said, scratching his head and moving closer to examine the canister. They untied it, lowered it carefully, then placed it out by the light plant in back of the lodge. Don recorded the numbers stencilled on metal and put them in his wallet.

A call came over the radio for a charter to Anchorage. Within minutes the Cessna 180 was airborne, headed up the coast. Once he arrived, Don went to the flight office in the private air terminal to shoot the breeze over a cup of coffee. He found it amusing to repeat the bomb story. One of the personnel radioed the tale to a buddy at the Coast Guard office. It was then relayed to Almendorf Air Force Base. Within minutes a harassed demolition officer from Almendorf airfield called the Anchorage flight office and demanded to speak to Don Johnson.

His attitude was irritating in itself, but the combination of his audacity with a Brooklyn accent really capped the issue. Don's ire rose.

"Mr. Johnson, where did you find the bomb?"

"On the beach."

"Why didn't you leave it alone?"

"I was curious."

"Goddamn it, man, anyone knows better than to mess with an unexploded bomb!"

It appeared to be time to rattle the know-it-all; in fact, there was nothing Don liked better. "Oh, yeah. Well, what kind of bomb is it?"

"Mr. Johnson, that is classified material," the officer replied in clear Brooklynese. "Now, what are the numbers on the canister?"

Don read off the numbers he had written on the paper.

"Oh, Jesus," he heard on the other end.

"That bad?" Don asked in an impish voice.

"Goddamn it," he heard again. "Where is the bomb now?"

It was time to have some fun. Don grinned broadly. Everyone in the flight office was listening. "Oh," he answered nonchalantly, "the kids are playing with it."

"Jesus Christ, are you crazy? You get that thing a half-mile from your home and rope it off. Do you hear me?" he shouted.

By now the pilot was having a good laugh, goading the officer and enjoying every minute of it. "Listen," he said in a sincere tone, "I'll try. I really will. But, hell, you know how kids are." Then he hung up and laughed all the way to the 180.

Anchorage to Bear Lake was a five-hour flight. Flying through the magnificent Alaskan range took him through Clark's Pass, over glacier lakes, past Naknek and inland harbors, finally emerging on the Bering Sea where the tundra flattened to wide beaches. It was always an enjoyable trip; Don relaxed. He had given little thought to the conversation with the Air Force bomb specialist and had just about forgotten the matter.

By late evening the Air Force landed at Bear Lake. The plane's occupants included the Brooklyn officer and two demolition men.

Striding into the lodge in an officious manner, the Captain asked, "Are you Johnson?"

"Yeah."

"Well," he huffed out, "where is the bomb?"

"Oh, that," Don answered casually. "It's out in back of the lodge."

The officer's black eyes flew to the ceiling. "I told you to move it."

Blue eyes widened over an innocent smile. "Yeah, I know. I forgot."

The Captain sucked air. His face reddened before he began. He talked interminably about secrecy, fear and danger. It reminded Don of the Navy and the hopeless nonsense of power often held by men who didn't know how to use it. This guy was on his turf, and the war was over. He lit a cigarette as the man concluded.

Then, turning, the Captain issued an order to the demolition men standing just behind. They rushed out of the building toward the rear of the lodge.

By now Don was curious. He had asked a lot of questions which always evoked the same answer, "That is classified." Don was beginning to think Warren had brought home an atomic bomb.

The uneasy conversation lasted for quite a while until one of the demolition people finally returned and whispered something to the Captain. Raising a saccharine grin, the man said, "It won't be long now." Then, he looked at his watch.

"What won't be long now?" Don asked, wrinkling his brow

and staring out the window toward the lake and the end of the runway where the demolition men had gone.

"The bomb, of course. We've detonated it." He seemed relieved.

"Oh!" Don gasped over widening eyes. "That's bad."

The captain reeled. "WHY?" he screamed.

"Because my son will be landing here any minute."

"Jesus Christ, man—what is the matter with you—why didn't you say?. . ." Before the astounded man could finish, the explosion deafened them. It rocked the lodge, rattling windows and dishes and knocking pictures off the walls.

Don eyed the man, whose nerves seemed to unravel with the blast. He turned white and with eyes bulging, gasped out, "Your SON!"

"Oh, he probably won't be here for an hour or so." Don paused, "I was just kidding."

****

Life was changing on the Chain. Aleuts, who once fished in small skiffs, were now using large salmon boats equipped with electronic depthfinders, radar and electric nets. Their catch was now amounting to hundreds of thousands of pounds of the coveted red salmon. Huge tenders steamed into the Bering Sea complete with fish-processing plants. The balance of the fleet's find went into the canneries dotting the Alaskan coast, most of which had been purchased by the astute Japanese. And while the price of salmon escalated, the price per pound paid to Aleut fishermen dropped yearly.

Don's children were fishing on a regular basis. He had a vested interest. A belief that stored fish, dumped onto the world market just prior to negotiations, drove the price down caused constant consternation. His Aleut friends, and now his children, were directly involved—he fought hard.

Fishing sites, costing some $150,000 for a small coastal area, and the sophisticated fishing equipment now necessary on the boats, made life difficult for some who really didn't understand what was happening. To add to the situation, foreign interlopers were hard at work denuding rich fishing grounds. The United States government demanded quotas, but Don didn't feel they were diligent in monitoring the sea. He felt the Russians took advantage of that carelessness, which ultimately would affect all those concerned. And although he was willing to stand by the fishermen as he had the Inuit in the north, it was a losing battle. Besides all that, the IRS had appeared, and the Aleuts just ignored their letters. Of course, eventually, they would confiscate the boats which were the only means of livelihood the Aleuts had.

Much had changed for the determined young Navy man who had arrived in the territory with few funds. Maintaining the taciturn facade and working with his usual fervor, he progressed, but deep down in his heart he knew a way of life was eroding.

By now he had built a new home for his family on the homestead, which had five bedrooms and a place for the exotic game collection. The expensive trophies needed a constant temperature to preserve the hides.

Record trophies were being displayed in airports throughout Alaska, in the Alaska museum and in sundry spots around the lower "forty-eight." The name "Don Johnson" had become synonymous with the words "bush pilot," and letters addressed only to "Don Johnson, Alaska" found their way to the homestead.

Fall and spring brought as many as 20 hunters to the camp annually. Of course, 16 guides would arrive simultaneously to accommodate them, and there was extra help for the kitchen and rooms. The hunters were each given a guide and then flown to the spike camp sites. Pick-ups were arranged for several days later when the hunter would be returned to camp, where flushers would prepare the hides.

Business was mushrooming and although it was lucrative, there were enormous expenses involved. Airplanes, which were in constant use, had to be overhauled regularly and from great distances. Pilots had to be hired and housed. Many of the ships were damaged in storms to the point where they were unusable—the cost of replacement was rising.

Don's fertile mind saw the potential of the future. As he flew the tundra or out over the sea, plans were forming which were carefully thought out and later executed.

There was no question that they needed and could now afford a new lodge. All of the smaller buildings which had cropped up were cluttering the land. Although tight and warm, they were inadequate. He envisioned a large dining room where everyone could gather for meals, and a bar for evenings. The scheme included a dart board, pool table, long bar overlooking the glacier and lake, comfortable couches, and a place to show the interesting films taken on numerous world hunts.

Joe Sanger, Don's friend since World War II, was available now that the Alice Communications Station, above Port Moller, was closing down. Joe would be moving to Bear Lake as head mechanic, builder and mentor.

In the meantime and during the long winter, Joe and his dog, Blackie, would dig out the basement for the new lodge. The Labrador learned from observing Joe and soon spent every day digging in the tundra enlarging the hole.

The dog and Joe were inseparable pals until one winter night when a pack of wolves came in close to the lodge. Somehow, Blackie had made friends with them and soon disappeared with the pack. Don spotted him running wild for almost a year. The matter concerned Don. He had been acquainted with wolf habits for a long time and knew, eventually, Blackie would fall out of favor with the predators and would be killed. Later that year, Don saw the pack, and the black interloper had disappeared.

Joe began making plans for the lodge which were quite elaborate. The building would have two bedrooms, a bath, a laundry and a large workshop-storage room in the basement. The first floor would contain a much-needed kitchen, pantry and a large dining room which would seat 20 persons at a time. On the second floor, they planned two baths side-by-side in a hallway which would house all the hunting and fishing gear, a bedroom and bath and a beautiful bar which overlooked the glacier lake.

Don's brother, Quinten, a carpenter by trade, was planning to fly in to supervise construction. But Joe was already hard at work making plans to salvage lumber from a sunken barge in Port Moller Bay. Joe had been in the Aleutians for a long time and had learned to utilize every bit of salvage.

Later that year, a huge icehouse at the cannery blew down in 125-mph winds, strewing thousands of 3x12s all over the beach. Joe diligently collected them. He patiently extracted the nails and hauled his find to the runway. The icehouse insulation would make a cozy lining for the new facility.

Don and Joe enjoyed disagreeing with each other. One incident came about as the result of a Crown Royal battle during an Aleutian storm. The battles were regular occurrences and eagerly anticipated as record winds confined the pair for days on end. After finishing the mundane chores, there would be little to do. They would prepare dinner and in a little while would get out a bottle of Don's favorite whiskey and begin to talk. Inevitably, the conversation would get around to camp problems, for which each had a different solution. To say that they were both stubborn was an understatement. All that was left to do was to prove their point. Sometimes that would take a long time, as was the case involving the wood in the sunken barge.

Joe had a trackster the size of a Sherman tank. The iron monster could roll over the tundra in snow or mud without complaint, and Joe intended to use the big vehicle to prove he could salvage the wreck. The very fact that Don had told him it was impractical and couldn't be done spurred him on.

The barge was deeply embedded in a muddy bank where it had been thrown in a storm. It might as well have been in cement. Don was certain that after the winter freeze the barge would be immovable, but Joe was of German heritage; he was determined. Each beam, some as long as 36 feet, evoked a satisfied grunt as Joe dragged its weathered form up onto the beach. He couldn't wait until the feat was accomplished just to win.

Joe knew the 36-foot 8-x-10 would make an ideal center beam in the big bar-game room. With salvage from the barge and the icehouse remnants, he would surely have enough lumber to build the lodge. They were Alaskans and a long way from the wood mill; besides there was nothing Joe liked better than to be inventive.

Actually, the day he won the argument, there was a strange occurrence.

Don had been ferrying fuel from the Port Moller airstrip to the lodge in the Super-Cub. He stopped on the cannery runway after the third trip for a chat with Joe.

The mechanic had spent the better part of the day dragging huge beams three miles from the port to the airstrip where visiting helicopters would later be asked to haul them over the mountains to Bear Lake. As Don landed, Joe watched furtively. His hands were busy untying the last of the lumber from the trackster's side. Neither of them acknowledged the completion of Joe's controversial feat, but instead were distracted by the sound of a Northern Air Cargo C-182 twin, tall cargo plane roaring onto the runway.

A 180 had crashed near a mountain in the vicinity. It wasn't unusual for planes to crash in the Aleutians, and Northern Air Cargo, out of Anchorage, had made a good living from their salvage.

Bobby Shulton, owner of the company, leaped out of the plane and waved a greeting. "I brought my nephew, Joe," he yelled into the brisk wind. "Thought he might get a moose while we are here."

After a brief chat with Don, the trio left in the trackster headed over the tundra for a three-mile trip to hunt. Don took off in the plane with two more barrels of fuel. By the time he returned and reloaded, he decided to over-fly the area where the hunt was taking place to see if the boy had been successful.

During his flight, the trackster lumbered across the bog, groaning up a knoll before the men climbed out and hiked about 150 yards. Joe knew the area well. Being familiar with the game, he could usually locate what he hunted. He paused on a rise and glassed the area below. A big bull moose was grazing lazily.

Bobby handed his .300 Savage to his nephew and grinned, saying, "That's a good one—go to it." The boy took aim and fired. A bullet lodged in the animal's lower front leg before the magazine fell out of the gun. Joe swore.

While the men scrambled on the ground awkwardly, the moose started running. Without hesitation, Joe pulled out his Gerber knife and raced down the hill just in front of the animal. Then, leaping at the rack, Joe's right arm ringed the moose's neck. As the big bull fled with the German attached, Joe slashed its throat with the knife. Blood gushed out, completely covering Joe's face and glasses just as the moose hit the creek. The Super-Cub roared over the comic scene. Blinded, Joe let go and fell headlong into swift water as the animal leaped across.

Laughing hard, Don was so engrossed in the action below he almost failed to see an upcoming peak and narrowly avoided crashing into it.

The water, washing Joe's startled face, cleaned his glasses as he rose out of the creek just in time to see Don's plane roar straight up. He laughed hard watching the pilot barely miss the mountain top.

By now everyone was doubled up with laughter, and the game was lying dead on the opposite bank. Joe scurried across the clearing, headed for the vehicle and dry clothes. After Bobby and his nephew skinned out their quarry and salvaged the plane, they loaded up and flew out.

That night Joe and Don fixed supper at the lodge and decided to celebrate the extraordinary hunt. It took a few Crown Royals before they actually got going. Finally Don said, "Okay, you son-of-a-bitch, next time we have a moose hunt, all you get to hunt with is a bag of salt and a knife." That night there was no arguing, only celebrating.

On another occasion, they had been cabin-bound for some five days while outside a gale was in full force. About 2 a.m. Joe announced he could make a fortune floating empty oil-drums down the torturous Bear River to the Bering Sea, a distance of some 10 miles. He said that if he tied them together, when they reached the ocean all he would have to do is have a salmon boat tow them to the cannery. Then, when the next freighter came in from Seattle, he would crane them to the hold. They were worth $55 per drum.

After all the years Don had been flying into camp, there were hundreds of them piled near the lake. Joe had figured he would make at least $20,000 on the deal. They had another drink. Don was adamant—it couldn't be done. The clash lasted until four. Don went to sleep on the couch, and Joe left for his rendezvous with destiny. As Don was dozing, he imagined Joe might make it six or seven miles downriver. A soft chuckle escaped, and he fell into a deep sleep.

Around nine, Don awoke. The clouds were low, and soft rain oozed down the windowpanes. He definitely needed coffee. Shortly, cup in hand, he headed for the Super-Cub and took off. It was time to round up Joe, who he imagined by this time was very cold and wet. Within a few minutes, he was miles up the Bear River, circling an island down below. There was Joe, asleep and curled up into a fetal knot in the island's center, surrounded by a cluster of red gas barrels strung haphazardly about.

No one ever did retrieve the barrels; they are rusting in the river to this day.

Both men always agreed that Bear Lake needed a Caterpillar. The big machine would be invaluable in moving game, hauling equipment and dragging trash to the dump a mile from the lodge, but it would be especially useful in repairing the runways. In fact, on this one occasion their only quarrel was how long it would take to get it to Bear Lake after its arrival in Port Moller aboard a freighter.

After it was craned to the dock, Don drove it to the runway, and they started out across the tundra. The trip was a 20-minute flight over the mountains—on the ground it would take much longer. Bets were made, but they were both wrong—it took three years. Of course, movement was done on an occasional basis when someone could be flown to the spot where it had been left. They would spend the whole day moving turtle-like across the bogs and gullies, rising slowly up to the mountains. Eventual arrival at the lodge heralded the feat, and a party ensued.

Although life was difficult, great friendships were forming. Yolman and Carpa Orloff, the two Aleut fishermen, were now brothers to Don. He became their mentor as he had Allan Rock in Point Hope.

The following spring, in 1966, on a routine flight into camp, Don turned off the sea and started flying upriver. Further up the coast, he could see a crowd gathered near Yolman's fishing site. It puzzled the pilot. Banking deep, he over-flew the scene. Down below he saw many familiar faces, and in the middle of the crowd, a body lying on the beach. Upon landing, he learned it was the old man, Yolman.

The Aleut was 75 at the time and still fishing regularly. The seas were raging furiously after a storm, and the 118-pound Aleut had lost his footing and fallen overboard. Becoming hopelessly tangled in his nets and unable to climb out, Yolman drowned. Danny Lynch, one of Don's guides, found and recovered the body. By the time Don arrived, everyone at the village had gathered at the spot.

The tragedy affected everyone who knew and loved him, especially his son, Carpa, the other man Don had once seen standing and staring out at the sea. Don's anguish was acute. He had come to love the old man as he would a father. Never again would he over-fly the village without picturing the slight Eskimo standing by his small house staring out at the sea he loved so much—the sea which ultimately claimed his life.

Carpa ordered his sons to take the boat to a nearby island and burn it. It was their custom. He and his family never returned to the ancient village, which today stands in decay. It had been in existence for hundreds of years and had been actively inhabited until the flu epidemic of 1919 almost wiped out the entire tribe.

There was great sadness on that part of the Aleutians. The villagers took up a collection for a tombstone which would mark the spot of Yolman's grave alongside his beloved land. It was the only Aleut gravestone in the Aleutian islands—a tribute from those who cared.

After the old man's death, Carpa moved his family to a fishing shack near the cannery and later to a trailer home mounted on a pad at the foot of a mountain just beneath the huge Alice Communications Station. The station faced Russia. The government had built the concrete structure for housing electronics, outside of which was a mammoth metal radar barrier. Down below, on a desolate road, were old military barracks. Don had purchased them with the intention of housing hunters there during bear season. The barracks included quite a bit of waterfront property and huge oil tanks which Don would later fill with aviation fuel to sell and use in his business.

Having been located at the site beneath the Alice station, Carpa needed a truck to drive the 20 miles to the cannery where he moored his boat.

It was a costly undertaking to fly vehicles to the islands in a C-183 which could only transport two at a time. Since Don needed trucks at airport stops, he offered to buy two and share the expense of the $8,000 shipping bill with the Aleut. Carpa was frank—he had no money. The statement shocked the pilot. Fishermen regularly made several hundred thousand dollars during lucrative salmon runs. Carpa said he had been told the purchases in the company store by his family and relatives from Nelson Lagoon, a nearby fishing village, had eroded his funds from the catch.

Don's rage rose as he went immediately to the Japanese accountant at the cannery office. A heated discussion resulted, but from that point on, Carpa Orloff's payment was in the form of a check made out to the two men. Shortly thereafter, Carpa's bills were paid, and money was allocated for expenses—the balance of the fortune was invested in an inland bank. In the future Carpa's children will reap the benefit of that astute kindness.

Don would have preferred to ignore the issue after it had been settled, but Carpa, who made home brew and enjoyed sampling it rather heavily, decided the world should know of his good fortune. And in the state he was in one particularly stormy night, he got on his radio to tell friends and relatives and all the ships at sea just what his friend had done.

The only problem was that he used some rather unflattering comments about the foreign owners and gave Don complete credit for the matter. Don was eating his dinner at the lodge when the broadcast started. He said, "I damn near swallowed my fork, and it took quite a while before I could get in the plane and stop him."

On another occasion, after realizing that his Aleut friends were using their considerable incomes to buy liquor to help pass the time during idle frozen months, Don became concerned. He also learned that catalogues, which arrived in the mail, resulted in thousands-upon-thousands of dollars worth of purchases, which were often unusable in that remote place. However, catalogue sales soon dwindled as Don said, "Somehow, the damned things just fell out of the airplane while I was flying over the Bering Sea."

Don's generosity extended to trips for his adopted brothers. On several occasions, he took Carpa to Las Vegas; the Aleut had never been off the Chain. And one year he took the entire family to Disneyland.

By now, the Johnson children were grown; Don took immense pride in their accomplishments. It was the end of the '60s. He bought his daughter, Lori, a fishing permit and enjoyed her prowess. In time she would captain her own boat and crew. Audrey, the youngest daughter planned to marry Mark Hodgins. Don gave the young couple land on the homestead, where they started building a home. His son, Warren, had been flying since he was 15 and began flying regularly for Kenai Float Plane Service. Ultimately, he would take over its management completely. Between flights and during the summer, he fished on the Bering seacoast in the Johnson's salmon boat.

The camp was running smoothly, and cooking for the guests was an integral part of the operation. Five or six loaves of fresh bread were baked daily for ravenous guests who were enticed by the scent; a soup pot simmered on the sideboard daily for incoming visitors or guests and, of course, the bottomless coffee pot was always available in the big dining room. In the afternoons, desserts were baked, and a constant supply of cookies filled the pantry. The trappers, guides, pilots and guests were usually hungry.

Dick Remur, the bartender, kept a truck garden watered and free of marmots whose energies were spent digging beneath the fence to get at the plump harvest. It was a rare treat to have fresh produce from their tundra garden.

Game was the principal entree served in the lodge. Fish, caught no less than an hour before dinner, was flanked by two or three kinds of meat along with sundry vegetables, canned fruit and warm bread.

Finding the ingredients for all the delicious dishes wasn't simple. Much of the time storms plagued the area, and fresh eggs were unavailable. Don made flights to sand spits off the coast where seagulls had hidden their spotted eggs away from prying eyes of marauding foxes. The yolks are salmon-colored and taste exactly like chicken eggs, although much larger.

Milk flavored as if it just came from the dairy was now available in cans which could be stored for indefinite periods of time. That really saved the day in the camp kitchen.

Preparing a grocery list for a six-month period at Bear Lake took some doing and much experience. Upon arrival on a freighter from Seattle, supplies were craned to the dock at Port Moller, and trucked to the runway three miles away where bush planes waited to ferry them to the lodge. That chore alone would take two planes three full days to complete. The bill was a hefty $10,000.

In season, grateful crab fishermen would supply Bear Lake with a Super-Cub full of the leggy catch. A waiting water-filled oil-drum would boil on the tundra. Then, after everyone left the lodge to unload the plane, the crabs were boiled, lifted out with long tongs and carried to the kitchen where picking, cleaning, tasting and bagging provided an entertaining evening. For some, it was a first-time experience which would long be remembered.

Oil companies studying geology in Alaska eventually found their way to the Aleutian Islands where they planned explora-

173

tion. It was not uncommon for 20, or more, geologists, helicopters and pilots to arrive at Bear Lake. Actually, there was no other place in the vicinity to house them. Their arrival doubled the work. Unlike hunters and fishermen, the oil explorers got up and out by 6:30. The help in charge would wash, dry and fold the mountains of clothing these young professionals would wear.

By the middle '70s, Don had installed a light plant in the new lodge. Bear Lake then had its own electricity, powered by the roaring river, which ran freezers, lights in the compound, washer and dryers, a record player, portable "canned" television, radios and electrical appliances for the kitchen and the essential windometer.

However, Tim Okonek and Slim Gale, Don's guide-trappers who also work as caretakers in camp during dormant winter months, prefer a more primitive life. Unlike their compadres, they still wash their clothes in the Bear River, anchoring the items with heavy rocks. Of course, on occasions when a good blow hits the Chain, they have found their laundry miles downriver, and after having been tumbled in the racing current, clean but in pretty bad shape.

The pair, both in their late 20s, live in the old lodge and spend a lot of time filming animals. They decided a long time ago that they needed very little to live on. Don explained their salary is usually deposited, untouched, in an inland bank. Once in awhile, when Don is leaving on a long flight to Anchorage, he will ask if they need anything. Sometimes they will request a new trap for their lines or special thread for the fur boots they make. They are, perhaps, the last of the mountain men.

While the crowds arriving at Bear Lake became larger, the demand for airplane fuel increased. The choppers used barrels of it; the bush planes on regular runs were constantly in need of refueling, and during hunting season there was the business of ferrying clients and supplies to spike camps. The chore was an arduous one, but Don believed he should be the one to do it since it was always dangerous.

The demands on his time were increasing, and running three

businesses was all-consuming.

Over the years, clients who came from sophisticated environments often became angry with the pilot-guide for not answering letters or invitations. And he was notorious for not being where he was supposed to be at any given time. Few stopped to consider his time clock depended on game sightings, weather and airplanes.

He had lived in a world without telephones for so long he rarely used them even when they were available. But the most important matter was the unequalled turmoil in his life. There were so many challenges, all being handled at once, that it was nearly impossible to accomplish them—let alone keep on schedule.

Legendary storms in the "Birthplace of the winds," or the frozen arctic, were never predictable, a fact which probably would have driven a businessman to distraction, but Don took it all in stride. None of it could have been achieved had he taken the time to discuss the matter with anyone. He rarely explained his actions, and when confronted with the request to do so, merely shrugged and walked away. And yet, in spring, when the lodge was being readied for clients and the gunsmiths, workers, cooks, bartenders and sundry friends who would fly in at his invitation, he would have them take time out for fun.

There were wonderful flights over the tundra to spot game. In an instant he was spiraling over a bear chewing contentedly on a dead walrus or soaring low over the seal rookeries, while laughing at the excited comments coming from his passengers. No one ever refused a trip to the caves where the seagulls had stashed their eggs. Most guests eventually were taken to scavenge on the treasure-filled beaches, or offered a line to catch a plump, red salmon. It was obvious he loved to fly, loved his land and was happy to expose it to those who appreciated that rare treat.

The Aleutians in winter from the air.

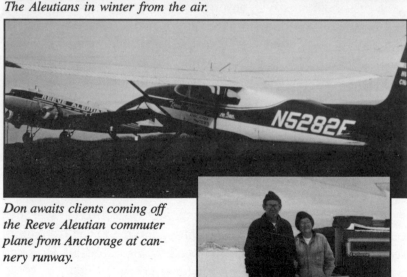

Don awaits clients coming off the Reeve Aleutian commuter plane from Anchorage at cannery runway.

Friends, Joe Sanger and Rachel Rogers, watch Don's take-off on the Port Moller runway.

Chapter 21

Hunting Marco Polo Sheep in Kabul

T he penchant for hunting increased as did Don's exotic game collection.

In August 1966, he left for Afghanistan at the invitation of Gazi, the King's brother, whom the guide had met on a previous hunt in Africa. This particular hunt promised to be interesting. They were after Marco Polo sheep, which roost high in the Hindu Kush Mountains on the Afghanistan-China border. In fact, the magnificent rams are only found at 18,000 feet on the Pamir Plateau, aptly called the "Roof of the World."

Much care would be taken of the hunters since a thin needle of land on their proposed route, 100-miles long, was in the Primeres in the USSR, and they were guests of a monarch.

The big interest was game, but the geographic location also elicited intrigue. A land of unrecorded peaks, of the romantic Khyber Pass, of giant cliff-carved Buddhas, of Bagram ivory carvings, of the great Mosque of Junsma Masjid begun in the 12th Century, and of women in purdah and voluminous chadris. This was a place where the national sport, Bozkashi, is played by teams of Moslem horsemen who try to retrieve a beheaded goat. But it was also a place where poverty is the rule and rampant disease a fact.

And, since Don was being accompanied by Nicoli Franco, a Spaniard he had guided for polar bear at Point Hope in 1959 (who was the nephew of General Franco of Spain), much thought was given to the state of their health—so much so that Don telephoned the problem to a specialist in Los Angeles. The result of the call produced a kit from UCLA Medical School complete with instructions. Don added two huge bottles filled with blue and pink baby aspirin purchased in Anchorage to the black suitcase. He had hunted the world experiencing the needs of simplistic people. Reassured, Nicoli asked one proviso— General Franco wanted the bag when the hunt was over. UCLA Medical School enjoyed a special respect in the world medical community. The General was anxious to have it.

Nicoli was a devotee of the hunt, and as anxious as Don to acquire the treasured trophy. Both men were experienced; they even shared a rather ribald sense of humor. There was, however, one major difference between them—Nicoli's family were dictators, and, as such, had to exercise constant care against assassins. So, when the 727 they were flying to Kabul made an unscheduled landing at Istanbul, Turkey, Nicoli became extremely agitated.

Don had been sleeping. The plane was still at flying speed when they touched down, which brought the Alaskan bolt-upright in his seat. Having raced off the end of the runway, the big jet thumped awkwardly off into a field, stopping abruptly on the edge of a cliff.

No one on board seemed the least bit perturbed except the two hunters who glared open-mouthed at each other. While they tried to regain their composure, rickety buses lumbered out across the field to meet deplaning passengers. Nicoli loudly refused to get off. Hurrying back to the cabin, the pilots started to harangue him.

After such an unusual landing, Don interceded saying, "Let's get the hell off this thing. It isn't safe." He had been flying for over 20 years and had never experienced a landing like this one. He certainly didn't want to give those two a chance to do it again. The Spaniard blanched before gasping out, "We wouldn't live the night out here. I'm not getting off this plane."

Shrugging, Don went back to sleep, leaving his friend arguing in French. Eventually an agreement was reached—there would be a four-hour delay for repairs, and then the flight would continue on to Iran. By morning, the 727 with a new crew landed in Tehran, a long way from Kabul. Don was prepared for the usual hassles over guns and ammunition, and while he started to battle, Nicoli left to call the palace.

The Shah of Iran and his brother, Prince Alvarez, were close, personal friends. It paid to have friends in court—a limousine appeared shortly to take the pair to the Spanish Embassy on the outskirts of the teeming city.

The arms and ammunition, sans their actions, were stored safely until departure, and the hunters were treated with new respect.

Later that evening, the visitors were invited to the palace to see Prince Alvarez's game room. The collection was reputed to be one of the finest in the world. The Prince and a few of his hunting companions were preparing to go on a water buffalo hunt in Australia. They invited the newcomers to join them. The Spaniard agreed; Don remained mute. A lifelong habit of finishing whatever he started prevented any other course. 'Besides,' he thought, 'I don't want to offend Gazi.'

After dinner they returned to the embassy. Don sought the aid of a secretary in sending Gazi a wire. It read: "AM STUCK IN TEHRAN STOP NO PLANES AVAILABLE FOR KABUL STOP DON."

Within two days a wire arrived from the Prince of Afghanistan. "AM SENDING A 727 TOMORROW STOP EXPECT YOU FOR THE HUNT STOP GAZI."

Arrival in Kabul was thankfully uneventful. Gazi met them with a car and a driver. They were escorted to a plain, but comfortable, hotel where they immediately set about acquiring essentials for the hunt. Oxygen was a basic for survival at 18,000 feet. They ordered 112 bottles, plus 15 cases of U.S. Army C-rations, available only on the black market and which Gazi said was important. Food in that part of the world was scarce. Their hospitable host made all the arrangements. There was one other very important matter. Don and Nicoli each put up $500, and

Don took a cab to the nearest bank. Inside, he motioned to an official and pointed to piles of currency on a shelf behind the counter. A broad smile and 10 crisp $100 bills lifted the banker's eyebrows. Obviously impressed, the man began collecting the cache of red, blue, purple and yellow puls and afghanis which he dropped into a paper bag. Returning to the hotel and after entering the room, Don impulsively emptied the contents of the sack onto the bed where his companion was lying half asleep. Eyes bulging, the hunter bolted upright and exclaimed, "Christ!"

"Here, it's half yours," Don said chuckling. It was enough to fill two suitcases. At least, they would not have a problem tipping their carriers.

A knock brought a message from Gazi. "The King will see you for tea at four p.m. tomorrow. His car will call for you."

The meeting was in an impoverished government building which Nicoli said looked like a jailhouse. The room, reminiscent of army mess halls, contained walled maps of the country showing selected hunting cabins at 10,000-foot elevations. Army units protected the camps which were close to the Russian and Chinese borders.

During tea, the King explained through an interpreter how the hunt would be accomplished. They were to ride yaks to the pinnacle after having left the 14,000-foot campsite at midnight. At daybreak they would be where the sheep roost. He suggested they fly a government Otter to Falzabad and take Land-Rovers into the Primeres. Horses and yaks would be provided for transportation from that point.

Don listened attentively until the King finished, then he leaned into Gazi whispering, "Can I shoot two sheep?" Nicoli elbowed Don, "Get me two." Don remained mute.

The interpreter spoke humbly to the monarch transmitting the request. The answer was firm. "Additional sheep will cost six-thousand dollars apiece." He asked for paper and wrote something briefly. Without further adieu, he rose, bowed silently to the two men and left. Immediately, the interpreter approached Don whispering politely, "There is a message for you."

Puzzled, the hunter stared at him. "Well, what does it say?"

His host seemed reluctant to speak. Instead, he handed Don a note which read, "Mr. Johnson may get more than one sheep." Showing his gratitude, Don mumbled, "Thank you."

The Otter roared into the desert oasis of Falzabad where steamy temperatures of 115 degrees encased them as they descended to the airport. A band of ominous-looking horsemen waited to escort them to a village. They were taken to a stone building, devoid of furniture, where they were introduced to the Army commander in charge of the borders. Pillows arrived, and the officer motioned to them to sit down. Once they were cross-legged on the floor, Don told the so-called interpreter what to say. His English left much to be desired; however, he made a valiant effort to converse. Suddenly he said, "Where is your permission to hunt?"

Staring over at Nicoli, Don explained awkwardly, "Hell, I got the note from the King but no permission."

The interpreter went on, saying, "The Colonel is very sorry, but he has orders—no one goes into the Primeres without permission."

Nicoli said, "Well, you tell the Colonel we're sorry as hell about his problem, but if he doesn't let us go in I'll get his ass fired."

Struggling with the language was difficult enough; the man turned pale and became obviously frightened. "I cannot tell him that!" he gasped.

Don's impatience was showing. "Christ, Nicoli, this guy's got his orders, lay off." Then, turning to the interpreter he said, "Please ask the Colonel to send a wire to the King."

It took 10 minutes to discern the fact that there were no wires, no telephones, no communications—just runners on horseback which the Colonel would gladly send. Meanwhile, they were served hard-boiled eggs and tea. After a bit, the interpeter said they were going to their hotel.

When they arrived and viewed the structure, Don chuckled at the look on his companion's face. Except for the Colonel's office, it was the only building they had seen. There were holes for windows but no panes, no door and a dirt floor. The bedroom contained two reed beds with no mattresses, and crooked willow branches served as slats.

"I'll be damned if I'll sleep in that pig-sty," Nicoli bellowed as Don stood by laughing. "Aw, come on, let's take these beds outside and put our sleeping bags in them."

Nicoli was right—the place was filthy, but they had no other choice. The night turned out to be long and hot, but by mid-morning the messenger galloped into camp with their approval.

For the next three days they moved across a barren desert in Land-Rovers. Natives, who appeared from nowhere, were used to building temporary bridges across washed-out roads and ravines. They were approaching Russia and had traveled 150 miles. Soldiers accompanied the caravan. Women with children appeared dressed in rags, trailing their men and horses, behind which were animals. It was a grand parade.

A half-mile from the Russian border, they saw a nice bungalow on a promontory surrounded by a three-foot stone wall. Two Afghan soldiers guarded the entrance. It turned out to be the King's hunting lodge which had not been used for 15 years. Inside was a comfortable living room with homemade furniture, two beds without mattresses and a door to a locked room. Don pried open the lock, exposing a big bathroom with no running water, but which contained an enormous bathtub. "Well, that's more like it," he said, winking. Pulling out some of his "play" money, he handed it to the interpreter. "Okay, tell them lots of hot water."

Outside, a campsite was being prepared. Don peered out calling to his companion, "Holy shit, will you look at this?"

There were 30 soldiers and horses, 15 natives, 100 sheep and goats and two Land-Rovers. The two men laughed for 10 minutes.

After a refreshing bath with hot water, two bourbons and C-rations, they felt human again. It was a pleasant sojourn, and they were eager to hunt.

The trek would become more difficult from here. Sargus was two days away at 14,000 feet. By now, yaks had replaced horses for the long, perilous climb up winding, rocky trails. At 15,000 feet they would use masks, sucking at precious oxygen for two minutes out of every half hour. And, of course, the protectors would have to wait for them where the air was not so rare.

Somehow the contents of the hunter's black bag became known. Before long, word had spread throughout the hills of Afghanistan and, like Jesus, Don was being greeted at every hamlet where the sick had been called out. Farsightedness really paid off. These people had never had medicine; antibiotics could have killed them, and the baby aspirin satisfied their curiosity. By mid-trip "Doctor" Johnson could see it was the "in" thing to do to get in line, sick or not. His life among the Eskimos had been keen preparation for dealing with primitives. At each stop, the head man would offer him tea and hard-boiled eggs before making the request. Then, the good doctor would start dispensing his pink and blue healers to the whole community.

By the time they reached base camp, the entourage was enlarged by 20 more, and they had lost count of the animals that were multiplying like flies. At least, they were not alone. The suitcase full of play money melted into eager hands, and Doc Johnson was becoming a hero in the hills.

The yak ride to the valley where Marco Polo sheep graze was dangerous, but a sheer drop from the trail became less ominous after dark. By morning the hunters were at 18,000 feet, on top of the world in a beautiful valley. The hunters flipped a coin to see who would get the first shot. Nicoli won.

They had been warned not to cross the peaks—the other side was China. Once they were on foot, Don scoped 17 beautiful animals bedded down on the crest of the mountain. Excitement rose as the men studied the herd for their quarry. There was much conversation about which was larger. Nicoli raised his rifle, but before he could use his scope, the herd got up and raced into China.

"Oh, shit," was heard loud and clear. They were both disgusted. For the next 10 days they searched the valley desperately without a sighting.

On the eleventh day, they made their perilous midnight climb, reaching a spot near a glacier by eight a.m. Sniffing the oxygen frequently and stalking their prey all day left the pair exhausted by nightfall. Just before they returned to base camp, Don glassed the herd bedding down near the top. "I'm staying here," Don said as he handed Nicoli the binoculars. "I'm going to retreat a mile or so—we don't want to scare those sheep again."

The guides became nervous. They told Don through the interpreter that it was very dangerous, and they were running low on oxygen. "Okay, send the yaks back for gear and more oxygen—but I'm staying."

When they ran out of the life-giving gas, they were plagued with severe headaches. A biting wind raced across the top of the world, chilling them to the bone.

At last, the yaks returned with food, extra bedding and the oxygen. Taking a good whiff, Don crawled into his bag and slept soundly until three a.m. Upon waking he felt famished, but even more eager for the oxygen.

They loaded their weapons on the yaks and moved quietly up the valley toward the glacier. Just before dawn, they were a half-mile from the herd. Leaving the animals with a carrier, they tracked on foot. Fierce, crying winds battered the two down-covered figures moving with stealth across the remote plateau in darkness. The temperature dropped to zero every night on the "Roof of the World." In gray light the landscape appeared captivating and unreal. Don's mukluks barely marred the glacier. Up ahead a treasure awaited, and by daybreak they topped out on the peak. A new day glistened and reflected against ice. Don squinted, then grinned. Down below the glacier was a lush green meadow where 17 Marco Polo sheep slept.

The cold was forgotten as he pulled off down mittens and took a firm grip on the .300 H&H, after first glassing the herd. He had the advantage. All the years of flying and guiding the Wrangells had sharpened his eye. Nicoli sighed impatiently. They knew the first shots would frighten the game. Each man scoped, poised for the volleys. Don used 220-grain magnums and "aimed for the brisket"—bang, bang, bang. He snorted as they fell, and his companion finished firing. They laughed, running hurriedly toward the meadow and watching the remaining sheep flee to China.

By now, the newness of a clear, crisp morning flooded the pinnacle, and below, China unfolded before their eyes. There was almost a reverence in the place, shades of Shangri-La. And now, sunlight warmed them.

The guides brought the yaks to the summit. Photographs were taken, and the group headed for an interim camp one last time.

For Don, all the inconvenience melted into oblivion. He had shot a beautiful snow leopard at 14,000 feet and a Chinese ibex. The King had said, "Mr. Johnson may have more than one sheep." He had three: one for his collection, one for the Alaskan museum, and one for his son—a gift from Asia.

Back at the 14,000-foot camp, they were treated to hot showers in canvas tents with water relayed up thousands of feet by carriers, then boiled over open fires. Camp followers flushed and salted the hides before putting them into burlap sacks. After dinner and a few bourbons, the satisfied pair climbed into their sleeping bags anticipating a good night's sleep. Around midnight, Nicoli bolted into a sitting position. "What the hell is that?" he growled.

Shaking his head, Don tried to awaken as he pulled open the tent flap and peered out. Turning back, he squinted one eye before saying, "There are six of the meanest-looking guys out there I ever saw."

"What they hell do they want?"

"Hell, I don't know but I'll bet we'll find out pretty quick. Here comes our interpreter."

The little man bowed a lot. He was so polite and so apologetic at having disturbed them, but the leader of the tribe in a nearby village was ill. They wanted the doctor-hunter to come quick.

"Oh, Christ! I knew it," wailed the Spaniard. "You and that goddamned black bag are going to get us killed."

Don shrugged. Climbing out of the sleeping bag, he started to put on his clothes.

His partner looked startled. "Don—you can't go. You are no doctor. I'll never see you again."

"Well, shit—that's a mean-looking crew. You go out there and tell them no."

Within half-an-hour, Doctor Johnson was dropped off outside a white yurt. Inside were two women cooking over a dung fire on a raised section against the wall. The smoke floated lazily overhead escaping from a hole in the roof. In a submerged pit in the center of the one-room house, swathed in fur skins, rested a man.

Kneeling down and laying a hand on the sweat-bathed forehead, Don mumbled, "Jesus, you are really sick." He sighed at the futility of his mission. The body, shaking with fever, looked emaciated under a fur coverlet. Two glassy eyes rolled back in his head until only the whites showed, and his pulse was very weak.

The women watched quietly, their black eyes overwhelming in veiled faces. There was no sound except for the wind and the sick man's labored breathing.

Opening the bag, Don removed the instructions. Most of them were too complicated to use on anyone that sick. 'This guy has never had medicine in his life,' he thought. 'But, what the hell—he ain't gonna make it anyway. So, here goes. I'll give him something for the trots in case he's got them and something in case he don't. I'll give him Terramycin for something really bad and some aspirin in case he's got a headache.' Then taking out a hunting knife, he cut all the pills in half. It seemed a reasonable thing to do. Finally, he asked for water in sign language and when he received it, he forced the pills down the man's throat. Preparing three piles of the pills, he showed the woman his watch and described time passing, advising as best he could to give patient medicine every few hours. The woman's tarry retinas glistened with appreciation as she nodded her understanding. Whether she understood or not he would never know. When he left it was two a.m., pitch-black outside, and the band of yak riders had mysteriously disappeared.

Don cursed as he hiked along the dirt trail toward camp. When he finally arrived and entered the tent, Nicoli yelled, "God, am I glad to see you—I figured you were dead."

Caustic laughter oozed out. "I might be yet. That poor bastard is really sick," he sighed. "But, I did what I could, and I'm really tired." In seconds he was asleep.

When Don awoke, Nicoki was standing over him. Fear laced his look. "They're back," he said nervously.

"Oh, yeah?" Don answered. "How do they look?"

"Meaner than before," the man paused and lowered his voice. "Don't go."

They stared at each other for an uncertain moment. Don reached for his rifle, thinking, 'Well, if I'm gonna get killed, I might just as well go down swingin'.'

Outside the interpreter bowed deep. "Please, sir, they want you to come."

Don smirked. "No, I don't think so. I don't know what's goin' on."

Nicoli screamed, "I can't stand much more of this!"

The interpreter's pleasant smile grew on swarthy skin. His eyes lit appreciatively. "It's all right. Their leader is better."

By now Don was feeling giddy; his luck had held again. He went out and climbed onto the yak. The entrance into the village was reminiscent of Palm Sunday in Jerusalem. The entire village had amassed, smiling broadly, making animated sounds and waving. It was the Afghans' version of a ticker-tape parade, and Don Johnson was the hero.

Outside the yurt, their leader rested against a doorjamb on a fur rug. He was still sick but smiling gratefully as the doctor knelt beside him to feel the now-dry head. The fever had broken; he was weak and humbled. His women brought yak yogurt as an offering. Don remembered his Eskimo friends. Smiling broadly, he bowed before dipping a hunting knife into the pot and pretending to sample it. They all cheered in unison. Finally, the townspeople formed a long, unruly line in front of their savior. And, one by one, they were given the precious pink and blue pills now famous in Afghanistan.

This time, Don returned to camp in triumph. Leading the scruffy band, sitting high on the yak and waving a greeting, he rode in.

The Spaniard's eyes flew heavenward. He would indeed be thankful when this hunt was over, and they were both safely back in civilization. But, 'for now,' he thought, half-amused, 'we'll have a whiskey to celebrate.'

As eventful as the trip had been, it wasn't over. On the arduous trail down from Sargas, one of the pack animals went over the side, careening thousands of feet to its death. The experience sobered everyone as they exercised extreme caution moving down the steep, rocky trail.

Six days later, they arrived at Falzabad. They were met by the Colonel who had a message from the King. One of his soldiers had been wounded in a town near the Russian border. He wanted Don to fly the Otter in to pick him up. There was one rub—they would have to over-fly Russian territory to the spot without permission.

By this time, Nicoli realized there was no use arguing with his stubborn friend. They had no radio equipment on the plane, and the maps were inadequate at best.

Flying the bush in the arctic prepared Don, and he considered the request a challenge; immediately, he climbed into the Otter. Being a careful observer and given the carelessness with which these people lived, he was certain the kerosene used to fuel the craft wasn't pure. He asked for chamois skins and personally supervised the straining of 175 gallons. They certainly needed every advantage.

Meanwhile, the Colonel drew a fairly decent map detailing where the wounded man was, where they were at present, and just how much of Russia lay in between. It meant flying around the peaks and down walled canyons while staying beneath radar.

For Don it was just another bush run and an exciting one at that. For Nicoli it was suicide. Fortunately, the weather was good. The scenery added zest to their flight through giant crags. The canyons were magnificent; unspoiled rock cathedrals finally opened onto a plateau where a crowd gathered by a long dirt strip. A huge sigh escaped the Spaniard's lips as they touched down and raced toward them.

They were both unprepared for what happened next. After the wounded man was carried on board by military personnel, the crowd surged in behind. Don gaped. He yelled at them to get off, but to no avail. Soon both Caucasians were screaming, unheard in the noisy throng. Gunning the engines, the pilot forced the plane down the strip. One of the crowd pulled the door shut. They were seriously overweight. Don taxied as far as he dared, turned around and forced the engine wide-open, hoping they would clear the mountains. The plane rose swiftly—tension mounted in the cockpit as the plane cleared the unforgiving rock.

Hours later they landed safely in Kabul. Once they parked, utter confusion broke out on board. Nicoli and Don were escorted off the ship while the horde was detained by soldiers. After questioning an officer, the two men learned there was a fee for the ride which amounted to $3 American. Apparently, the interlopers had no money. Shaking weary heads, the men eagerly climbed into a waiting truck while their gear was removed from the Otter.

Back at their hotel and following a hot shower, clean clothes, a good meal and drinks, the pair started to laugh. It was a hunt to end all hunts.

When they unwrapped their trophies, they found them teeming with vermin. Don quickly filled the bathtub with scalding water and dunked the hides into it. Drying them was another matter.

Gazi called and was reassured of the hunters' pleasure. Later the same night, they made reservations for London and prepared to leave.

As had always been the case, extra cash changed hands along the route. By the time they arrived at Heathrow Airport, Don had paid out $800 to people who saw the trophies as a means to steal. Frustrated and running out of cash, he headed for the airline shipping office. The man behind the counter was very

Pamir Plateau, "Roof of the World"—home of the Marco Polo sheep. Afghan-China border.

British and conscientious, and he was also a hunter. After a brief conversation regarding the hunt, he raised a wry smile, saying, "Blimey, govnor, hi'll get those skins to Halaska or hi'll know the reason why."

"How much?" Don asked with apprehension.

"Twenty pounds."

The hunter relaxed, thanked the man and left.

Alaska was a different story. Officials made a scene as the hides were brought in. Don was at wit's end. He'd come halfway around the world, had spent a fortune and now his own people were refusing him entry. Raw anger surfaced. At one point, he said later, he almost set the damned things on fire.

After a long tirade, an official appeared who agreed to seal them and send them to the taxidermist where they could be sanitized. Then, he stared at the hunter and said, "If I were you and had been where you've been, I'd go home, strip down on the front porch, burn my clothes and use disinfectant on my body." Don laughed. It was not the first trip which hadn't been ideal—it wouldn't be the last. And now, he had the prize of the Himalayas for his collection.

Don with Marco Polo trophy, Afghanistan 1966.

Nicoli Franco with his Marco Polo trophy on Afghan-China border.

The Prince of Iran poses with an average black bear he took on a hunt with Don Johnson.

Chapter 22

Some Bears Are Harder To Track Dead Than Alive

Promise of an early winter blew snow squalls across Austria in the fall of 1968 as Doctor Fritz Wechselberger left his home in Linz bound for the Aleutian islands.

During the long flight over the North Pole, Fritz had mixed emotions. It was time for the annual red deer stag hunt, and rutting season had already begun. Pangs of nostalgia surfaced as he pictured his snug, snow-ladened Jaghutte near Hinterstoder on the banks of the Gams Jagd River. Mathias, his professional hunter, would take some of the doctor's friends instead this year. Wrinkling a brow, the Austrian considered the contrast of mystery and drama which lay ahead. He had always wanted to see Alaska. And, if the guide he'd selected was as good as everyone said, there would be a Kodiak trophy for his game room.

A day later, Reeve Aleutian's commuter pulsed through a melancholy sky heading Down Chain from Anchorage. Between low hanging clouds, the doctor could see slag heaps, volcanic cones and barren tundra prairies below the cabin window. His excitement grew by the time they landed.

A quick glance at Port Moller International Airport raised a grin. There were three brightly-painted shacks, a pickup truck and one red Super-Cub. The primitive spot and biting Aleutian winds, which almost carried the big man away, were acceptable, but he was unprepared for the greeting. A man, who turned out to be Don Johnson, climbed out of the truck and yelled, "If you are Wechselberger, get into my plane."

The doctor said later, "It was as though he was telling me to get into a car."

Once the hunter was on board, the pilot joined him. After ignition, they lifted off swiftly and banked deep over the tundra, soaring toward the mountains without one word of conversation.

While the weather left a lot to be desired, the doctor was uncomplaining and accepted Don's daily invitation to fly. He marveled, as did everyone, at the spectacular scenery he observed from only a few-hundred feet above the tundra. Of course, the game astounded him.

Doctor Wechselberger enjoyed prestige among his peers in Europe. He had only recently been a consultant to ailing Leonid Brezhnev of Russia. Hunting was his special pleasure and was done with the usual European formality and a great deal of conviviality, for which the Austrians were well-known. But after a week of flying the bush, the doctor was curiously impressed by the taciturn pilot-guide who was, unfortunately, still very silent.

The doctor was packing a German Air Force three-barreled Drilling, which had belonged to Hermann Goering during World War II. One night when they were camped, Don had picked it up and admired the weapon while studying its unusual tooling. The doctor volunteered the story of its acquisition.

Fritz frowned, remembering. The war had been ugly and the Nazis hated, but Austrians were pressed into service under pain of death to family members, and the doctor was no exception. However, when it looked as though the Allies were making inroads into Europe and Germany was losing, the astute Austrian had escaped. He spent many months hiding and moving through the frozen Alps on his way home.

The Drilling, he said, had belonged to the German leader. During the Nazis' organization, an astute German had insisted Air Force officers carry a particularly good weapon. They were 93x74 millimeter rifles with an excellent scope. The one which had been the property of Goering was given to the doctor's commanding

officer in recognition of meritorious service during fierce air battles over France. When Fritz Wechselberger decided to desert,
he commandeered it. The story was interesting, although it was
a painful memory for Wechselberger. Somehow, that campfire
evening cemented their friendship.

After that, the hunt took on a new dimension. Fritz had been
counting bear sightings—37, to be exact. And, as if that wasn't
incredible enough, he could not believe the flying being done.
Fritz marveled at Don's ability to take off and land within no
more than eight meters on just about any terrain. Also, they were
airborne in weather which would not have been tolerated in
Europe. It was obvious that the guide meant for him to have a
good trophy.

At the end of a week and during a routine flight, Don spotted
a strong, old Brownie which he decided might please his client.
Very shortly, they landed. The place, a narrow stretch of beach,
was alongside the turbulent Nelson River. Early the following
morning the pair began the track. By midday, they sighted the
bear headed toward a hill which he easily climbed and disappeared over.

Urging the Austrian to hurry, Don moved parallel to the man
as they followed.

At the top of the hill, Fritz Wechselberger met the bear eyeball-
to-eyeball. He was so shocked, he forgot to shoot. Startled and
frightened, the animal started running downhill and was quickly
swallowed in the tall grass.

Don and the hunter raced after him. Naturally, they moved
with stealth in the thicket, tracking for a long time.

Fritz could hear a roaring torrent which grew increasingly
louder. Finally, Don stopped and nodded ahead. The bear was
no more than 20 meters away, lying unconcerned on a riverbank.

"Don't shoot," Don cautioned.

Hearing an enemy, the bruin reared on hind legs, growling
furiously. The Drilling recoiled—bang, bang. The doctor gaped
as his trophy tumbled into the current and sank momentarily,
then rose and bobbed unevenly downriver.

Anticipating the problem, Don was already sprinting ahead, trying to keep pace with the bear. As he ran, he yelled over his shoulder, "Have you got a rope?"

It was awkward, but the client rifled his pack for a pair of shoelaces and a roll of gauze which he tied together. Then, hurrying down the bank, he caught up with Don and hastily passed the lead to eager hands.

Unfortunately, Don was only too familiar with the situation. There was no denying it—retrieving the hide would be difficult. Once wet, deadweight became almost impossible to extract from racing water. He was quick to tie the lead to his rifle. Bounding forward, trying desperately to beat the bear to a bend upstream, he ran parallel to the quarry, threw his weapon over the protruding stomach and jerked. The animal, who looked bizarre floating outstretched, slowly nudged closer. Loping alongside it, Don tugged cautiously, impatient for a chance to lunge at the fur. It was tedious, but efficient, until the gauze snapped, and Don's rifle sank. Once the rifle disappeared, the bear floated away.

They were both tired. Adrenaline rose with determination as the chase continued downriver. Once again the guide beat the animal's route to a deep cut in the bank. This time he leaped down onto a rocky flat and rushed into the water directly in front of the animal. Puffing hard, the doctor eventually caught up and hurried into the cold water. They were both straining to drag the heavy beast up onto the beach when they heard a comforting sound.

Dick Gunlogson, one of Don's pilots who was guiding a hunter, was returning from a spike camp when he saw the men below. Within minutes, they landed close to the spot where the struggle was taking place. Shortly thereafter, six experienced hands were skinning the bruin.

Don stiffened as his eyes scrutinized black clouds lowering above them. "Leave it," his voice yelled into the wind.

The doctor was puzzled until he saw the guide making the sign of cutting his throat.

Dick had been at Bear Lake for several seasons. He

immediately heeded the caution knowing Don had good reason. All four men flew upriver to Don's plane, which they saw rocking helplessly in the wind. Soon they were aloft, heading for the lodge, a hot bath and a good meal. The doctor was satisfied as Don explained on the way back, "We'll get your trophy as soon as the wind lets up."

As it turned out, that was several days later, but when the treasured hide was safely in the flushing shack, the Austrian was delighted. He later said, "I had my dream trophy—a beautiful hide which measured nine feet in length and nine feet in width and had a wide head."

Time was passing rapidly, and both men seemed more at ease with each other. There were meals in the warmth of the big dining room where the doctor relished the taste of moose, caribou and salmon delicacies. And it was even more exciting to hear Don rehash the hunt with other clients over a drink in the bar. Everyone laughed, the doctor included, as Don said with a twinkle in his eye, "And, I whispered, 'Don't shoot,' and then I heard bang, bang and the damn thing went splat into the river."

There was, however, one regret. Don had lost his rifle in the Nelson River—one which the Austrian was certain he liked.

A few days later, after breakfast, they flew over the Bering seacoast. Fritz spotted a seal coming in and tapped Don on the shoulder. By now, he rather enjoyed the unexpected landings. But by the time they were on the ground, it was a long shot to the mammal in a hefty, damp wind. He aimed the Drilling and fired twice. Turning, he could see Don was impressed as the animal fell.

"I knew he wanted my gun," the doctor admitted during an interview. "He had given his weapon to save my trophy. So, I gave it to him. Years later I saw he still liked it—that pleased me."

By the time the doctor left Bear Lake, he had a new friend. Issuing an invitation to hunt in Austria, the doctor talked about his Jaghutte. Don accepted and made a date for later that year. It was the start of many hunts on both sides of the ocean and a friendship that would offer both men much pleasure.

Dr. Fritz Wechselberger with his stag in Austria.

Chapter 23

End of an Era

L ife in "The Great Country," as the Eskimos called Alaska, was spectacular by its challenge. Being ready for the unexpected became a way of life.

In the late '60s after a particularly good hunt, Don left Point Hope for the hour-and-forty-five-minute flight to Kotzebue to pick up airplane parts. Flying low, he scouted wolf packs along the way. Finally, spotting a good-sized group of canidaes, he circled and landed.

The ship was loaded with supplies for the rented camp, meat for the tribe, an extra set of landing gear and sundries. His rifle rested far to the rear, just out of reach. Ignoring that fact and climbing out of the cockpit, he glassed the pack which was quickly disappearing over a heavy snow ridge.

The shewolf angled around behind a crusted foothill, moving surreptitiously up behind the plane. Unaware of the predator, Don continued scoping. Suddenly, he was startled by a loud metallic sound and reeled around. The wolf had charged the underwing of his Super-Cub, growling fiercely in repeated futile attacks, which raised awesome sounds. Failing and becoming more vicious, she raced to the tail fin. This time ivory connected with metal, bending and tearing. Anger fused into Don who leaped into the back of the plane, swearing loudly at the predator that continued its assault on his lifeline. Within seconds, he was out on an ice-pack blasting a shot into the wolf. Soon it was quiet. Snarling, Don checked the damage to the fin. A cold wind tore at the lone figure kneeling on the ice. Pulling off his gloves, he struggled to force metal with cold fingers and one knee, trying to bend wrinkles into flying position. Accomplishing that, he rummaged in the cabin for surgical gloves which were kept in abundance for daily chores. The shewolf was probably rabid and the precaution necessary.

When at last he was aloft, a furtive glance raised a caustic laugh. The skin was a big one. It would bring a good price, or, perhaps, could be bartered for something useful from his friends, the Inuit.

By now, the tribe had accepted him; they were like family. And, when he returned each December a potlach was held.

An indication of the depth of that friendship came in the form of Jimmy Killigruk, a 75-year-old Eskimo. Among artifacts collected around Point Hope was a stone slate, four-inches long and an eighth-of-an-inch thick with a hole drilled near its edge and what appeared to be file marks on the surface. The superstitious Inuit deemed the item a good omen which provided its bearer safety from harm.

Early in Don's polar bear career, the old man presented the amulet to him, repeating over and over the need to carry it on his person during every hunt on the ice. After each hunt, the old gentleman would ask, "Do you have it, Don?" The pilot's words were touching. "That artifact meant more than diamonds or gold, or any gift I ever received because he cared so much for my safety."

Don carried it for 19 years. Later he expressed his feelings in poignant terms. "They were such good friends, you felt they would die for you."

Although the Caucasian hunter generally accepted Inuit customs, some matters caused distress.

When life ebbed in that culture, there was a dog team and sled which arrived to take the elderly on the last journey. The act was unheralded. People like Jimmy just disappeared on that silent trek across the frozen sea where wind and barking huskies and the singing hum of runners were the only sounds. After the sobering ride, the lone figure was left on the ice. Cold, arctic winds brought on a long, endless sleep. Death with dignity was their way, and they accepted it without complaint.

Other practices caused silent consternation. Whaling was a privilege reserved for the strong men of the village. The captain received much adulation, while the crew remained fairly anonymous. During the winter of 1959, Allan Rock captained his crew on the Chukchi Sea.

For weeks they were camped on the lead, sheltered in white tents, wearing snow shirts, hiding behind tombstones of ice. "Whales have small eyes, see far—whales have large ears, hear far," the striker said.

The midnight sun's lazy descent melted siku (ice), raising excitement among Point Hope's inhabitants. The men launched their skin-covered umniaks, moving out cautiously through chunks of shorefast ice. As it lost its grip on the land, a slush called genu formed on the surface, which was constantly poked with a long striking pole by the man in the bow. Jagged submerged icebergs could be lurking just beneath the surface waiting to damage the boat.

Allan sat proudly in the stern, eyes riveted on the deathly, black water where a beautiful beluga had just surfaced. The bowheads would not be far away. His black eyes squinted in the glare of a golden path lighting a blue-gray horizon. It was dangerous traversing narrow channels which widened into ponds and lakes between the huge pans shifting with the tides. They might open and shut at whim, crushing boat and crew or sucking them into deadly water.

The bowheads were on their yearly migration moving north in a steady course. Allan awaited the telltale dark vent of steam as crewmen sat mute in the boats behind him. The rest of the fleet moved in relative silence.

After a long search, several giants broke the surface. Whispers of "agvig" (whale) were repeated down the line. They crouched in silence as the mammal neared and dove beneath them. It was 30 minutes before it resurfaced on the starboard side with a loud gush. "Puhhh! Puhhh!" was heard as it rose from the sea, exposing one great castigating eye. Simultaneously, Allan's harpoon gun exploded, catapulting a spear and charge into the tough blubber and tearing a mortal wound into the biggest whale ever taken at Point Hope.

Electric cries of "Aghvengukuut!" ("We have struck a whale!") echoed over the sea as a feverish pace began. Allan's heart pounded. The whale's blubber could yield a hundred barrels of lighting oil. In the jawbone were two tall, fringed mouthplates offering 1,500 pounds of valuable baleen. Its enormity would be appraised later—over 60 feet long, weighing upward of 70 tons and enough meat for the village for three years. He had waited a long time, and it had been worth the wait.

The crews manacled the beast, then headed for shore eager to hear the cheers of the families waiting for the triumphant cry. And, for Allan, there would be a place of honor at Nalukatuk (the whaling festival). Don felt pride at the invitation to attend.

During the celebration, he was shocked to learn the tribe would take away the captain's most valuable possession—his home. This custom was a ritual beyond Don's comprehension, but nevertheless an accepted fact for every captain after taking his first whale.

Later, Allan brought his brass harpoon gun to the camp, politely requesting it be taken to Anchorage for repair. It was the wrong caliber and had to be redone in a machine shop. Don agreed. When he returned it the following winter, Allan said it was now the best whale gun in Alaska. And it enjoyed that notoriety from that point on.

And, yes, the "grass-is-always-greener" syndrome dominated Eskimo women also. Don regularly brought them gifts. Of course, fresh produce was the ultimate item during the winter months, but as their friendship cemented, he would acquiesce to requests for discarded fur coats from affluent hunters' wives. Mink, fox, beaver, lynx—even rabbit fur—found its way to Kenai via the

U.S. mail. The largesse never failed to raise broad smiles as he doled them out to the women as soon as he landed. Then, grateful seamstresses would make special jackets and boots for the hunter in return.

Artifacts dug up along the coastal bogs were, perhaps, the most valuable presents he ever received, with the exception of a beaded parka, which is a museum piece.

The tribe had lived on the coast for over 1,000 years. Bone shovels, which were used for making sod houses, arrowheads, spearheads, bone masks and stone tools all became a cherished collection. But the most valued gift, aside from Jimmy Killigruk's amulet, was a priceless jade ax three-inches wide by two-and-a-half-inches deep with a carved caribou handle.

Sadness envelops Don when he talks of these items; they were all stolen from the Kenai homestead while he was away and were never recovered.

It was the pilot's nature to collect things. During the 19-year stint in the north country, he became enamoured of the handcrafts. Besides artifacts, there were beaded mukluks from urine- and saliva-cured seal and caribou skins, and beautiful parkas furlined with the fruits of their hunts. Baleen baskets woven from the tough, dark strips found in the whale's mouth were treasured, and ivory carvings grew into a special collection. Allan Rock built Don a dog sled which still hangs in the bar at Bear Lake Lodge.

Margret and Salmon Killigruk were the flushers in the Point Hope camp. That job, so important to the hunt, was carried out in their modest home. Salmon cut a hole in the ice, roped the hide and rinsed it in the Chukchi Sea. Ignoring the cold, the Eskimo would then beat it with snow until it was dry and return it to his wife for salting. The task was worth $25 during the early years and $50 later. Margret and Salmon enjoyed the work, but their greatest enjoyment was an invitation to the parties celebrating the hunt. There was always excitement, camaraderie, good liquor and Don's embellished, witty hunting stories.

The guide considered them both cherished friends. He

celebrated the birth of their first grandchild, a girl, and often brought gifts from Kenai for the couple.

The firstborn girl was by custom given to the grandmother to raise out of respect. For many months that winter, Margret carried the infant in a caribou case on her back as she moved about the village or went to the hunting lodge. One evening, during a blinding blizzard which ravaged Point Hope, Margret became snowblind and lost. Before frozen sleep overtook her, she removed the case from her back, sealed it against her body and curled into a fetal knot. When they found the pair, Margret was dead—the child had miraculously survived. Don wept when he was told.

Polar bear hides had brought a good price that year. Margret's loyalty had been intractable. She had warned the guide that Salmon had seen telltale signs of a poacher on the ice. That fact sent Don into the air to investigate. Fearful of being caught with too many skins, the poacher had anchored his cache on ropes just under the frozen sea in a three-acre area. Don waffled the ice in the Super-Cub; gaping holes marbled the sea. Now certain that Salmon's suspicions were correct, he returned to camp. Before he could do anything about it, a blizzard moved into Point Hope, transforming the landscape. The hides are, no doubt, resting in the deep, lost forever.

Remembering the Eskimo woman, Don told one of his hunters how she had handled a slightly-overzealous game warden who found her with an untagged hide. Salmon politely asked him if he could give it a good wash before the official could complete his duties. The skin accidentally slipped beneath the ice to which the pair merely shrugged. Salmon and his wife were stoic, explaining the incident—only their eyes smiled.

Spring arrived early that year. There were almost 22 hours of daylight. The midnight sun's reflection softened the ice quickly, causing it to split and slip away. Sounds of calving and tearing ice rolled over a silent land. Stiff winds swept across the landscape, pushing the drifting pack-ice toward the Arctic Ocean. The hunting was extremely dangerous. Occasionally, the wind stopped. Everyone agreed it was pleasant at times to go out on the ice, sometimes in a sweater or light jacket over boots and down, wearing sunglasses against the brilliant glare as the pilots raised a face to warm sun on hungry skin.

All Inuit homes rose only three feet above the ground. Their roofs were sod-covered. A 30-foot entrance tunnel prevented cold air blasts during long, bitter winters. Being airtight and warmed by a grease-barrel stove fueled with unctuous seal oil or blubber, the family stayed snug and warm. If hunting had been slow due to storms or heavily migrant seal populations, kerosene was used.

Bureau of Indian Affairs (BIA) officials, after a careful study of the matter, decided the Eskimos would be better off living at an inland lake six miles from the sea where fresh water was readily available. In their infinite wisdom, they ordered new homes constructed on stilts, allowing fierce arctic winds to chill both top and bottom.

For over a thousand years, the village of Point Hope had existed on that spot. Supplies came in once a year on the freighter North Star, its appearance a much-heralded occasion visible from the shore. Point Hope's 200 residents, always eager for news and visitors, rushed to the greeting. Potlaches were held by tradition, and pulsing gaiety ensued. Once they were settled inland, the tribe was deprived of more than their homesteads. After that time, the mukluk telegraph brought news of the occasion, and the elderly, sick and young were unable to witness it.

There were other changes being brought about by interfering bureaucrats. Frostbite, which happened to Don's hunters occasionally, almost never touched the tribesmen. The Inuit, who had driven dog sleds for hundreds of years, seemed immune to frostbite under their thick polar bear and caribou robes while moving at slow speeds with blubber-smeared faces. With the advent of snowmobiles (snowgo) introduced by "intelligent" Caucasians who were ignorant of the problem that speed would present, tribesmen raced across the ice becoming exposed and burned. Few of them stopped to figure out the reason. Don would see the telltale signs of pure white skin which would burn, then redden and peel. Some cases were so acute, gangrene and loss resulted.

Don never fully learned the Inuit dialect, but he did know the 80 or 90 words which covered his needs. Each tribe's dialect was different, and the Inuit spoke gutturally, using one-syllable words, or two to three at the most. Language in the north or down on the Chain was not a problem for Don. For as well as he came to know the Inuit, who welcomed him as family, he would also come to know the Aleuts.

Knowing them, loving them, and concerned for them when they were taken advantage of, Don tried to offer protection from the growing avarice which threatened their culture and economic security. It was an old story. They had survived Russian domination, and they would survive the BIA interference, but not without irreparable damage to their ancient culture. They were, by nature, docile and trusting, prey to greedy, unthinking white men.

BIA officials sorely resented Don's presence. Some of those people were absorbing the handcrafts for profit. And, as insidious tentacles reached from Washington to remote villages, Don's bitterness grew. Voicing an appraisal of corruption and ignorance at council meetings with tribal leaders, he hoped to advise them, but gradually, Don realized the futility of his efforts. The officials, who viewed him as a threat, made a supreme effort to run him out of Point Hope.

Don had served his nation valiantly in World War II and had received Bronze Stars for the European, African and Middle Eastern campaigns. He held medals for bravery from the Asiatic and Pacific theaters of operations and a commendation from the British Admiralty. He was a loyal American watching his government destroy his Eskimo friends.

They were naive, and gradual socialization made them completely dependent. By 1972, federal law restricted hunting for mammals, except to natives for subsistence. Don's comrades were caught in the trap, consumed by alcohol, and finally, drugs. Their incentive lost, the once-happy tribe turned sad; an innate warmth

Margret and Salmon Killigruk flushing a polar bear skin in Don's Point Hope camp.

had been diluted until they were indolent and angry.

Now they rarely hunted and turned to "Big Brother" for every need. Don regularly spotted them waiting at trading posts for welfare checks which were, more often than not, spent on liquor. By the time he left the North Country for good, it was with a heavy heart.

Jimmy Killigruk, the old Eskimo who gave Don the amulet.

Muktuk strips waiting for takers.

Cutting up the whale in the Chukchi off Point Hope.

Allan Rock and another boatman in front of their boats at the end of the hunt.

Chapter 24

Novice in the Alders

Most of the people who came to Bear Lake were eager for the hunt, arriving in used outdoor clothing and properly equipped. Occasionally, someone showed up in the latest Abercrombie and Fitch splendor who really wasn't ready to face the world's largest carnivore. This type of hunter might even get buck fever at a close encounter. Even if they weren't the best shot, they always had the determination to bring down their game. With the exception of hunting camp food or in the case of real danger, the guide rarely fired his gun.

So, when Don met the trio from Oklahoma City for the spring hunt and one of them was wearing a Hart, Shaffner and Marx suit with Italian shoes, he was mighty surprised.

The guide's normal facade includes a serious stare and a quick, warm smile which deletes conversation unless necessary. Living by his wits allows for fast appraisals. 'Pretty strange hunting outfit, but what the hell,' he thought, as he loaded them into his plane in Anchorage.

During the initial evening of the hunt, it was customary to play cards, drawing for high card to see who would get the first bear. The man in the city clothes had ever-widening eyes as he nervously fingered the King of Hearts. Silent for a moment and staring in disbelief, he found voice and stammered, "What the hell do you do if a bear charges—climb a tree?"

Amusement crept into Don's eyes. Pursing plump lips and look-ing up over his glasses before chuckling, he said, "No, you jump in the lake."

The others broke into loud guffaws while the questioner nodded soberly, his damp face an astonished mask.

By now, Don realized this poor guy had been talked into going on the hunt. He was as green as grass. For a moment he pic-tured the cocktail lounge where it must have happened, and where, after a third martini, macho stories of bagging an Alaskan bear in a remote camp enticed. As the fear intensified in his face, Don imagined him still gin-courageous, climbing on a jet eager for the adventure. At this juncture, he was sober and had never fired a gun.

Early the next morning, the pair headed down Bear Lake toward the alders where Don knew they would find a bear.

The hunter looked more believable in a loaned ducking jumper and down jacket. A boot tapped regularly on the rib of the boat as Don maneuvered it toward the glacier. Handing him a rifle, he called loudly over the outboard's roar, "You've got 14 rounds." A smile widened knowingly before he continued, "That ought to be enough."

Nodding, the hunter clutched the stock with wet palms as nausea rippled through his stomach, pushing bile into his throat. He swallowed hard. Ignoring the sensation, he thought, 'Johnson seems determined. Christ, how did I get into a situation like this?'

Once the boat nudged the shore, Don jumped out and anchored it. Motioning with one hand for the hunter to follow, he led the way around a pebbled beach curving toward a dense thicket. Halfway around, an unsuspecting bear rose out of the alders right in front of them. "SHOOT!" the guide yelled.

'He looks like King Kong,' the astonished hunter thought, pull-ing the rifle to his shoulder. Closing both eyes, he flinched with each explosion.

The first bullet pierced the bear's backside; the second caught his gut and he raced away frightened by the incessant reverbera-tions from the .338. During the rest of the barrage in which the hunter used up most of his ammunition, the bear disappeared into the alders.

Don raced up the beach after him, yelling to the hunter to follow.

By now, the bear was in a rage. Tearing bushes out by the roots, he thrashed violently while clearing a huge area around him. Growling, the huge beast's great jaws widened. The bushes erupted in the air, exposing his position until he smelled the enemy. A guttural shriek rending around them rose to a terrifying pitch.

Behind him, Don heard a thump. The unusual sound pulled him around sharply. The hunter had dropped the gun and was running like hell in the direction of the boat. In his mind he was screaming, but no sound escaped from the stretched lips.

Taken aback, the guide paused before racing down to the beach where he found his client already sitting in the back end of the boat, cowering in his down jacket. The man's face peered from beneath the collar, and he was crying softly.

Don's brow knitted together, culling a scowl which preceded his wrath. "Goddammit, get out there and shoot your bear!" he demanded.

The face scrinched. Garbled words tumbled out pleading, "Take me back to camp."

Rooted to the spot, the guide stood spreadlegged on the shore leaning forward slightly, hands pressed against his hips while a livid face opened. "I'm not takin' you back. Get out. You shoot this bear!"

Curling further into a down knot, the hunter replied weakly, "You earned your money, take me back." There was an eerie silence until the hunter whispered hoarsely, "I don't want the bear anymore."

Being a guide presented many situations, some more ludicrous than others. In all his years on the tundra or out on the ice, Don had never faced one like this. There were rules about hunting. This guy had wounded an animal who was suffering, and by God, he was going to kill it. Turning away, Don stared silently up the lake where the animal had gone quietly and was sitting chin deep. When he finally found his voice, it pulsed with rage. "Goddammit, I'm not shooting your bear. You're gonna do it."

Humiliation crept into the hunter's soulful eyes as he stood up, nodding slowly. "All right!" he yelled. For a second he stared at the guide defiantly, then, lowering his voice almost to a whisper, he said, "there are only three shells left, and the only way I'll go is if you shoot it."

They were standing eyeball-to-eyeball. The glare in Don's blue eyes frightened him, but the carnivore scared him more. Relieved, he watched as the guide turned and started back toward the alders. Then, slowly, he followed.

Once they were close to the area where the bear had retreated to safety, Don dropped to his knees, demanding the hunter do likewise.

It was damp on the tundra. Underneath clawing bushes, a sharp snapping could be heard as they moved through them. Don kneed his way along, lifting the rifle and setting it down rhythmically until, suddenly, he felt a hand grab his ankle, holding him fast.

A pleading voice behind said, "I can't go any further, I have a cramp in my leg."

"Quit that baloney—keep goin'," Don growled before jerking his leg forward.

By now, the guide's mouth contracted over clenched teeth. His anger was reinforced every few feet as the clammy hand reached for his ankle.

Stench from the bear was growing stronger with each move in the alders. They couldn't have been more than 15 feet from the animal. Suddenly, Don whistled. Raging fur came growling up, talons flailing against an unseen enemy.

Just beneath him, the two hunters crouched. Don rolled over, flinging the rifle at the startled man behind him. "Here—shoot your bear!" he yelled.

The hunter rose on one knee. Fearfully clutching the gun, he fired rapidly without a target, expending the last three shells into the air. Then, without missing a heartbeat, he jumped up, ran to the high bank and leaped into the river.

By the time the guide reached the bank, he was laughing hard. The client was up to his armpits in mud, wallowing like a shrieking sow. Extending an arm and finally grasping at the stock being offered, he moved along the bank's edge to a place where he could be helped out. He was a sight. Dark mud oozed down his clothes. The skin around his eyes and mouth was wet and caked, and his hair resembled seaweed. Glazed eyes studied Don.

"Okay. Get in the boat," was the order.

This time there was no contest. The muddy frame raced ahead gingerly before leaping into the boat.

Once they hit camp, the hunter raced up the hill and into the lodge where he grabbed a bottle of Scotch and swilled it. Their arrival surprised his buddies. It was silent for a moment until they surveyed the clothing and began to razz him. The hunter's heart was pounding. He could not believe he was still alive. Oblivious to the heckling from the other men, he took another gulp.

It became quiet in the cabin. The other two men watched fascinated as Don stomped around the room collecting guns and ammunition. His silence and apparent determination caused the novice to panic. The quizzing began again, only with increasing laughter. Don's resonance raised, "We're going back." It sounded final.

The hunter stared at him, feeling steel burning his soul.

Immediately, they left in the boat.

They were silent cruising down the lake. Don glassed in the bow, searching for telltale signs of a wounded animal. Inevitably, they moved toward the shore. In the stern, a down jacket stiffened. It was deathly quiet until the hull scratched on sand, distracting them.

They both saw the animal simultaneously. "There he is." Don handed him the rifle.

Wooden steps took the hunter onto the beach. The bear reared up at 200 feet. The novice appeared to take careful aim and fired. The bear took a bullet in the heart and died. It had been a lucky shot.

The hunter grinned softly, feeling panic subside as a chill breeze flowed over perspiration. He turned slowly, greeting the guide's satisfied smile. This was an experience neither of them would ever forget. And Don always wondered what he told people when they saw the trophy.

Chapter 25

Bears

"Talking about bears brings to mind their tenacity," Don said, sobering as he remembered. "There are three things which make them dangerous: A sow with her cubs is very protective (if she thinks they are in danger, LOOK OUT!); if you wound a bear, he will turn vicious; or, if a bear is cornered and scared. Polar bears will, more times than not, circle around and stalk a man. I've had many polar bears charge me," he grinned. "So far, I've been lucky. If an animal is charging, there isn't much time to think because it could really be all over in seconds. There have been times when I didn't have time to aim; I just leveled my rifle at the bear's neck. So far, the closest I've come to real danger with bears are the times they've fallen dead at my feet."

The hunter leaned his chair against the wall. His look tightened thoughtfully as he remember an incident.

"Last spring, there was a lot of tall grass in the alder patches. Another guide I know well headed out with a client. His hunter fired on a big brown who was still encased in the alders. Normally," he went on, "the bear would have run off, hiding deeper, but this one just stayed put." Don's hand unconsciously smoothed his short, gray mane. "The guide went in and almost stepped on the bear. He was just trying to flush him out for his hunter. The grass was so tall that time of year, they met point-blank, glaring at each other for a second or two. They were both startled. They were so close, the bear put his claws right through the guide's stomach. His guts were hanging out." Don's face twisted sideways for a second before continuing. "The guide screamed, and the hunter fired a shot right over them. It worked. The bear dropped the guide and took off over the mountain. That was lucky." He grimmaced, staring ahead pensively. "The bear just pushed those talons in and pulled them out—but if he had raked, which they usually do, he would have disemboweled him."

Prior to Bear Lake's present sophistication, it was affectionately called "Bear Camp." "Bears were as thick as flies," Don recalled. It wasn't uncommon for them to go on 15- or 20-mile nocturnal strolls, smell food in the camp tents and saunter in.

Don's cook recalled several occasions, after the big lodge was built and he was staying there alone, that bears began to hover around the building. One of them even came into the lower level and looked around. The guns were on the third floor, which has access through a stairwell passing the entry where the curious animal was standing. The cook banged pots together. The noise frightened the animal, and he took off.

During hunting seasons when there are skinned carcasses hanging on game trees outside the lodge, bears often come in. Don's bartender, Dick Remer, amused everyone by telling a story of Don luring a big brown away from the tree by uttering guttural sounds as the bear listened and moved. The hunters in the lodge stood fascinated up on the third floor deck, safely away from danger.

Bears prefer meat after it has decayed. They are, however, extremely curious. They can smell spoiled carrion for over a mile and will clamor to the site. On the run, they can get up to the speed of a small horse, but cannot maintain that speed for long periods. And, since there are no trees in the Aleutians—forget about climbing a tree.

Super-Cubs are used to spot. The engines and sight of the planes disturb the game; no flying and hunting the same day is the rule. If hunting and the weather are good, clients are often dispersed in a launch down the eight-mile lake to an alder thicket just beneath the glacier, especially in fall after the salmon have come upstream and spawned in Bear Lake. The shores and streams, thick with decaying fish, attract the bruins and after gorging on the delicacy, they dig holes under the alders to cool themselves and prepare for a winter respite.

Usually, guides direct a hunter to a knoll where glassing is done. "Patience is the key—always staying downwind and still concentrating on dark patches in the bush looking for movement. If it is cold, hunters take turns walking in small circles behind the knoll, out of sight, to keep warm," says Don.

Before leaving on the hunt, clients are encouraged to eat a five- or six-course meal which includes several kinds of game and fish, hot gravy, biscuits, potatoes, homemade bread, vegetables, fruit, coffee and dessert. Hypothermia is no joke. Climatic changes are swift on the Chain, particularly on the fall hunt— October 10-25—when winter, at her whim, makes an entrance.

Once the game is sighted, stalking begins. The guides move up parallel to the hunter. Clients usually agree—if their first shot fails—"Back me up." But most of the guides said that rarely happens. "A wounded Brownie will charge, and you'd better stop him right now. He intends to fight to the death."

Early in the fall stay high above them, and in evening get on a rise; they will always come down to feed just before dusk. Stay close to easy access; they are fast. If they've been laying in their cover to cool themselves, their scent is strong.

In spring, after hibernation, bears work their way down just below the snow line and start feeding on new grass and berries. Eventually, migrants will move to the river, gullies and lakes in search of fish and then on to the seas for a tasty meal of dead walrus or sea lions which wash up on the Bering coast.

After the fatal shot, approach the animal with caution and, "kick him in the butt." If he isn't dead, you've got a second to fire. One game warden's quote seemed apropros: "If you've only got a handgun with four bullets, make sure you save the last one for yourself."

The guides are all trained to skin with finesse. "It is critical to our clients to determine beforehand what he wants: full mount, a head, a rug, or in the case of other game, a rack." However, after 30 years at this game and knowing people sometimes change their minds, Don instructs the guides to skin for a full mount.

The flusher is in base camp and in season is a busy man. Bear Lake's annual take on a fall hunt is usually around 21 bears.

Turning the ears inside out and splitting and salting the lips, he then takes the cartilage out of the nose. Some hunters take the hide with them, while others expect the outfitter to bag it with his tag and ship it out for taxidermy. The flusher works with the hunter to guarantee satisfaction. After a good hunt, they are usually generous with tips, if he is competent. A flying box-car arrives after the season in Nelson Lagoon (30 air-miles away) and hauls hides to Seattle to the taxidermist. Of course, European, Asian, Australian, Mexican or South American hunters would probably ship their hides to Anchorage where there is an International Airport.

Most hunters do not want game meat. Bear Lake annually grinds up about 2,000 pounds of mooseburger, which is distributed to a grateful Aleut community. But, since Bear Lake Lodge has crisscross runways a mile long, some clients fly their own planes into its strip and are anxious to go home with 1,500 or 1,600 pounds of game and fish.

Shooting the bear is not the only problem. A bear hide weighs in the neighborhood of 200 pounds. One man cannot carry it for miles. Guides try to track and acquire bear in decently-acceptable spots.

Ground humps, called digger heads, rise irregularly all over the tundra and were formed by glaciers. Track vehicles, which have been walked into Bear Lake over mountains after having first been shipped from Seattle by freighter to Port Moller, are of little use on most of the rough terrain except in occasional open areas and out on the tundra near the sea. Airplanes and launches on the lake do most of the hauling. Rubber rafts are used on the rivers.

The Bear Lake preserve encompasses 100 miles. That area contains tidal flats, mountains, a glacier lake, rivers, the coastline and the tundra. Such diversity allows for interesting hunts involving a broad range of animals and birds. Don has built 27 spike camps which house bunks, a camp kitchen, potbelly stoves and wood, canned goods and sundry needed supplies. They are accessible only by plane and are often battered by marauding bears who crash through one side and exit the other. While inside, destruction is total. Most canned goods are bitten in half and the contents devoured. The remnants are haphazardly strewn about the building while the playful felons bash and break the interior. After they leave, Aleutian winds manage to reduce the house to splinters, leaving, perhaps, only a cast-iron stove standing nakedly in the wind.

In order to maintain the grandfathered preserve, some of the sites must have a building. It is a full-time job keeping them stocked and in repair. If one is destroyed, helicopters, which come by regularly for a visit, will often ferry men and equipment to the spot where rebuilding will take place within a few days. The sight of a chopper rising over the lake with metal siding and 2-x-4s attached to the skids reminds the visitor of the difficulty of living in a remote area.

Most authorities consider the Alaskan brown bear and grizzly to be one and the same, the only difference being their feeding grounds. The browns vary in size enormously. Inland, the average adult bear will weigh about 400 pounds and will measure 6½ feet over the back from nose to tail, about 7½ feet across his front arms—claw tip to claw tip. Females will average 30 to 40 percent less. If size is really the question, old records go as high as 1,100 pounds for inland bears, but that is rare, and they are getting smaller with time. Eight-hundred pounds is about tops, presently. Bears store up considerable weight for hibernation.

Big coastal bears achieve enormous poundage, going as high as 1,200 pounds with females weighing up to 800 pounds—live weight. Don's largest polar bear went 1,600 pounds, while the biggest brown bear was 12 feet, eight inches, and weighed 1,700 pounds—a record trophy.

Much exaggeration exists about the size and danger of a stalk and kill. Don offered laughingly that cocktail hunting stories often increase all of the hunt details, but figures the hunter is entitled.

Bears are extremely powerful and can be mean—especially a bear with an injury, abscessed tooth or one recovering from an old gunshot wound. In one case, Don's hunter brought down a bear which had been put into a firehose tracking collar that was too small and had rubbed its neck bloody. Fish and Game had collared 48 of them; they all died. That animal was suffering and was, naturally, in a rage. Bears often bluff rage, but only a guide or truly experienced hunter would take that chance.

During a siege, Alaskan browns will huff and puff, teeth gnashing, uttering blood-curdling growls while frightening eye-contact reduces the enemy. Yearlings and two-year-old cubs can be very devilish. Having lost their timidity, they are curious and outgoing and may go where angels fear to tread. That combination is dangerous.

Harvesting in Alaska runs around 800 a year from a field of about 15,000 to 20,000. A hunter may take one every five years. Kodiak and peninsula bears are generally considered to be the largest.

Mountain grizzlies are scattered throughout the interior and usually run smaller than their coastal cousins. They are considered more aggressive because they lead tougher lives. Food is not as plentiful; in fact, they may not den because they are hungry all the time. Their hides range from Toklat blonde, medium brown and dark chocolate to an occasional silver-tip with long, gray, guard hairs closely resembling a blue-gray panda. Coastal bears exhibit similar colors. The most unusual one Don ever shot was an albino, which he took about 100 miles south of Kenai on the McNeil River on the Kenai Peninsula.

Spring bears, just out of the den, have prime pelage, are glossier and longer-coated. Don's advice was to glass the animal carefully; he might have rubbed off a spot while confined to the den, which would naturally spoil the hide.

Ursus arctos has a bad temper and is tough, especially at absorbing shock from rifle wounds when the adrenaline is up. In some seasons his body is fat-belted, protecting his vitals from all but the most powerful loads. Front shoulder shots break them down and anchor the beast which can then be finished off in safety. Breaking down the hindquarters will not stop them when they are in high gear, especially on a downhill run. On that note of caution, the hunter should avoid shooting the bear directly uphill of him. The bear may ball and roll directly into his adversary.

If he is wounded, beware. Try at all costs to get a clean, humane kill. Since the hunt is usually a one-time experience, the hunter should try to be prepared—gun, bullets, personal fitness, proper clothing and old boots—and, of course, be in the right frame of mind.

Cartridges of .270/.30-06 have killed many a bear but .338 and .300 Magnums have cartridges allowing 3,600 to 4,000 pounds of muzzle energy. When one is hunting in a fairly open area, heavily-constructed bullets using 175 to 250 grains should do the trick. In thick cover, the hunter needs to stop him immediately. If the hunter only wounds the bear he better have real knockdown fire power—the Winchester .338, 300 class Magnums or the .375 H&H Magnum. Heavy-duty 200- to 300-grain bullets will blast two tons of muzzle energy and break up the thickest bones. Naturally, widemouth wound channels result leaving a bloody track. If you are thinking this is overgunning, ask the guy who has scrunched in the alders listening to a bear's rage.

Fish and Game authorities arrive in the middle of the season. The seal has to be recorded. A ringed canine and skull measurement determines the bear's age. Bear galls, the size of a softball, are sold frozen to Koreans for heart medicines and aphrodisiacs. Bear skulls are trophies in Europe. They are mounted on a plaque and proudly displayed. Bear talons bring $400 a set.

****

European hunters are a different breed. For one thing, they prepare for the hunt by donning traditional attire. Green woolen coats, leather lederhosen and a wool Jaghut of green or gray, adorned near the brim by a twisted cord and chamois brush. Some carry a very straight alpine stick (Bergstock), which is carved from a hazlenut tree. It is good for uphill hikes or to support the rifle. Baron Eltz had one made which could be disassembled, making it easy to fit into the Super-Cub.

Since hunting is considered an honored profession, they are prepared to hunt more than once for the same animal without actually shooting any game. After selection is finally made and the trophy shot, a ceremony ensues. It is a tribute to man and beast. After flushing, it is not uncommon for the satisfied hunter to present the outfitter with his rifle.

On one hunt, a German arrived who was quite stoic. While having dinner the first evening, he admitted to Don that this was his fourth hunt for bear, and he had never taken a trophy. He then asked when his hunt would begin. Cracking a wry smile, and in an offhand way, Don said, "Oh, tomorrow, I guess." He had paid for a 10-day stint, and the guide wanted him to enjoy it.

A poker game put most of the group to bed late. At five a.m., Don was startled awake by the sound of a Bergstock banging on the floor at the foot of his bed. Springing into a sitting position and squinting through somewhat bleary eyes, Don growled, "What the hell?"

The German in full regalia stood glaring at his host mumbling, "It iss time." A quick glance at the clock left Bear Lake's owner stunned. "Well, it ain't my time," he ragged out and returned to the pillow.

At 10:30 after a hearty breakfast in the dining room, Don studied the European, still rigid, at the end of the room. Swiftly, the guide motioned to the hunter to follow and grabbed gear from the long hallway collection on his way out.

They moved in tandem out across the runway on foot. Heading for a small promontory no more than a mile from the lodge, they moved at a rapid pace. Don smirked. Flying in from Port Moller the previous evening, he had spotted a good-sized brown bear moving up from the sea. Aware of the animal's travel habits, the guide figured the bear would be close to the lodge about this time.

He positioned the man and told him to wait. Then hurrying over the hill, Don perched to glass on a knoll overlooking the river. Brownie was sauntering along collecting salmon and chewing contentedly. Chuckling, the guide slipped down and around and drove the bruin toward the waiting client.

It was silent longer than it should have been. Running up the hill, Don yelled, "What the hell are you waiting for?" The surprised German took his trophy with two well-placed shots. Determined strides brought the guide to the prey. He stared at the client.

"I am astounded," the hunter gasped. "I haf only been here one day."

"Well, you were in such a damned big hurry, I figured we ought to get it over with," Don answered.

"But, vat vill I do now?"

Shrugging, Don answered, "I guess that's up to you."

Later that evening, after a few drinks, the embarrassed man confessed that former outfitters had led him a merry chase, always disappointing him. He was frankly mistrusting and regretted his manner.

"Hell," Don quipped, recounting the tale, "I'm certain that guy thinks I had the damned thing tied to a tree."

In the spring of 1965, two first-time bear hunters arrived. They were eager and for three days roamed Bear Patch and the surrounding mountains spotting several average bruins. Perhaps, they admitted later, it was the height of confidence, but it paid off.

Late on the third day, they spotted a trophy. In 20- to 30-mile-per-hour winds, the bear scented the trio and moved off. They stalked him for two miles, always staying on his right flank and downwind. The approach was deliberate, and the bear finally collapsed on top of a draw. Suddenly, he stood and shook himself. Joe Rasmussen blasted him with a .338 Magnum. The bear fell, got up, staggered, took two more shots and dropped. A fourth

Warren and Quinten Johnson try to remove a can of cooking grease this cub stuck his head into outside the lodge kitchen.

shot confirmed the kill. Fur and flesh rolled headlong into the bottom of a canyon. It was a long struggle getting the heavy skin out, but at camp he was measured at a prime 10 feet, eight inches.

Within the next few days, Don took the pair down to the beach. It was windy. The sea, murky over volcanic sand, swelled and ebbed, flushing a black sea lion lying deathly still on its edge. A bear, heading for the tasty, rotten blubber, hurried out to the dunes. Just before lunch and with stealth, he turned to peruse his flank. Hunter and beast were 60 yards apart glaring at each other. The .338 spoke twice, and the bear fell.

Don yelled to his smiling client. "Pete, I know he's dead but hit him again. I never have no trouble with a double-dead bear."

Lying down, the bear looked enormous. Pete Alport felt real exhilaration. It took an extra day in the flushing shack back at camp because of the size. After measurement, the hunters were incredulous—he went 11 feet, two inches—this one was number two for the record.

Chapter 26

Bruno Scherrer —
The Ultimate Bear

Bruno Scherrer was in the Westward Hotel in Anchorage waiting for the guide who would take him on his first Alaskan hunt. He was very excited, anticipating his trip and the trophy he hoped to acquire. While sitting there, he overheard a conversation at the next table. The men were discussing an outfitter, which piqued Bruno's interest as he strained to hear the man's name. Finally one of the men said, "Don Johnson." Bruno had never heard of him, but if their praise was that lavish, he was definitely sorry that wasn't the guide he was awaiting.

By 1972, Bruno returned to Alaska for another hunt. During the ensuing years, he had forgotten about the conversation he had overheard in the Anchorage hotel. On his way home from the hunt, while waiting in the airport for his plane, he ran into three fellows from the East. They were dressed similarly and struck up a conversation.

"How about letting us see your trophies?" one of them asked.

Seeing their interest, Bruno capitulated. They were polite but offered some advice. "You were hunting with the wrong man," they said. "Next time you had better hunt with Don Johnson." 'There's that name again,' he thought. 'This time I won't forget it.'

But it wasn't until 1974 that Bruno actually had the opportunity to meet Don. He arrived at the annual Safari International Convention in Las Vegas, determined to find the guide whose name was becoming a legend to him.

After finding Johnson, Bruno began his conversation by saying that he had already shot an Alaskan bear, but had never connected with a really big one. He said he was defintely interested in going on a hunt with Don. "I want a 10-footer," he said firmly. "And, I want it bad." They talked on for a while and suddenly, in the middle of the conversation, Don walked off.

Bruno stared after him. It occurred that maybe he had forgotten something and would return. He waited for 40 minutes, but to no avail. Bruno reproached himself—he must have said the wrong thing.

Two more years passed. Bruno went back to Las Vegas for the convention with the sole purpose of finding Don Johnson and giving him a deposit for a hunt. Once he located Don, Bruno launched into a conversation, making it very clear that he wanted to go to Bear Lake for a hunt.

While they were standing there, Bruno reached for his checkbook to write out a deposit. He wasn't going to take the chance of letting him get away without a firm commitment. In his excitement, he forgot to ask about a date, merely saying, "Listen, Don, whenever you have an opening, let me know."

Don nodded yes, smiled politely and left.

For the next four years, Bruno saw Don Johnson at every convention. Each year he would decide that this was the time the guide would offer him a hunting date. Bruno's quote was, "He remained like a rare Bongo—'shy and elusive'."

By January of 1980, Bruno had booked safaris in both Ethiopia and the Central African Republic. He was eagerly awaiting his hunts. Once again, he made plans to go to the Las Vegas convention, but before he left for Nevada he learned that Ethiopia's government had closed all hunting. Once he arrived at the convention, he learned the Central African Republic was doing the same thing. Bruno was very disappointed; all of his carefully-laid plans had fallen through. He was standing in the middle of the convention hall, feeling very dejected, when Don Johnson walked by. Bruno hurried to intercept him. This time he wasn't going to slip away.

"Don," he called, "I need to see you. Come on into the coffee shop, please."

Don looked at him, smiling. He said, "You'd better come up to Bear Lake this year. I saw a few good bears last fall."

Bruno's shock was evident—he laughed as he felt his excitement mount. At last, he was going to get his trophy.

It was only a month later when Bruno arrived at Cold Bay. Warren Johnson flew in to pick him up. Bruno was surprised and pleased at the accommodations at Bear Lake. "It's probably the finest hunting lodge in the world." Bruno appreciated the man and the skills he was famous for. He was a hunter—he knew what it took to produce that place in the middle of the remote Aleutians. He also believed that the food was the best he had ever enjoyed on any safari.

The following morning, Don flew Bruno to his Hot Springs camp. During the flight, they spotted a huge bear.

The camp is a secluded spot, surrounded by bubbling springs hot enough to boil an egg in and surrounded by tall grass which fans the air under stiff Alaskan winds. Along its perimeter is a broad beach which curves to an inlet.

Don landed, and they began a 30-mile hike just one day after they had spotted the trophy. There was no trace of him. They hunted for four more days; he had literally disappeared. They returned to Bear Lake Lodge.

Bruno was surprised to find three hunting friends from Los Angeles there. Steve Noday, Jim Assad and Pete Bello greeted him cordially. For the next few days, they all rested while enjoying the wonderful meals and their friendship in a very special place.

During the day, Jim and Bruno liked to meet in the dining room for a visit. Dinner was being prepared as they joined Don for a conversation. In the middle of the chat, Don got up and walked away from the table. Jim was startled, "What did I say?" he blurted out. "Is he mad at me?" He looked really alarmed. "Is this guy nuts?"

Bruno was a past master at dealing with Don Johnson's erratic behavior. He laughed hard. "No, no, don't worry, Jim. That's just the way Don is." Jim was still staring at him when Don approached and said, "Okay, Bruno, the wind's died down—let's go."

The hunter followed, unquestioning, leaving the puzzled Jim staring after them.

They went to another camp and stayed for four more days. Bruno had seen bears—quite a few—but he was haunted by the huge bear he had seen at the Hot Springs. After all, he reasoned, when he knew the king was out there somewhere, what good would any of the others be?

They went back to the Bear Lake Hilton, as Bruno was wont to call it, for a few more days and then went to another spot. Bruno figured he had walked at least 500 miles, and still no bear. Twenty-two days went by. Bruno was determined—after all, wasn't he with the greatest guide in Alaska? He had dreamed of it for 10 years—he relied on the man—but even with all of that confidence, his spirits were beginning to lag.

Two days later, as Bruno and Don flew back to the lodge, they passed over Hot Springs. Bruno's .375 Magnum Winchester rested in the tail section. He was anxious to use it.

Down below, he saw the bear. Bruno was ecstatic. He yelled for Don to go down. It was incredible—on his first day and his 22nd day, he saw him—the ultimate bear. Don lowered, landing on the beach in the ominous twilight.

Bruno couldn't wait for morning. The night was full of trepidation—suppose the bear went on another walk, disappearing for 22 more days. It was a long night. The next morning Bruno stalked and shot one of his most cherished trophies. As he ran toward the slain animal, his heart was pumping; he was bigger than even he imagined, and he scored 10 feet, 11 inches—a real trophy.

Bruno went away from Bear Lake happy. He felt that he had made a friend of "a great man, a great hunter, and perhaps the finest pilot I have ever flown with." The rest of his words also

Bruno Scherrer with his long-awaited trophy at the Bear Lake Hilton.

bear repeating:

"I shall always cherish this hunt and the friendship I have with this fine, humble man—sometimes humorous, sometimes serious, always as elusive as the wild creatures he seeks. Don may laugh when others frown, frown when others laugh, and perhaps he is, as Jim said (a little nuts), but aren't we all? In my book, he's the greatest hunter in the Far North."

Don's record Kodiak bear, 1700 lbs. PHOTO COURTESY OF THE COMMERCIAL
PHOTOGRAPHERS, SPOKANE, WASH.

Chapter 27

Newcomer at Bear Lake: Getting Acquainted

T he Aleutian weather gave its usual performance for Dr. Ron Norman's first hunt in that part of the world. He was not yet acquainted with Don Johnson except by reputation. Arrival at Port Moller International Airport was in itself a surprise.

The setting is unique, and the three-mile airstrip on the shores of the Bering Sea fascinated Ron. Located a few miles from Port Moller Cannery, it is serviced by a black volcanic-sand road where the constantly-shifting, wind-created tarry dunes are deep enough to envelop a four-wheeled vehicle. The long runway is bordered by green lights, behind which are bright orange signs in various stages of disarray. (A trapper from Bear Lake later informed the doctor that the signs had been pummeled by passing bears who obviously resented their color.) With the exception of three storage shacks and a few trucks, the airport was deserted. This was undoubtedly the end of the world. Wind pressed his body, driving the doctor into the shack's shelter. He shivered as he watched a truck coming slowly down the runway toward him.

Tim Okonek, one of Don's guides, jumped out and offered the doctor a seat in the cab. "Don will be here shortly to fly us back to the lodge."

The wait gave the hunter ample time to absorb his surroundings. A stiff wind, racing across the runway, bent the bear grass

231

double. Just past the baroque-colored sea, beyond the airport, were distant bleak mountains. The sky had become ominous, darkened by heavy rain clouds which were lowering fast. Ron couldn't believe how quickly the fog appeared. Just then, they heard the throaty roar of a Super-Cub which wasn't visible until it was almost on the runway racing toward them.

After a good dinner and a warm night's sleep, Ron was taken upriver with a guide and dropped. Their supplies included a large rubber raft, which proved to be effective transportation to a deep valley where a moose herd had been spotted. They hunted all day until they sighted a group moving lazily over tussocks which obscured their view most of the time.

In the late afternoon, the doctor slumped into reed grass behind a small rise. Lifting the .380 Winchester Magnumm he aimed at a large ungulate. The 200-grain Nosler shell popped four times before the prey fell.

The animal had a good-sized rack, but a hefty wind had risen around the hunters, chilling the pair as they hurried to skin the moose.

"Better get to the raft," the guide instructed. "The weather is not too good, and Don will be coming for us soon. We've got to get downstream before dark."

They abandoned the skinned cape and meat on the edge of the river and climbed into the raft. Wind and the incoming tide swirled water, tossing the raft as they moved toward the sea. Ron wasn't daunted; instead he held fast to his camera snapping photos of an unusual, bright pink sunset contrasted against gray rain clouds. As he clicked the camera, squinting to focus, he could see the guide struggling to light his cigarette with the last of their matches.

Suddenly, they heard a plane approaching. Staring up they saw the Super-Cub's doorless side banked over them and heard Don yelling into the wind, "Beach the damned raft."

After a few minutes, they were on foot climbing into waist-high bear grass. By now their clothing was wet, clinging to cold skin, laced by bone-chilling high wind.

Don returned, yelling, "Follow where I fly, and I'll pick you up where I circle."

Ron assumed that everything was going according to plan. He was uncomfortable but eagerly anticipating the warmth of the plane. In his mind's eye, he pictured the space heater in the huge dining room at the lodge. He would warm his hands there while the cooks served up a bowl of homemade soup from a simmering kettle along with some of that wonderful bread which was baking as they left.

Looking up, he noticed the guide moving in the opposite direction from the pilot's signaling spiral. "Hey," he yelled, "where are you going?"

Keeping the same pace and without turning, the guide yelled, "I know a shortcut."

After an arduous hike, Ron saw the guide stop on a promontory over a deep cut in the river. As he approached, the guide's head rotated, and he was mumbling inaudibly. Puzzled, the doctor hurried to join him. The shortcut was now under 12 feet of roaring, incoming tide and completely impassable.

A glare passed between the men. "Well, the tide's in, damn it; we can't cross now," the guide said defensively.

For a moment frustration set in until the guide fired into the air to attract the pilot's attention. Dusk was fading fast. Repeated explosions exposed their position; unfortunately, the bullets were the last of their ammunition.

It worked. Don flew toward them, circling at 50 feet and dropping two sleeping bags, one can of Spam and a Coke. Anger fused through Ron who thought, "I certainly expected much more than this—my God—this guy enjoys a big reputation as a hunter and a guide. What the hell is this?"

It would take quite a few months to cement the long friendship between these two men and a long, alcoholic evening before Don would tell Ron that there was more food on the plane, but that Don had thought, "Okay, if they are that stupid, then the hell with them."

The night was immediately dark and cold. Sounds of the plane faded quickly, leaving only the tearing wet wind. Ron's naked form curled into a fetal knot in the loaned sleeping bag. His thoughts of the man called Don Johnson were more than unkind. In fact, instead of counting sheep, he thought of every rotten word he knew to use on the guide. It helped pass the time. By morning, he was furious after a restless, fitful, cold sleep. When at last he heard the plane roaring above his head, he rose up like a bolt, eager to unleash his pent-up fury.

Don's raspy voice emerged over the engine's throaty sound. "Go upriver with the raft and float your moose down."

The plane floated away, returning shortly over Ron Norman's red face. He waved excitedly before demanding, "Get your ass down here and pick me up!"

Banking deep, Don returned, hovering just above the two men. "Are you hurt?" he shouted.

A furious wail escaped from the hunter's mouth. "Your ass, I'm hurt. I'm near pneumonia, get your ass. . ."

The Super-Cub's engine drowned out the rest of his words as it went straight up, banking deep for another pass. This time Don's instructions were clear. "Go down the beach a quarter of a mile, cross the river and I'll pick you up there."

Later, after a long, cold hike in damp clothes, Ron met Don face-to-face.

"Are you hurt?" Don called as the doctor approached.

The hunter blanched. "Your ass, I'm hurt. You leave me out all night with this dummy and a can of Spam." Rage flooded his body as he shook clenched hands.

They glared at each other for a long moment until Don began to laugh. From that moment on, they became fast friends.

Back at the lodge after a hot shower, a good meal and time to reflect upon the experience, Ron was more amenable. They joked about his ordeal, during which Don explained that he had sent a raft after the prized trophy.

After all that trouble, Ron definitely wanted that moose. Don listened attentively, feigning concern, before he spoke. "Well, listen Ron, I sent a guide upriver with the raft, and the antlers tore a hole in it." He paused, sobering for effect, before going on. "The damn thing sunk, and it was lost in the current."

With widening eyes, the hunter stiffened in his chair as anger renewed itself. He began to swear, finally exclaiming, "I'll kill you!"

Don's laughter rose in the big room. "I'm only joking," he finally admitted.

For the rest of that hunt, Don showed the hunter a particularly good time. He acquired a record caribou, a big wolf and fished for red salmon. During the time they hunted caribou, Ron saw a beautiful moose. "Should I shoot it?" Ron questioned.

Don shrugged, "I don't know, you are the hunter."

"Well," Ron demanded, "is he good?"

Don answered, "Ugh."

Later in the bar, Don told everyone that Ron refused a bigger moose than the one he had frozen his butt off to get.

The laughter that followed was a regular occurrence. They all knew Don's penchant for jokes and usually enjoyed them. It would not do to be at Bear Lake without a sense of humor. Don Johnson loves life and lives it to the hilt. His clients return year after year, anxiously looking forward to the camaraderie as much as the hunt.

During Ron's first stay at the lodge, Don kept repeating stories of his European hunters who always left their rifles with Don as a gesture of brotherhood, signifying a particularly good hunt. Ron ignored the good-natured ribbing, until Don began to wear his European tam to the table at meal times. Finally, at dinner one evening, Ron leaned close to his host and stage-whispered, "You aren't going to get *my* rifle, you turkey!"

By 1977, Ron Norman was in the habit of returning to Bear Lake yearly. On this trip, he brought a fellow colleague along— Dr. Charlie Christenson.

Bragging to friends about Don Johnson's prowess in the plane, Ron had exhibited great enthusiasm. As it was with everyone who knew him, Don was an extraordinary pilot. That fact relaxed Ron during hair-raising flights in Aleutian storms.

During the first part of the hunt, Don's son Warren flew the pair to the sheep camp in the Wrangells. Warren was a product of Don's capable tutoring; he handled the plane exceptionally well. Since it was customary to hunt high for the beautiful Dall sheep, the Super-Cub was climbing fast. Suddenly, it turned upside down and began cartwheeling toward the ground, eventually righting itself and starting back up. The pale guest, Christenson, gasped out, "What is going on?"

Warren nonchalantly called back, "Oh, I thought I saw something brown moving by the lake."

The doctor stiffened, exclaiming loudly, "If you saw something brown, it probably came out of my pants!"

They finally landed high on a peak and had a successful hunt, bagging two large Dall sheep.

That evening Danny Lynch, a guide at the Wrangell Mountain Camp, celebrated the success of their hunt with some of Don's whiskey. It had long been an amusing bone of contention between Don and his friend Ron that some pervert had unloaded cases of that terrible stuff on the pilot.

The freshly-butchered sheep ribs were roasting over an open fire high on the mountain, the air was crisp and clean; the hunters were completely content, enjoying the aroma, anticipating satiating their hunger with a drink to celebrate. Ron Norman raised his glass to his comrades. "If Don Johnson ever has dirt thrown in his face, I intend to give the wake. I'll have a large gathering and toast him with this rotgut booze."

On the following day, Don met the group in the camp town of McCarthy. He landed in a larger plane piloted by an acquaintance. He was bringing the two doctors' wives with him. The group planned on flying down to the Kenai homestead and on to Bear Lake Lodge where the women would hunt caribou. The pilot who flew the plane wore a perennial smile while flying daredevil stunts. His antics had been described to the doctors as they sat by the fire the previous evening by Warren, who was being roasted for doing the cartwheeling to see a moose.

During the flight, the clouds dropped lower and lower. The pilot reduced his altitude accordingly until they were at treetop-level heading down a box canyon.

Ron's eyes were bulging until Don got up and went to the cockpit. "Turn this damn thing around and get us the hell out of here," he yelled at the pilot.

Donna, Ron's wife, had been so convinced by her husband's awe of Don's flying capabilities in the air that she assumed all was well until he explained it to her weeks later. Don wasn't piloting, but his accustomed eye took care of the problem. Don then told the pilot to land at the nearest airport, where he chartered a plane and flew them all to Kenai.

That evening, as luck would have it, the group decided to go to Rachel Rogers' Casino Bar in Kenai. Sitting at the bar was Howard Wilson, the Eskimo cook who had been at Bear Lake for years. His stories of Bear Lake were worth the price of admission. He cautioned the women to wear their cement shoes as a protection against being blown away in 100-mph winds. Before the evening was over, Howard explained that he had a wife who disappeared at Bear Lake, and she had been "wearing her cement shoes."

In the morning, two planes raced off the Kenai runway headed for the lodge. Ron and Donna flew with Don while Dr. Christenson and his wife, Debbie, left with one of Don's pilots. During the five-hour flight, a storm developed. Sixty-mph winds raged outside the cockpit as they landed in King Salmon to refuel. Don instructed the other pilot to stay the night. His concern for his clients was genuine, but he was accustomed to the wind and decided to continue.

Back in the air, he entertained the newcomers by low-flying over seal rookeries and the Bering Sea shallows where playful whales cavorted. This sight, as well as the herds of beautiful game animals, never failed to excite his passengers; it was a rare treat.

The wind outside was savage. Flying close to the shoreline allowed proximity to the ever-curving beach just 150 feet beneath them. About an hour out of King Salmon, they began to smell something burning. Don's hands smoothed the instrument panel; it was hot. He immediately gained altitude over the spongy tundra bordering the beach. Suddenly, the engine stopped; the prop drifted around slowly and followed suit. The only sound was the raging wind and a sizzling noise.

Donna's eyes flew open as fingernails dug into her husband's flesh and she gasped. Ron comforted her quickly, saying, "Don't worry, Don will handle it. I have great faith in Don."

He made a beautiful, soft-field landing in deep volcanic sand, coming to rest near the shores of the Bering Sea. A calming voice soothed the passengers. "Better get out and hunt for logs or rocks to tie us down." The radio seemed lifeless, but the pilot decided the signal was just blocked by the mountains.

After examining the nosecone, the men decided it had burned just below the prop, sucking the heat and debris into the carburetors. Don assured them they were only 45 minutes from the lodge by air and that someone would come along to help them.

They prepared to spend the night on a desolate stretch of beach after taking the seats out of the cockpit and tying the plane to beach debris.

Donna's composure had returned; she was feeling benevolent toward their guide, until she learned that there was no survival gear in the plane. "It's a damned good thing you are stuck here with us, Don," she said half-laughing. Then, as if it suddenly occurred to her, she added, "What about bears?"

A wink preceded a quick assurance. "Bears never come near the water's edge at night," he said dryly. Placating the lady seemed advisable at the time.

They slept cramped, but they slept nevertheless. By morning, Ron left on foot to search for some small game. He failed to find any, but he did scavenge some glass balls from Japanese fishing nets. When he returned, he met with Donna's ire. "There are bear tracks all around this plane," she wailed. Her eyes pierced her husband's before she reeled to confront the pilot, who was suddenly busy searching for a can of mixed nuts which he was certain he had hidden in the plane.

It wasn't long before they heard the cover plane nearing. Donna felt relief as she listened to the pilot contacting Don on the radio.

Port Moller International Airport runway.

The Cessna circled to ensure everyone was all right. Then, Dr. Christenson got on the radio. "Tell Ron and Don we had a good dinner, a couple of drinks and a warm bed in King Salmon last night." They could hear his laughing for a long while.

An hour later, a helicopter from Bear Lake arrived to lift the group out and fly them to Bear Lake. They were unharmed, and the adventure would be interesting in the telling. Donna now knew why her husband had been so taken with the colorful bush pilot. She would long remember her first trip into the bush and would return for many more hunts.

Typical spike camp.

Spike camp after bears and Aleutian winds destroyed it.

Chapter 28

Australian at Bear Lake

A rnold Glass had hunted all over the world. He especially loved hunting dangerous big game, and he wanted a bear. At a Safari International Convention in Las Vegas, Don Johnson was pointed out. "There's the man who'll get you a bear," a friend said.

His opinion of guides had diminished. Arnold was sick to death of safari operators promising the moon and failing to perform. Alaska was a long way from his home in Monte Carlo or his business in Australia, and he meant to question the proposed guide. After a few minutes of questioning during which Arnold wrote down all of the answers, he realized the guide had told him very little in an offhand way and was rather harsh with his answers. Arnold was really impressed. It seemed to him that Don Johnson was more anxious to go off to the casino for a game than he was to discuss a $14,000 hunt. Nevertheless, the pair agreed on an October date in the fall of 1979, then Don disappeared.

It was the middle of the night when Arnold connected in Seattle with his friends Joe (Castaway) Kulis, the Cleveland taxidermist, and Sandy Satullo, Arnold's racing and hunting partner. The Australian had come far; he slept on the five-hour trip to Cold Bay while his friends discussed other hunts and the promise of this one.

In the morning after being picked up, the group was flown to Bear Lake. They were equally impressed with the lodge, especially the bar upstairs overlooking the lake and river where Don's memorabilia hung. 'One can see the man has been here a long time and knows his business,' Arnold thought. That prospect enhanced his view of the forthcoming hunt.

Three guides were assigned and taken to their respective hunting areas. Arnold left in a jetboat for a trip down Bear Lake. The weather had soured, and Don's metal boat crashed heavily over the waves, soaking its occupants. For the hunter who considered hunting a second occupation and who was usually completely equipped, there had been a problem. He was without waders. Don provided a pair into which Arnold was, literally, stuffed. That fact concerned him greatly as they crossed roaring rivers newly swollen with melted snow. After a while, they climbed a huge mountain, then climbed down the same mountain which was an exhausting march for Arnold. They never saw a bear, and walking through the streams pulsing with salmon nearly upright against the current required a supreme effort.

Arnold's sense of humor prevailed, heightened by the constant sightings of half-eaten salmon carcasses strewn everywhere, which he knew had been discarded by wandering bears.

The following day, Don flew Arnold and a guide into a small mud strip adjacent to a spike camp and a stream. The arrangements were for a two-day stay which turned out to be nine. The weather included 30-mph winds in 38 degrees and rain. "Shocking weather," Arnold told his guide, and he meant it.

After several days, the prepared moose sandwiches became stale, and Arnold was introduced to Bisquick, which he readily admitted he had never heard of. There were no lights in the camp so bedtime came at six p.m. with reveille at seven a.m. To Arnold, no bath or shave seemed a bit much, but he toughed it out, growing a moustache which ultimately became part of his normal facade.

During the hunt they came upon a prize moose, but it was the last day of the season and Arnold was without a license. They saw plenty of tracks, but not a sight of bear. Five days later, Don flew in to pick them up to move them to a new camp.

The 200-foot runway was reduced to mud after five days of rain and sucked at the plump Super-Cub's tires, skidding the plane sideways as they taxied for take-off. Arnold, who hadn't mentioned his flying skills (30 years, to be exact), recoiled as they slid. "Johnson, you are leisurely dour," he cracked in his Australian twang, wondering at the same time if they would crash straightaway.

Don's silence amused the hunter who laughed as they cleared the alders and rose into the sky. The experience assured Arnold of Don's flying skills. 'Now,' he thought, 'if he can just get me a bear.' By the time they landed at Hoodo Lake at a 20-degree angle on shale, Arnold had new respect.

The spike camp was larger and better-equipped than the other. It was warmed by a large cast-iron stove. Don had brought new supplies and a guide named Mike. Things were looking up.

Arnold had been racing in the Grand Prix, hunting all over the world, and racing boats between business ventures for a long time; the experience had sophisticated his tastes. Admittedly, his view of Mike, the tall, bearded guide, was jaded; however, he soon reversed his opinion. Michael's mooseburgers intrigued and satisfied—it was the beginning of friendship.

Their particular encounter was to last four more days. They saw a wolf and beautiful foxes, but no bear. On the fourth day out across the river where Mike had already strung a guard rope, Arnold spotted one of his trophies. The big caribou lumbered along across the clearing on the other side of the stream. Pulling his .375 Holland and Holland to his shoulder, Arnold dropped the animal with two shots at 300 yards. He grinned at Mike before fording the stream.

After the two men reached the other side, they grabbed the horns, dragging the caribou like a sledge. Its enormous weight produced a lengthy struggle and exhaustion. Finally, they dropped it into the boat.

Back at the lodge, Don welcomed Sandy Satullo in from his

hunt. The hunter was happy after having filled out with both bear and caribou. They went up to the bar where Don proceeded to fix drinks.

"What's this guy like who is with Arnold?" Sandy asked.

Don laughed. "Oh, he's a hippy."

Sandy stiffened. "You'd better go get him; that bloody Arnold will kill him," the Sicilian retorted.

Don knew Mike, and the comment amused him. His young guide was unusual—a big man with shocks of dark, wiry hair who lived in the wilds absolutely without a sense of material gain. His entire catch from the previous winter's trapping was made into a fox coat for his mother. The money Don paid him in wages was deposited into a bank account which Don prepared and which was rarely touched. Don knew Mike and Arnold would ultimately be compatible.

Later that day, the Super-Cub landed at Hoodo Lake.

"Hi, Arnold," Don called from the doorless cockpit.

The hunter's face staved off questions; his caribou was what Arnold would later refer to as a good animal, and for Arnold that was high praise. Arnold had decided a long time ago that record books were not necessary, but if he shot an animal it had to be a good one.

"We spotted a bear in the next valley today, and tomorrow we'll take you in. So, pick up your gear and hop in."

Early the next day, Arnold and his friend Joe Kulis were flown to Port Moller. One of Don's guides would drive them up the beach toward the alder patch where the big brown had been sighted.

Eventually, the trio abandoned the truck to begin a three-hour hike. Joe was a big man who carried his video equipment on his shoulder. He had already completed his hunt, and his animals were being prepared for shipment to his business in Cleveland where he would perform the taxidermy. It would be a double hunt, only this time he would record Arnold's hunt for posterity.

During the long hike, they happened onto two fishermen whose crab boat was anchored in a cove away from the heavy seas. They began a conversation regarding their plight—the fishermen were bored. Four months on the open sea, slowed by constant storms, were just about enough. They had rowed in to shore for a walk, plain and simple; it was a great luxury.

Late in the day far up the Bering seacoast, the hunters began to glass. The guide saw the alders move. Pointing toward the spot he urged Arnold to prepare. They watched the bear move from one alder patch to another. Arnold's opinion was that the bear was heading for the stream for an evening salmon.

They climbed up on a grassy knoll where Arnold poised with his rifle. He was uncomfortable after about an hour. Just behind him, Joe readied his video equipment which rested on his broad shoulders without complaint.

Since it was almost evening, the guide moved away suggesting that he try to spook the animal out. "If I don't hear you shoot," he said, "I'll fire a shot. You'll get a 250-yard running shot that way." The guide's experience allowed for a projection. Occasionally, one of them failed to perform as expected—bears were unpredictable—but he imagined that the animal would run for the stream when spooked.

They waited a long time. Suddenly, the bear rose up full-height. Joe became excited as he saw it. "He's there, Arnold."

Arnold's scope had already found its mark. The guide fired.

The bear charged out of the alders moving like a train about 175 yards in front of the men. "Bang," Arnold's H&H exploded into the carnivore.

The bear spun around just as the hunter fired again. This time, the big bruin disappeared into the alders as the daylight was fading.

A big smile rose on Joe's face as he patted his camera. "I got it all, Arnold. Did you hit him?"

"Yes, Joe, twice and I hit him good."

By now the guide had returned, and a serious discussion began as to the bear's whereabouts. There was some disagreement involving a lengthy search for the 10-foot wounded killer in murky light.

The search started and lasted for half an hour. Arnold was certain he had really damaged the bear. While crawling through the alders, crushing brush with his head and shoulders, dragging his rifle and swearing, Arnold had mentally reconstructed the hunt. It brought him out of the alders where Joe, who had been doing the same connoitering said, "Look! He ran here—see the blood—and went right in at that spot." Joe pointed to the alders.

Arnold nodded, following his lead. When they found the bear, he was only 10 feet into the brush, dead from two heart shots. He was a beauty.

Within 40 minutes, in semi-darkness, Joe and the guide skinned the bear. They were all dreading the walk back. Finally, they retreated in darkness, following the guide's suggestion that they send a track vehicle in the next day to pick up the trophy.

Before the party departed Bear Lake, Arnold confronted Don. "I'd sure like to go on a polar bear hunt with you, Johnson."

"Yeah, so would a lot of other people." Don grinned and stared at them knowingly. "The government closed it to everyone but Eskimos. Who knows, when they finally are up to their asses in polar bears, they may open it again." Don winked. "It's happened before."

Arnold Glass had a 10-foot trophy which ultimately would find its way to his office in Sydney. The hunt had been a huge success for the three friends. However, there was one regret—Joe Kulis had tripped during the excitement of the bear hunt and severed the cord from the video recorder.

Chapter 29

Muzzleload Hunt and Caribou

A s the Reeve Aleutian Electra made its descent into the Cold Bay airport, Perry Null felt mounting excitement. Glancing over at his hunting companion, he remarked blandly, "It looks mighty cold out there."

Paul Christenson's many trips to that remote place to hunt, and further north to Nome and Kotzebue for polar bear, prepared him for what lay ahead. For a moment, he stared past Perry to the Quonset-hut hangars just below them.

"The only concern we have is whether Johnson or one of his pilots were able to fly out of Bear Lake to pick us up. The weather here leaves a lot to be desired, and it's over 120 miles Down Chain."

To Perry, the trip was a great adventure, not the least of which was the gun resting in the cargo bin of the Electra. He had personally selected the special parts, and the gunsmith who would carefully assemble them, beginning the challenge of hunting game with a .54 caliber muzzleloader.

Prior to this time, his use of the gun had been confined to his New Mexico deer hunts. Becoming proficient with powder in that dry climate was one thing, but looking outside the plane to the gray, threatening sky (which was obviously a norm for this part of the world), he wondered if the climate would create special problems.

247

During the five-hour flight from Seattle, Perry had time to ponder several serious matters.

"Aren't you concerned that Johnson won't be here?" he asked pointedly. "He didn't answer any of our letters."

Paul's laughter startled Perry. "That's just Don. He'll be here." Then, glancing out toward the tar runway, he pointed to a red Piper Super-Cub parked near the hangars. "There he is, waiting for us."

Relief flooded Perry's face. His adventure was about to commence.

The flight up the coast of the Bering Sea exposed the Aleutians to the newcomer. Flying beneath the clouds for the first time, he could see the majestic Alaskan Chain unfold: snow-covered cathedrals, raw, burnished tundra, wildlife in such abundance that it seemed unreal, and the silence of the tenuous man in the cockpit whose hunting skills were now legend.

Finally he saw the lodge. The buildings clutched the shore of the beautiful lake at whose end a magnificent glacier rose to the clouds. He eyed the crisscross dirt runway where airplanes were parked, and beyond the runway people waiting to greet them. He really didn't know what he expected, but it wasn't this.

In years past, Perry had listened attentively to his friend Paul's description of the place he called Bear Lake. His discussions had always included the warmth of the people and their genuine kindness to him, but there was no way to explain it, as indeed Perry would learn when he tried to communicate that certain feeling to others after he returned home. 'It's like coming home to family,' he thought, glancing around and absorbing the atmosphere. He was to learn in the next 10 days that it was a special place.

Later that evening, Don's Super-Cub roared out of the clouds where it landed and taxied to the lodge. Perry joined the others as they hurried excitedly toward the plane. He was astonished as guides, hunters and bush pilots filled two wheelbarrows with fresh-caught king crab which were carelessly thrown into the back of the airplane. Don hurried to the water-filled gas drums already boiling over an open fire in the yard, calling to Perry to follow.

"Come on, Perry, we'll cook these now."

They stayed out there until midnight, dumping the irregular, leggy catch into the drums. Tongs were used to pull them out before they were hauled to the camp kitchen where everyone was cleaning the crabs, nibbling and laughing as they worked. Some of the meat was bagged for freezing while the rest was refrigerated for use in the meals for the next week.

"How is it?" Don questioned later.

"I've never seen one before, Don, let alone eaten one," Perry said, grinning. "It's a real treat."

Much of what went on at the lodge went unspoken, and for the following three days Perry and Paul fished the Bear River alongside the lodge. It was a luxury to fish in a place where putting in a line resulted in a fish, but Perry's eyes wandered constantly to the lazy herds of caribou which wandered by occasionally. Since his nature was reticent, he capitulated to what seemed to be a norm, supposing that the hunt was planned for later. He was, however, eager to try his gun, and there seemed to be some mighty respectable animals passing without question.

On the third day, he brought along his muzzleloader—just in case. They had glassed with the spotting scope in the lodge that morning, and the herd moving off the mountains toward the sea looked very appealing.

"Hey, Paul," he called to his friend, "there's a nice one crossing the river up ahead. Come on."

The game leaped across the water, lifting to a bluff on the other side, then disappeared. Perry rushed into the water.

The temptation was more than he could stand. On his back rested a pack which contained bullets, a powder sack, primers, patches and a ramrod. The rushing water felt cold even outside the rubber waders where its force pushed against his legs. He was anxious; the caribou had disappeared beyond a bluff on the other side, and there was no telling how far it had gone.

The water seemed to be getting deeper as he moved through it. Perry rose on tiptoes trying to avoid the crisp shock of water flooding into the waders. Suddenly he went down into the torrent, holding the gun high as he was swept away into the current. Paul raced into the river after him, pulling him up and out. They limped back to the lodge soaked. Perry's equipment, now wet, was unusable.

After dinner, sitting on the cot in his room and using a borrowed hair dryer, he worked diligently to dry the powder and patches. This process would go on for several days, but to no avail.

On the fifth day at breakfast, Don questioned him. "Perry, were you able to dry your powder?"

He seemed dejected. "No, I've done everything I can, Don, but in this humidity—I guess, it won't work."

Don jumped up from the table, motioning to Perry to follow. He led him to the second floor foyer where the supply cabinets were located. Once they were opened, Perry whistled. Inside was everything a guy could need for hunting. Don poked around for a few minutes, finally emerging from the back of the storage unit with a can.

"How about this?" he said, offering powder to the perplexed hunter.

"Hey, all right!"

The next day, they flew to Sandy River with Warren piloting. The spike camp was located in a valley near the mountains from where the caribou regularly filed down to the sea.

On the previous evening as they prepared for the trip, Don had teased Perry about his prowess. "How fast can you load that thing?"

Perry's expression had made them all laugh, which he took good-naturedly. "It takes about a minute," he answered with honest aplomb.

At Sandy River they glassed until Warren spotted the herd coming down the foothills nearby. Once on the flats, they moved off rapidly. "There's a big one, Perry," Warren said, handing him the binoculars.

Perry's eyes searched the herd quickly until he rested on the trophy caribou. "Wow!"

"How far can you shoot that thing accurately?"

The hunter now had a moment of decision. He had come a long way to a special hunt with an unusual gun whose range was probably 200 yards maximum. Naturally, he would have preferred a 75- or 100-yard radius. He looked over at Warren, his guide. There was no question about it; this was a trophy animal—more than he had dreamed—maybe a record animal of some note. He didn't want to miss him, but the herd was definitely moving away from them, and it was open country. There was no way to sneak up on this one. He was 250 yards away. It was now or never. Perry sat down fondling his rifle.

The herd was migrating, and right now the big caribou was broadside of him. For a second, he felt for the set trigger. A sweat rose in his palm—it had a hair reaction; he placed the gun against his shoulder slowly, not wanting to rush the shot. Paul stood nearby with Warren, each of them glassing as they watched the trophy. Suddenly Perry squeezed the set, preempting the explosion and the puff of black smoke which clouded his vision. The animal flinched. Perry became excited trying to reload within the promised minute. It seemed to take five minutes although it actually only was two, and the others razzed him as the time passed.

The trophy never moved. Perry raised his muzzleloader a yard over his back, aimed and fired. As the big animal took the shot, the hunter heard it pop. "I hit him!" he said excitedly. Then the animal moved 25 yards and lay down.

"He's sick," Perry said, "maybe preparing to die." Reloading quickly, Perry fired again, missing the animal completely. This time the hunter wasn't rushed; he felt secure in the knowledge that he had his game.

The herd moved cautiously off the hill. Then, for no reason, they spooked, running off toward the river. The wounded caribou got up and ran after them. When the animal reached the river, he rose up on a bluff and disappeared over the other side.

Perry was on his feet racing after him. Once the hunter reached the site he slowed, carefully moving up until he saw the animal

75 yards away just below him. The muzzleloader exploded again, and the bullet tore through the caribou's shoulder. He stumbled, then raced up the bank and stopped. The wounds were mortal, so the hunter finished him with a merciful neck shot.

For an instant, Perry admired him. He was a tough animal—a beautiful specimen—scoring 392⅜. He was to become number five in the Safari Club record book, bringing Perry a Bare Ground Caribou gold award.

The time that was left to them wasn't to be wasted. Don flew him to the sea where he would hunt goose. Leaving Perry on the beach, Don waved, calling over the engine's roar, "I'll be back for you in a couple of hours."

Perry watched the Super-Cub lift and float into the cloud-filled void above him. Standing on the rocky beach, he marveled at Don's flying ability. The tide was out, and the beach etched by the previous tides seemed barren. Its rocky surface clicked as he moved over it with waders. A hefty wind rose around him filling the air with clean, damp, sea smell. It was a lonely place, full of remote beauty, where the birds flew regularly, and although he would get his limit, he would long remember the spot.

Two hours later, Perry hurried for his catch as he saw the red plane lowering toward him. "Get in quick!" Don yelled as he raced by. "The tide's coming in."

He hadn't noticed, but the beach was getting smaller very rapidly. Perry rushed along, climbing into the open cockpit as fast as he could. They raced down the beach feeling the spray splashing against the fuselage as they turned out to the ocean. By now, the wheels were under water. Don shut down the engine and yelled, "Get out, quick. We got to turn this thing around." Perry dropped to the beach. He was wearing waders which sufficed; noticing Don's low shoes he rushed ahead, trying to turn the plane away from the incoming sea. It took about five minutes of exacting work before the plane was high enough to move out without being sunk.

"I don't know if she'll start," Don yelled as he climbed in. "It got wet back there—but—we'll see." Perry was apprehensive, wondering if they would go into the drink or spend a wet night on the beach. On the first crank, the engine sputtered and caught, roaring loudly; its sound was music to their ears. Don pushed the light plane down the beach, one wing barely above the bluff where tall grass fell beneath the thrust. Within a few minutes, they were airborne, skimming the cold, gray Bering Sea, headed for the lodge. Perry sighed, then laughed, as Don turned and grinned. Later that night, they all had a good laugh as Perry recounted their adventure. Bear Lake was never dull.

Caribou

Caribou herds do well in the Aleutians. Naturally nomadic and more at home in less-timbered regions, the species is comfortable migrating across bog.

Lichens, affectionately called caribou moss, grow sparsely on tundra, and in order to be well-fed, the herd must travel great distances. Their hooves, proportionately larger than those of any other antlered animal, contain thick, rounded cushions which offer adequate support on spongy or snow-covered turf. The hollow hair provides insulation against the bitter weather and is exceptionally buoyant in water. All in all, the complete package prepares the animal for subzero winters as far north as Cape Lisburne, Alaska, where they feed on arctic birch and a rare type of grass found on permafrost soil.

Early in this century, their numbers were estimated at a million animals. Of course, by now they are at less than a quarter of that figure. Overkilling by natives north of the Brooks Range and a huge wolf population have taken their toll.

Generally, classification is by habitat: Barren Ground, Woodland and Mountain. Although they are found everywhere in Alaska, they avoid timber and will rise above forests. Feeding grounds seem to determine their size. There are many subspecies, and much argument ensues as to which species goes where. But occasionally, a record Barren Ground animal shows up weighing 700 pounds.

The species itself is circumpolar. Herds stretch in a wide belt from northern Norway and Sweden through northern Eurasia on across northern Alaska and Canada to the islands of Newfoundland and Greenland. Throughout most of Europe and Eurasia they are called reindeer, until one reaches Siberia where the name caribou emerges. Taxidermists have settled on *Rangifer tarandus* as a tag.

Whatever they are called, the rack and head make for an impressive physical trophy which is displayed prominently in most game collections.

Naturally Don flies the bush constantly, either on mail runs or ferrying passengers or hunters. Being used to the game's habits, he keeps a keen eye on herds. It is not uncommon for weak calves to become mired in skag along tundra gullies. Fortunately, capable bush pilots can land just about anywhere. At least three or four times a year, he has occasion to save one. It seems once the calf is stuck and foundering, the herd will abandon it. Incoming tides often drown the animal. After picking it up, Don will fly over the herd, land and allow the calf to re-enter.

One would never discuss this particular trophy without mentioning the prime reason for selection—the rack. In the arctic, a bull with 30-inch antlers is considered large. Osborn caribou, a subspecies of Barren Ground variety, develops one of the largest bulls, which can go well over 600 pounds—he may even have 54-inch antlers. The ultimate prize has double shovels—that brow tine usually present on one beam.

Eskimos hunt seals regularly. Since they shoot caribou for meat and hides, they are expert marksmen with severely-limited resources. That is to say—one gun, one grain. If a bear happens onto the scene, they can also down him. However, game hunters, although fairly proficient, need heavier weaponry, especially when trying to place a long shot on the tundra.

Caribou are regularly in areas flush with bears who enjoy caribou offal. It is smart to have an adequate rifle and equally powerful bullets. Of course, at Bear Lake the guides will back up the hunter if needed. Wolf packs seeking old or weak caribou will cull out ungulates, then kill and ravage, leaving remains for trailing bears. In that case, the hunter would want to be prepared.

Proper skin-out and care may well result in the trophy of a lifetime. His great white neck and mane stain easily so washing blood and grime away in a clean stream immediately is wise. Guides and flushers at the lodge are experienced, but it always behooves the hunter to show personal interest in his trophy.

Meat is of special value in this case. Since it ages faster than most game, steaks can be eaten within three days of killing and cooling. But hunt seasons usually coincide with mating seasons during which bulls become worn and thin due to excessive sexual activity. Also, they eat little and drink cow urine as well as wallowing in their own. Needless to say, your prize will be reeking like an old diaper pail, and your steak—well, need I say more?

The plumper this fellow is the better. If it is lean, Don says, "It is your decision." The trick is to hunt early before all of the above happens—that is, if you are bent on a caribou steak from your own trophy over an open fire after a long hunt. Certainly, that would be a well-deserved treat.

Caribou ribs are considered a delight at Bear Lake and are prepared often.

After being washed, they are put into a pressure cooker which is heated to about 15 pounds for 10 minutes. Once removed from the steamer, the rack is placed in a shallow pan, smothered in tangy barbeque sauce, seasoned to taste and baked at 375 degrees for 45 minutes. That succulent aroma drifting out of the camp kitchen draws even the casual diner to the table early.

Bush planes are used to take hunters and guides to a spike camp from which the hunt begins. The bulls, during the rut, will have as many as eight or 10 cows in the harem. They move great distances, and hunting is difficult. And while a bull caribou might normally be predictable, during the rut he will behave like a looney on a binge.

The first-time hunter might be poised for a shot when his quarry, who seems to be grazing, will suddenly dash away from the cows, cartwheel in the air, dash back, nibble awhile, then race away again. Caribou antics during the rut are worth filming.

Perry Null with Barren Ground trophy he shot with 54-caliber muzzleloader.

Bear Lake client with a beautiful caribou prize.

Once he's on the move, he's nearly impossible to keep pace with.

Even walking, the animals can outdistance a running man, so be prepared. However, he is curious and doesn't have keen eyesight. If he isn't manwise, he might even fall for waving or "tolling." Glancing over quizzically, he may lope toward the hunter, sweeping to pick up a scent. Almost elegant, he moves with a high-stepping stride, tossing a classic head and lifting white-stockinged feet, his white beard flowing against a gray-brown body. Most hunters consider it a sight to behold.

Chapter 30

Africa

Hunting in other areas of the world offered a pleasant respite from guiding and flying. Africa loomed large on Don's personal horizon. He wanted a record game collection of his own and decided he would start with a hunt on the Serengeti in Tanganyika.

It was a blustery, winter day in Anchorage as he departed for the Dark Continent. The last leg of the flight was from Cairo to the capital city of Tanganyika, Dar Es Salaam.

When the Germans colonized East Africa, the city became an administrative center, and although the politics had changed by the middle '60s, the architecture still bore their unmistakable hand.

A delightful breeze wafting in from the Indian Ocean washed over the nearby island of Zanzibar and into the most-aesthetically perfect harbor in Africa. Viewing it, Don smiled. He had expected a hot, humid atmosphere and was surprised at the weather, which was nearly ideal.

After settling into his hotel, he received a message from his Dutch guide saying he would be a day late, so Don took the opportunity to tour the cosmopolitan city. The exotic streets of the Arab-Asian sectors provided much color for his camera as he busily snapped photos of minarets above gleaming white mosques. The smells of ancient foods and the hordes of white-clad pedestrians were intriguing as he melted into the city's pleasant turmoil. Still, he was anxious for the hunt.

Within two days, the Dutch-born African arrived.

Brian Hern had immediate appeal. Don expected a good time from all of his hunts, and after meeting the 32-year-old guide and experiencing his broad smile and quick wit, Don felt reassured. In fact, their friendship cemented quickly. Later, Don would take several more safaris with him.

Over lunch they discussed the hunt. Don was patient and listened carefully as the guide explained that the Serengeti was most famous for its lions. But the Alaskan wanted just one animal this first time out. And, after learning a little more about his client, Brian knew why.

The Cape Buffalo was the unquestioned top contender for dangerous big game in the bush. Brian said he was tougher than the lion, leopard, elephant or rhino. "Masters at the art of tracking say the brute has marvelous vision, supernatural hearing, a near-perfect sense of smell, and for his enormity, incredible speed and maneuverability." Don listened intently, feeling excitement growing. He had long since lost the thrill of hunting the Alaskan game. It was old-hat. This was different!

Brian continued: "After goring his prey, which often includes vehicles, and getting the old adrenaline up, the Cape will keep charging. He has been known to put a three-foot hole in metal. Less formidable opponents, such as humans after they have been speared, will be ground into the earth by wide razor-sharp hooves. The final act will be continuous rolls of the near two-ton body over the carcass, leaving the victim unrecognizable."

Don remained stoic but felt his pulse race. He was certain the hunt would be exciting. This trip was a beginning, and he was content that the animal should be a fierce adversary.

The morning was sultry as they loaded the Land-Rover in the busy street outside the hotel. Brian remarked how welcome the sea breeze would be on their return. Don just laughed; he was eager to get started and not in the least concerned about the weather.

As they rolled toward the Serengeti's 5,500-mile preserve, Brian explained that the term "safari" was Swahili for trip and had become the most universal word in that language.

The heat had immediately become oppressive, but the Alaskan was too fascinated by the scenery to notice. They rolled through lush green rain forests and great scenic plains until finally they sighted the magnificent mountain immortalized by Ernest Hemingway's book, *The Snows of Kilimanjaro.*

Brian cast a sneaking glance at his client. He always enjoyed the reaction foreigners had to the country. The Alaskan, he knew, was used to grandeur but Africa was, to his way of thinking, something special. Don's silence amused him. He saw the flash of approval in the man's eyes. "And that's not all," Brian said with a grin. "Wait until you see Ngorongoro Crater."

The crater, largest in the world, was more than nine miles in diameter. Its floor, some 2,000 feet below the lip, contained a fantastic profusion of wildlife. Don stood high above the animals, adjusting binoculars and grinning. He whistled as Brian explained that during the dry season, the animal kingdom fled to the safety of the crater floor where there were lakes and feed. Down below, it looked like an African bonanza. There were Cape Buffalo, elands, wildebeests, antelopes and elephants.

They had been out eight days before they camped in the crater and planned the track.

That evening after dinner, Brian's happy facade faded as he answered some personal questions. It had been a pleasant journey thus far. Don was interested in his young friend and certainly not prying. In fact, the Alaskan was greatly surprised when the conversation suddenly turned bitter. He had asked the Dutch guide if he was married; it seemed innocuous enough. Brian's handsome face darkened before the angry words poured out.

"I live in Uganda," he said. "It is a politically shady country, and dangerous undercurrents are building hatreds. My whole family are Dutch farmers, and we are deeply resented by the powers-that-be. My wife had been a nurse in a local hospital there for several years before I married her. Several months ago, she was taken ill with a sudden attack of appendicitis. We rushed her to the hospital where she underwent surgery. It should have been a routine operation, and the doctor was certainly qualified." Brian's black eyes flashed with hatred. "She died on the table."

Don was taken aback. He stared at the grieving man quietly, certainly not expecting what came next.

"They murdered her," the guide said cryptically.

Much later, Don would learn that Brian had been kicked out of Uganda and the family farm confiscated by the government.

The next day, they drove to the foot of Kilimanjaro. Little more had been said about the political climate in that area. And, in the excitement of what promised to be a special day, Don quite forgot all about it. He was therefore unprepared for what happened next.

The drive was down a dusty, single-lane road in dense brush. The Land-Rover stopped at a little clearing.

Brian elbowed Don, pointing ahead to a big bull almost hidden in the thorn thicket. Don took careful aim and fired. He was certain he had hit the Cape Buffalo in a critical spot. It ran off deeper into the conbretum.

Hopping out of the machine, the pair stalked slowly, one on each side of the trail. Suddenly they saw movement. Don said, "It was maybe 100 feet to my right. I caught a glimpse of the Land-Rover out of the corner of my other eye on the left."

In an instant the animal turned, faced them and charged like a freight train. At 15 or 20 feet away, Don fired and heard only a click. He couldn't look down; there was no time. The hooked head was up but lowering methodically. It seemed unreal. The huge horns—usually corked first, then outstretched—were straight out on one side. A great MuSassa tree hung shade over them as the wild snorting increased. The head was still cocked as the massive horn crushed into Brian's ribs, breaking them and tearing a wide oozing wound in his stomach, then breaking the stock off his gun. The beast's belly swiped Don, knocking him off his feet. He was agile and scared. Quickly rolling into a ball, he did a flip and came up on his knees.

Brian's screams echoed in the dust of the animal's flight. Hitting the earth, the guide threw a handful of cartridges at Don. They both knew death was imminent.

The air was flush with sounds of bawling and bellowing so ferocious as to raise a sweat on the bearers yelling in unison. The bull had gone only about 20 feet, turned with the grace of a ballet dancer and was crashing back for the kill, fish-hooking toward them. His huge head with that abnormal bloodied horn flashing and lowering was accentuated by the fury-filled eyes as he bore down with unbelievable speed. One bullet exploded into the neck, snapping the vertebrae and severing the main artery. Don was on the ground directly in his path. Miraculously, the ponderous body went down between them. Then it was silent except for the distant excited cries of the natives. Don couldn't believe it, but Brian's pathetic moans soon overcame his shock.

Sweat oozed through his clothes as he rushed to the guide who was bleeding profusely where he lay, twisting on the ground.

Don leaned close to the wounded man's caked lips and heard him utter, "Brother's farm—two hours away—hurry."

While the bearers went to work on the Cape, Don and an assistant lifted Brian as gently as possible into the Land-Rover. They roared off.

Alaska was primitive; Don had been well-schooled in first aid. He worked diligently as they bounced across the Serengeti, listening to the cries of pain from the guide.

Fortunately they had a radio on the dash, and the message prepared Brian's brother who had a doctor waiting.

In the excitement, Don had not had time to fully realize what had happened. While Brian was recovering, his brother took the Alaskan hunting. Don learned that the natives had deliberately stolen the cartridges from his gun. In the future, he would never allow the rifle out of his sight. He was a prudent man and had had a really close call, but Africa was definitely a challenge that he welcomed.

Once mounted on the wall at the homestead, the trophy was a constant reminder of the death race which had almost cost two men their lives. For Don it had been another adventure and the unusual horn an added bonus.

****

Eventually there would be nine trips to the Dark Continent. They would include: the Sudan, Chad, C.A.R., Kenya, Tasmania, Uganda, the Belgian Congo, Gobia and of course, Tanganyika.

As the time went on, clients who came to Alaska to hunt and who viewed his growing collection at the homestead, or who were privy to the movies which were taken in Africa, began to make requests for Don to guide them on African hunts. That matter became a constant source of entertainment, for while he was able to go on the hunt for his own game, he also took along a paying client.

He began to know the countries and kept abreast of the political climate, which was steadily worsening in a land where there were no norms. There was no way of predicting what would be happening before they left on the safari. News reports were carefully scrutinized, but still there were times when matters became volatile during the flight over. Such was the the case involving a 1971 hunt in Chad.

The client was a doctor from Los Angeles who had been to Bear Lake many times. He was an experienced big-game hunter.

They left Anchorage around midnight enroute to Paris. Paris, the City of Light, was always a treat, and Don encouraged his clients to make the most of their visits by spending a few days seeing the sights and enjoying the fabulous night life. From France they flew to Athens. The Greek flight went directly to Chad, making a stop at Fort Lamy. Their destination was Fort Archambault, the rallying point for safaris into the bush or plains.

The plan included a month-long stay to hunt Lord Derby eland and leopards, among others on a long list.

There had been a savage uprising in Tanganyika after the hunt with Brian. Central African Republic was at this juncture experiencing sporadic skirmishes, and Chad was not without its problems.

The experience in Tanganyika had left a vivid impression. Don was not about to get killed, and if trouble came he was prepared to give as good as he got. He had plenty of ammunition in his carry-on luggage. He had also brought along several rifles, just in case.

As they cleared Customs his eyes sharpened, watching every move in the immediate vicinity. The client seemed unconcerned and was busy gaping at the airport, which was reputed to be the best-equipped in Africa.

Fort Lamy, the lively capital of the landlocked country, had almost 50,000 inhabitants. It was a city of picturesque anachronisms of camels and polanquins. There were quaint mud huts adjacent to white-walled European buildings surrounding the runway. Doctor Goodman was extolling the praises of the place just as Don saw an airport agent steal the client's gun and run off. Without a word, Don took off running and grabbed the man. Officials, used to the thefts, joined the hot pursuit. A huge harangue followed, during which Don produced a $50 bill which solved the dilemma immediately. The client was extremely grateful as the Alaskan returned his rifle.

It was New Year's Eve—Sylvestor's night, as the Swiss called it. And, as in every country which is rife with foreigners who live there, local customs prevail. Don and Dr. Goodman were invited to the huge costumed celebration which was to take place in their hotel that evening.

The men settled into their rooms eager for a shower and a nap. Later, rested and dressed, they anticipated the party which was in full swing as they descended the staircase into the lobby. The hotel was jammed with merrymakers, some in grotesque costumes which they learned were to ward off the evil spirits from the forests near the Alps. The evening promised to be fun as everyone ate, drank and danced with gusto.

At two a.m. Don heard what he thought were firecrackers exploding in the room. He laughed, thinking it was part of the show. Suddenly, everyone started screaming, and pandemonium broke out. Their French guide appeared at his side, grabbing both hunters and telling them to run for their lives. The sounds were rifle bullets being lobbed into the hotel by Arab attackers.

Escaping the riot, they fled to a waiting Land-Rover. Three vehicles loaded with their gear raced out simultaneously. They drove all night and the next day as if they were pursued. The trek was hard-going. When they hit the Iroca River, the guide called a halt to the caravan, and they camped on the edge of the river for five or six days. Due to their hasty exit, there were few luxuries and a minimum of food. The hunt had cost $10,000 apiece, and the client was extremely unhappy.

On a previous hunt, Don had been guided by Frenchman named Pierre. They had been quite compatible and had made arrangments for other hunts, but upon their arrival Don was informed that Pierre had been killed by Arab invaders. They were now in the hands of another Frenchman, a droll guide who had brought his girlfriend along and whose ideas about guiding clashed with Don's.

For the next 10 days, they followed tracks which the guides assured them were fresh. The Alaskan was silent and growing angrier by the minute. It was obvious the tracks were weeks old. The hunt was going nowhere.

The assistant guide had no power but seemed quite sincere. Don took him aside saying, "After 10 days, even a dummy gets smart." He cocked an eye at the man and asked, "What we want is across that river—isn't it?" The guide flushed and nodded before answering. "That is C.A.R., Mr. Johnson. We shouldn't cross. You have no visa or permits to hunt, and there is much trouble there now."

Raucous laughter followed. Don said, "Pick two of your best bearers. I'm goin' over."

On the following morning, the gun bearer, tracker and assistant guide climbed into a small boat with Don. Arriving on the other side, the party hiked for two hours. About three miles inland, they saw a spectacular lion. He was full-maned and the best specimen Don had ever seen. Reluctantly, Don passed him up. Since he was alone, he had decided to get his client an eland

and packing several animals out would be tough, especially this late in the day. They found several tracks and began to follow. At dusk, they spotted a dozen beautiful Lord Derbys. The hunter made his selection and shot two in thick brush a long way from the boat. Once they were caped out and strung, the group began running for the river. It wasn't safe to be caught in that country after dark for a lot of reasons, and they had no way of telling who had heard the shots.

They were all starved; it had been a long day. The tracker had thoughtfully cut out the eland's livers and had them in a sack hooked to his belt. They built a fire on the riverbank while the gun bearer cut strips of meat from the animal's head. After spearing the meat, they roasted it nervously over the fire and ate quickly. Once they were rested and fed, they stumbled along the bank in complete darkness. Locating the boat took some doing and several hours as they were extremely careful at each cut in the bank, worried that they might come across a snake. After finding the boat the outboard wouldn't start, and the party drifted and oared back to the other side. Everyone breathed easier when the camp's lights were sighted.

For the following three days they hunted elephants. The tracker relayed in sign language that there was a big one nearby. He seemed eager that the men have a good hunt. Don smiled after learning the men didn't want Don to walk too much. Elephants were scarce; Don agreed. He also wanted his client to have a good hunt, and so far the trip had been a bust.

The track was five-miles long, and the bearers ran all the way. Late in the afternoon of the third day, the big animal fell. The doctor brain-shot it with a .300 Magnum. There was much enthusiasm as they took the tail. The animal was skull-skinned and the ivory removed and taken to camp. On the following day, the body was buried in hot sand as it always was in torrid climates. In no time at all, insects had cleaned its bones. The head was salted and the ivory measured.

They had been out on the plains about 20 days. The doctor wanted a leopard. Don was eager to get one. He thought the spotted prey to be one of the most beautiful specimens on the continent, and he envisioned a prized one for his collection. Since the blind was already set up, he left early the next morning to shoot baboons to use as bait. The hike was hot in tall grass on a game trail. As they approached a huge clump of trees, he could see they were filled with the hairy animals. After he shot some of them, the trackers skinned them out, and the meat was strung on poles which were carried between them.

In Africa, night falls with a crash. Everyone was anxious to get back to camp before dark, but it was obvious they were not going to make it. The natives were edgy, fearing the trek through thick Tshani (grass). They began to run. Don could see them rushing ahead, their long strides silhouetted in the shadowy brush, sticks bobbing as the animals swung awkwardly. He was tired but kept up by taking a shortcut through the grass. Darting after the bearers, he was unaware of the snake until pain shot through his leg. He yelled and glanced down in time to see a pit viper pull away from his trouser leg. A native just alongside hollered the awesome words in his native tongue. The others repeated it down the line until the area was in turmoil. Several natives raced ahead to the camp to alert the doctor.

By the time the party ran across the sandbar, the camp was roused. Doctor Goodman was waiting for Don with a worried look. The Alaskan limped into the area, pain mirrored on a sun-burned face.

The examination took place in the main tent under lamplight. Although the hunter masked his pain, everyone was watching the knee swelling beyond belief. Shaking a concerned head, the doctor said, "There are shots available—26, to be exact. They should be given from the bite to your heart. But since you ran all the way in, it is probably dangerous to give them to you. You are lucky. He snagged your trouser with a fang. If he had bitten you directly, you'd be dead by now."

Don gave him a suspicious glance. He was starting to feel sick, and the leg looked enormous. It felt as if the skin would tear if it swelled any more. The bearers arrived and carried him to his tent with the doctor in tow. Don asked for a bottle of bourbon and began to take healthy swigs regularly. At last, he passed out.

As the sun's fiery glow raised over the parched African earth, Don awoke. A small groan escaped. He hiked up on one elbow to view the grotesque skin now taut over his kneecap. The area glowed cherry-red and as Don later described, "Hot enough to fry an egg on." The bourbon had had its usual effect. There was the cotton-mouth syndrome, a headache, fever, nausea, lethargy and pain in the immediate vicinity of the bite. The effects of the venom lasted about three days. On the fourth day he rose, limping slightly and swearing at the inconvenience, but more aggravated by boredom than anything else. There had been one bit of excitement. While he recuperated lying helplessly under the mosquito netting, he observed holes near the camp which the natives said were python huts. Stretching for his rifle, Don amused himself watching the openings. At last, one on the far side of the compound showed some movement, and as the big reptile oozed slowly out into the sun, he acquired another trophy.

By now, the client was reacting to all the trauma. There had been a lot of turmoil, and the trip was a disappointment. That matter caused some consternation. Don was used to providing a good hunt and intended that the doctor return home satisfied. It was true he had his eland, but he hadn't shot it. The elephant had aroused some pleasure, but then the accident had happened which prolonged the hunt. They had the baboon skins and with luck would get a good leopard during the remaining time.

The tracker suggested they go out that morning and spot the leopards as well as checking the blinds which had been set up within a two-mile area. After breakfast, they took the Land-Rovers and moved out. It was hot and sultry, and the insects were fierce. After a while, they started out on foot in an area where the big cats seemed to be moving.

Don stopped to shoot a warthog. The rifle was hard against his damp shoulder; as he squinted he could feel the crush of the stock against bone and flesh—it discharged. Don sighed while staring at his game which the carriers rushed to examine. Their mouths uttered alien sounds extolling the hunter's prowess. There was still the effect of the wound, and Don seemed out-of-sorts. Suddenly, a bird swooped toward his head. He was aware of anxious movement near his face. Don ducked, glaring at its retreat, only to stiffen as it turned to renew the attack.

"What the hell is wrong?" Don yelled to his guide.

"It's a honey bird," the tough-looking guide answered.

"Well, let's get rid of it," Don growled.

The Frenchman moved closer, waving his hands to ward off the onslaught.

"I've never seen anything like it. What's wrong with it?"

The guide grinned. "There is a superstition here in the jungle. I'll tell you about it."

Don listened, while keeping a wary eye on the intruder.

"It is a honey bird who cannot extract the food it wants. He will keep bothering you until you follow him to the place where his honey is." The man sobered. Don could see he was serious.

"Well, what's the superstition?" he asked.

"Supposedly, if you don't help it, you will not get any game that day."

The entire matter seemed ludicrous. Don grunted, thinking how bothersome the tiny bird was. He laughed sarcastically. "Well, hell, let's do it."

As the guide moved forward the bird flew ahead, stopping in mid-air, poised as if it were waiting for the men who followed steadily. Each few yards it flew on, stopping and returning to the group. Finally, the natives spotted a huge ant-hill sitting idly on the path. The bird settled on its apex, then anxiously flew around its top and resettled for a moment before repeating the performance.

A tall native, his oily skin shimmering as he moved, opened the top of the mound and dug into its center. Don watched him, amused at the entire matter, then scratching his head.

"Now, what?" he asked puzzled.

"The carrier will reach down into the heart of the ant-hill and extract old honey. It is thick and black and not fit for human consumption, but that little pest thrives on it."

By now, the native's arm was submerged in the ant-hill up to his shoulder. He spoke in excited Swahili then pulled up his long, dirt-caked arm exposing his hand which was filled with gobs of viscuous, dark honey. Again he dug into the fissure removing more honey.

The bird fluttered and lit on the nectar which rested on the top of the crusted mound. It seemed content and began swooping on the substance, taking bits in its mouth.

The scene had mesmerized Don who stared at the guide and said, laughing, "Well, if that don't beat all."

Returning to the hunt, the monkey flesh was baited in a huge, spindly tree. The men awaited their spotted prey looking for a nocturnal snack.

Don and the doctor groused at the flies while waiting. They were cramped and hot, not daring to swipe as they peered blearily through a tiny peephole above the green port. After several hours, two golden-green eyes glowed in the murky light. Dull white talons cut into bark as the leopard crept up on the branch. The sounds of the African night melted, overcome by the tearing, chewing sounds raising nearby.

Earlier, the pair had flipped a coin for the first shot—Don won. He savored the moment; it had been long-awaited. He picked out a rosette at the top of the shoulder. It was imperative not to miss—he had to break him down as the 300-grain .375 Silvertip exploded into fur and bone with precision.

He looked beautiful—150 pounds of perfectly-camouflaged dynamite under the elegance of that unique, slender coat. The great mouth gorged on the bait as his evil eyes seemed to peer into the hunter's soul. The steel felt sweaty under Don's hand as one finger slowly closed on the trigger. Upon explosion the great cat flew from its perch, disappearing into the dark night. The trackers moved immediately, spears in hand, calling alien sounds into the blackness until Don heard the cries of success.

The pair hurried to the scene. A lamp glowed over his kill.

Don stared down at the big cat looking even more exotic in death. Its coat was sleek and well-cared-for, not matted or tick-infested the way lions or other longer-haired animals were. There was no sign of lifelessness, just a stillness which added to the melodrama.

The doctor whistled and suddenly, Don realized the leg didn't hurt anymore. He hadn't noticed the heat or the insects, and the world looked enticing again for the first time in days. He thought of the hunt and what it meant to him and turned to his client and said, "Tomorrow you will have one just as good."

It wasn't long until they returned to Fort Lamy to prepare for their journey home. The skins had been salted and were packed for traveling. Don was certain he would cancel the check for the adventure. It had been poorly-handled, and had it not been for his experience, they would not have had any animals at all. 'After all,' he told himself, 'twenty-thousand is a lot of money.' Besides, it always upset him when his clients were involved. The bank at Kenai cooperated fully, and the client was pleased with the return of his funds. Bad outfitters had caused a tremendous amount of problems on every continent. Don knew better than most what they had done to Alaska.

Shortly after his return to Alaska, he learned that Brian Hern had been killed in Uganda. It was one of his great disappointments. Brian was the ideal guide and had been what Don considered a good friend. He never quite got all of the details, but imagined that Brian had had some pretty hefty enemies in that part of the world. It gave Don some cause for concern. In the future, he would pay particular attention to the political climate in the places he took his clients.

The hunting fraternity included some powerful figures who drew the hunter/guide/bush-pilot into exotic worlds in search of unusual game.

Aside from the royalty, there were innumerable businessmen from four continents, national political figures, American sports celebrities and hundreds of hunt lovers.

Within a 30-year period and between Alaskan seasons, Don

circled the globe. The places he hunted included every state in the U.S., Canada (except Quebec), Mexico, Panama, Brazil, Venezuela, Peru, Chile, Honduras, Argentina, England, Ireland, Scotland, the Orkeny Islands, the Shetland Islands, Denmark, Holland, Norway, Sweden, Czechoslovakia, Hungary, Russia, Germany, France, Spain, East Germany, Italy, Newfoundland, Bear Island, Austria, Mongolia, Sudan, Chad, Central African Republic, Kenya, Tasmania, Uganda, the Belgian Congo and Gobia.

On some of the hunts, Don guided as well as hunted, resulting in a magnificent collection of trophies which include:

Elephants - 4 (trunk and feet)	Zebra - 14 (head)
Cape Buffalo - 20 (head)	Lion - 1 (full)
Red Buffalo - 1 (head)	Warthog - 9 (head)
Cheetah - 1 (head)	Spotted Hyena - 2
Waterbuck - 1 (head)	Jackal - 3
Giraffe - 1 (half mount)	Crocodile - 1 (skin)
Greater Kudu - 1 (head)	Impala - 2 (head)
Lesser Kudu - 1 (head)	Grant Gazelle - 2 (head)
Baboon - 7 (full)	Leopard - 1 (full)
Springbok - 1 (head)	Python - 1 (full)
Common Eland - 1 (head)	Gnu - 1 (head)
Lord Derby Eland - 1 (head)	Hartebeest - 4 (head)
Wildebeest - 3 (head)	Monkey - 1 (full)
Ostrich - 1	Wild Dog - 5 (head)
Tohompson Gazelle - 1 (head)	Kilspringer - 1 (full)
Gemsbok - 1 (head)	Duiker - 1 (full)
Hippo - 1 (teeth only)	Bush Buck - 1 (head)
Dik Dik - 1 (head)	

Of course, these trophies do not include all of the American game animals, with the exception of the Desert Bighorn. The list is endless and embraces all of the Alaskan game animals and birds (most of which were record trophies and are now on exhibit throughout Alaska and in some parts of the lower U.S.). All of the Aleutian bird species are mounted and exhibited in the game room at Bear Lake Lodge along with smaller wild creatures found

1986—Transvol Desert, South Africa. Don and his friend, Tom Kamph, with a sable antelope.

Brian Hern who was later murdered in Uganda.

African leopard - 1967.

on the Chain.

In January 1984, the state of Alaska requested that the entire collection be put on permanent exhibit in the city building on Kenai Peninsula.

There was no doubt that the collection belonged on exhibit for tourists, residents and hunters—a lifetime of trophies whose very presence gave him comfort. Viewing them Don felt a nostalgic sadness, but in the end he would capitulate to the request.

Chapter 31

Hunt for the Tur
and Argolis Sheep

Darkness had settled on Leningrad long before the KLM jet lumbered onto the runway following its direct flight over the North Pole. It was October of 1982. The brief stopover was complicated by the usual red-tape and to Don, at least, unaccustomed militarism. After the long delay, passengers going on to Moscow were herded solemnly through stark corridors to the Aeroflot boarding ramp.

At midnight when they disembarked in the capital, Don felt weary and out-of-sorts. He was not looking forward to the next couple of hours. Moving guns and ammunition in and out of countries had always been difficult, and since he had brought an extra rifle along to be repaired by an Austrian gunsmith—for which he had no permit—he expected problems.

On international hunts, one gun was enough. Four packages of 180-grain bullets were safe in his carry-on luggage along with the bolt from his 7mm Weatherby rifle. Other necessities, such as a good down sleeping-bag, light-but-warm clothing and a specially prepared medical kit resting in the canvas bags, were carefully watched. He had learned long ago not to be caught at the mercy of bone-chilling cold in rugged unprotected areas, or to let less-than-competent doctors care for him.

After approaching a counter laden with a surplus of printed materials, he noticed none of them were printed in English. He then selected a German form and heaved a sigh before attempting to fill it out. When it was completed, his furtive observation drifted toward the Custom counters where Russian military performed thorough searches. A satisfied gaze settled on one good-looking young officer whose attitudes were reflected with an amicable smile. The Alaskan collected his gear and got into line.

Considering the hour, the thoroughness diminished somewhat, and after a cursory check the man waved Don through. To avoid problems later, he paused and gave the Russian a weak smile while pointing a finger to the permit specifying one gun. Quick hands moved to the weapons as understanding passed silently between them. The guard signaled the hunter to wait.

It took all of 10 minutes before a jolly, portly-looking official appeared and made inquiries. After the brief explanation, he said in an offhand way, "No problem. Just leave the broken gun with me. You can pick it up after your return from Mongolia a month from now." A broad smile erupted as he added, "You can't use it anyway."

Nodding, the hunter expressed relief. As was usually the case, he had made a friend. The Russian seemed curious, and Don would later learn the man was also a hunter and eager to talk to the American.

Unlike other airports, no one complained about the delay. Continuing the conversation comfortably, the official seemed reluctant to let him go. Don shifted feet and glanced around uneasily to the line growing smaller behind him as passengers quietly drifted away.

Suddenly, the Russian invited him to dinner on the following evening. The impulsive invitation was a pleasant surprise which was quickly accepted.

Later, after a much-needed rest in the sophisticated National Hotel overlooking Red Square, the Alaskan prepared for his visit.

There had been one other Russian hunt years ago, and his guides had taken him to their apartments. They turned out to be near-slums. Water, pumped from a street hydrant, had to be hand-carried up flights of dark stairwells for after-dinner tea and dishes. At that time, Don had learned that each leader had developed public housing which bore his name. Huge clumps of stark, cement structures in specific sections of the megalopolis attested to that fact.

George Yusarov was a middle-echelon government official bearing the title of Chief Customs Agent. He arrived at the National in a black automobile which resembled a Mercedes and was obviously a government car. The black background tags of the Soviet Union confirmed the matter. In the city of 7,000,000 residents, it was rare to see white background tags which indicated private ownership.

They arrived at a fairly new concrete apartment house serviced by a small elevator that slowly rose to the second floor.

The Yusarovs were extremely accommodating. Immediately, wine was served, and Don was asked to sit down.

Don thought the four-room flat rather old-fashioned by U.S. standards, but it was immaculate, and his host was obviously proud of it.

Mrs. Yusarov fussed over the lace tablecloth which held her well-matched china. Her language would have to be an eager smile and the tasty boiled dinner of pork, potatoes and tomatoes she had been cooking all day as she did not speak English.

Don watched the plump, dark-haired lady pouring tumblers full of the popular "Russian national drink" made from bread. She placed them beside the wine glasses while her husband went to get vodka for a toast.

George revelled in the Alaskan's stories after which he promised complete cooperation during the hunter's stay in his country. At the evening's conclusion, Don felt comfortable that he had at least one ally in this formidable land.

The thought turned out to be a gross understatement. Within the month, Don would have passed through the Moscow airport five times. The Customs Chief had alerted the entire establishment, and Mr. Johnson received what amounted to VIP treatment. His bags were carried by obliging soldiers who deleted all of the paperwork and outdid their comrades by getting him a car. Don had made quite an impression. All that was expected in return was to hear about Alaska and his hunting world through an immediately-secured interpreter.

Before leaving for the hunt, Don toured the city. Of course the Kremlin was the first priority, and afterward a cab driver suggested the famous Bolshoi theater. The U.S. Embassy was next on the agenda and finally, the Winter Palace of the Czars where Don's interest piqued at the unequalled gold collection on exhibit there. Actually, the hunter had never been much of a tourist. Seeing famous places was usually the result of being with some congenial companion who wanted him to have a good time. He really preferred the night life and, since he was alone and had time to kill, made the rounds.

Russia at night was unlike other major cities of the world. Most hotels of note had Victorian dining rooms with huge 1930-era orchestras, but an obliging cab driver suggested a trip to a "dollar bar" where loud Western-style music overflowed into the street. Don later said, "I guess I was drinking with some of the greatest alcoholics in the world."

On the fourth day, Aeroflot lifted him off from Moscow bound for Baku on the Caspian Sea.

Since the Soviet Union is a land of fascinating contrasts, the sun never sets on its gigantic kaleidoscope of people and geography. It is the largest country in the world.

Before each hunt outside the U.S., Don religiously studied maps of the places he would visit. Russia is 8,000-miles wide and 5,000-miles deep, and given his experience in the air, he imagined the flight to Baku would take about three hours.

At his destination, a waiting Intourist guide took the hunter to a large cafeteria whose sides near a high roof were rife with gaping holes open to the air. Hungry birds frequented the place, seeking bits of bread offered by diners. Being a high-paying guest, Don was given a table alone where he amused himself by tossing out breadcrumbs. The gesture attracted more winged creatures to his table than any of the others, which led him to conclude that he was more generous with the bread than the frugal Russians.

The lunch was quite delicious. He had pork Kiev (shashlik kebob), a bowl of borscht (which he didn't eat) and tea. The Intourist guide made the selection after which she brought a pitcher full of the "national drink" and a basket of bread. Being a seasoned traveler, Don had definite opinions about food. He considered the heavy, soft, gray dough concoction to be the best in the world. It was always served with plenty of butter and cold cuts, out of which the American could easily have made a meal.

In due time, the guide returned and ushered him to a waiting car. After explaining that he was the first foreign hunter ever to come alone, she gave the driver instructions, wished him a safe journey and left.

Baku is only miles from the Iranian border. They drove into rolling farm country for some three hours. Don believed they were going east, but the driver did not speak English so the journey was a silent one.

It was just after dark when they stopped on a secluded street in Kaspisches. The driver signalled Don to wait before disappearing into a dark building. He returned with an attractive young woman who said in perfect English, "Give me your passport." Her brusque manner and command elicited an immediate retort.

"Go to hell. I'm not givin' that away—even to you."

Taken aback, the young woman paused before smiling and saying in a softer tone, "I will be going on the hunt with you. I believe it would be safer to contain the document in our office safe."

Don's scowl faded; suspicion replaced the look as he reluctantly passed the precious document to the now-pleasant interpreter.

Taska Selenkov was, at 23, a good communist. After returning to the car she put her suitcase inside, climbed in next to Don and began a running commentary on the place—the terrain, the people and, of course, Mother Russia—a la Kremlin.

During the drive to the hunting lodge just outside Astrachan, which the young woman explained could house 60 guests, she told Don he would be the only one there now. Her smile broadened as she added, "The lodge is often frequented by prominent Soviet officials. Nikita Krushchev came here often. It is very famous in Russia."

Don, who had definite ideas about the Kremlin, just grinned. The hunt had cost $6,800. He wanted a Tur, which resembles the Dall sheep. In fact, one of his goals was the Super Slam of wild sheep. And by the time this particular hunt was over, he would have every one in the world except the desert big horn found in Arizona and Mexico.

It was a moonless night, but even in the darkness the hunter was impressed with the lodge. The huge stone and dark wood structure looked ominous and deserted, but once inside he was pleased to see a staff of six waiting to accommodate him. The hour was late—almost midnight; he was tired and hungry.

After being ushered to an elegant three-room suite, a polite request was made that he wash and rest while dinner was prepared.

Casting an approving eye over heavy hand-carved oak furnishings in the study, Don moved to the big bedroom where a comforting fire crackled in the hearth. A bounce on the bed raised a satisfied grin. Moments later, he actually laughed out loud after learning that all the plumbing worked.

The interpreter joined him for dinner in a casual but well-appointed dining room where a formal table had been set and where candlelight enhanced the setting. The cozy atmosphere was also succulent as bowls of thick cabbage soup called Shchi were brought into the room by servants.

Don was suddenly ravenous. He welcomed the hot stock and later praised the delicious chicken cutlet whose name he couldn't pronounce, but which Taska said was a local specialty. At the conclusion of the meal, waiters brought tea and ice cream which he refused. Of course, there was vodka for a toast—four, to be exact—which left him feeling mellow and sleepy.

A sound rest in the feather bed refreshed the hunter. After a huge breakfast, he and Taska toured the wooded grounds on foot. Don declined an offer to fish, so the pair walked to town. It was a brisk, damp day, and the promise of winter hung in the forest.

His interpreter was dedicated to the Party. There was a running commentary which started with her exposure of a statue of Lenin on a horse in the center of a hand-laid cobblestone street. In the next square of the antiquated town was a stone sculpture of the leader in uniform, and so on. All the government buildings were monuments to the same man who, Taska explained, was the first communist ruler.

The second day was about the same as their guides were not yet ready. On this trip, the interpreter drove a jeep. Stopping in the square, she pointed to the statue and said, "You may want to photograph our leader."

Don had just about had it. Grinning, he said, "Who the hell was this guy, anyway?" He later quipped, "That broke the ice, and the lady stopped trying to convert me."

There were rules about hunting out of the U.S. which were strictly adhered to. "When in Rome," was Don's motto. He had brought along two suitcases full of blue jeans and shirts in assorted sizes which the Russians were reputed to covet. And in his wallet was $1,000 worth of rubles. Guides, Don believed, were just people and usually poor people; if he treated them right he would get a good animal.

It was obvious they liked to drink, so he suggested they go shopping for vodka and beer to take along on the trip.

By now, the dialogue between the pair had reversed. No longer was Don beng inundated with propaganda. Instead, the young woman seemed fascinated by the American's freedom and the fact that he owned airplanes, cars, boats and several homes.

That afternoon, Don took her to lunch. After food and a few drinks, Taska became quite open about life in the USSR—good and bad.

On the following morning, they embarked on the hunting trip in an army jeep. The drive into the mountains was interesting. Being only a few hours away from the borders of Iran and Turkey in rugged terrain, Don waited as they climbed, hoping they would hunt on the distant peaks.

Before long, they arrived in a small village which the interpreter said was the driver's home town. The Russians had decided the American was generous and asked Taska to suggest he might want to stop for more liquor.

Don agreed.

The liquor store was in a private home. By this time, everyone was becoming quite jovial; they made the purchases and drove off.

Just prior to arrival at their hunting camp, the driver stopped at a shrine in an ancient cemetery. Don was instructed to throw a coin into the fountain near the gate for good luck. After that was done, the entire group toured the graveyard. It was unusual; all of the caskets were made of dark slate and were sitting on top of the ground. A closer inspection revealed etchings which were hundreds of years old. And while the tour was a bit strange, Don admitted it was intriguing.

Not too far away was a two-room stone house. He soon learned it was their base camp. One room, an 8-x-10 barren dark cave, raised a shiver. It was filled with mountain potatoes the thickness of a quarter, upon which the guides were to sleep. The other room was more appealing, but still pretty primitive. It contained a wood stove which was used for heating and cooking; however, there was very little wood. Even in his hunting jacket, hat and gloves, Don was cold. The place was extremely damp, and now it was obvious why the astute Russians desired so much liquor.

In the morning, horses arrived for all four people. For the following five days, they ambled up the steep, rocky Bol Soj Kavkaz Range, never quite achieving the summit. One mountain seemed to fold into another even larger one.

Don decided his generosity had paid off; the guides worked hard to track a good Tur. On the fifth day, he shot a beautiful trophy. Naturally, there was a celebration and much vodka was drunk. In fact, they were as dedicated to the celebration as they had been to the track.

Although Don liked a drink, he rarely took too much when he was in foreign territory, especially when he was alone with strangers, no matter how friendly they had become. Nevertheless, he marvelled at the ability of his companions to drink three or four quarts of vodka a day and still appear sober.

Eventually, they returned to the comfort of the hunting lodge. Don was surprised to find five men waiting whose duty it was to score his trophy. Their evaluation seemed endless—it took days. And at its termination, the hunter owed another $1,750, due to the size. Don contained his anger. The $6,800 did not include airfare, cabs or meals in hotels. Statements in the prepaid package clearly earmarked $800 for the size of the animal. However, there was little to be accomplished by discussing the matter, and the guides had done a good job. Besides, the five men, all in their late 60s, seemed to be having such a good time. Once the matter was settled, four days later, they all enjoyed a huge game feast, and this time the vodka was on the house—toast after toast after toast.

Wintry, damp winds accompanied their farewell. Don was generous with the rubles to the staff and guides. In a weak moment, he gave his down sleeping-bag to the head guide for whom he felt pity after a night in the stone house. The matter was later regretted as he was headed for Mongolia's Gobi Desert which turned out to be "colder than hell."

Taska's parents lived in Jevlach enroute to Baku. The compound, enclosed by a huge stone wall, contained eight homes. Don accepted an invitation to visit them briefly. Over cake and coffee and the watchful eye of the smiling Russian family, she gave him a gift. Of course, she explained in her native tongue and with a broad smile, the American had given her two $100 bills and 10 sets of the coveted blue jeans and shirts. Taska's life would be greatly enriched for the next few months while she figured out who would be the recipients of such treasures. And, while she beamed at the windfall, Don felt abject pleasure at her gratitude.

Back in Moscow, Don rested for three days, knowing the Mongolian trip would be an arduous one. Flying time alone was over 13 hours.

Departing Moscow, they stopped at Omsk and Irkutsk before crossing the Mongolian border and landing at Ulan-Bator.

Outside the airport the wind whistled. They were high—almost 8,000 feet, and winter seemed determined. The city was under-developed and populated by a half-million hard, fierce-looking Mongolians. They had been under Russian rule long enough to accept the fact, but Don thought they obviously resented it. The place appeared downright unfriendly, right down to the huge Soviet tank mounted skyward in a barren cement square which centered the city.

A colorful brochure had arrived prior to the hunt. Don had it with him. He blinked and scanned the photos with a grimace. Later, he said, "The Russian who shot those pictures must have been a genius."

The brochure showed sunshine and color, but the sky was blustery gray, colored further by a smoky pall which hung in the air and which made breathing difficult. Don learned that they produced electricity from coal. Constantly-belching smokestacks polluted the atmosphere day and night. He said later, "Hell, they must have given everybody a week off while they shot those pictures."

The architecture was a mixture of Russian-bleak and colorful Bogdo palaces, probably remnants of the great Khan. But the grim-faced inhabitants were a visual reminder of the great armies of costumed warriors who overran the known world during the time of Marco Polo, whose cruelty was legend.

All this might have depressed Don, but there was one bright note; a guide appeared wearing a pale blue blazer and expensive tailored slacks. Don decided they had been a gift from some generous American hunter—for it was not uncommon for hunters to reward those who served them well, and Americans were particularly noted for it. The matter served a lot of purposes and certainly left a good impression on foreign guides. His name was Purka. A dark, swarthy young man of about 30 who was extremely polite and dedicated to his charge. Don liked him immediately.

Once they arrived at Ulan Bator's one good hotel, life began to improve. The lobby was huge and surprisingly pleasant. In its center was a gracious Y-shaped staircase gently curving to a large balcony. Off the main room was an excellent dining room now filled with noisy Russian and Hungarian diners; behind that was a comfortable bar. Don roamed through the rooms while Purka took care of his reservation. He nodded thoughtfully and decided this was all right.

After a brief drink, Purka escorted him to a suite on the second floor. The rooms were clean and well-furnished, and while it was quite large, Don was amazed to find a 16 x 20 well-plumbed bathroom.

When the guide left, Don went down to the dining room for a meal. It was evident no one spoke English. He glanced around at the tables nearby, pointed to something which looked appealing, and nodded to the waitress. When it arrived it was tasty and hot, but he never really knew what he had eaten.

Later, he met two Americans in the bar. It was a seemingly pleasant surprise, and the pair invited him to join them. They talked for a long time as they were returning from a hunt where they had bagged two argolis sheep. Since it is the largest of the sheep family, its acquisition is considered a plum in any game collection. Soon Don was quietly grinning as his companions gave him full instructions. However, he was patient and polite. Later he said, "They made the goddamned hunt sound like work."

Eventually, Purka returned and told him they were ready.

An F-27, which resembled the old turbo prop Fairchilds but was bigger and heavier, arrived to ferry them to the desert. All 50 passengers boarded solemnly for the 400-mile trip. Beneath them, for as far as the eye could see, was a barren lifeless stretch of sand. There was no runway when they landed, and the big ship thumped awkwardly for a long way. Outside, Don could see 50-x-75 Mongolian Yurt houses inside a board-fence compound. As they exited, he was greeted by the sound of balking camels filling the wind.

Purka took him directly to one of the 20-foot canvas houses. They were eager to get inside and had to stoop to enter as the openings were only 4½-feet high. The house was pleasantly warm. There was an iron dung stove which rested on the dirt floor centering the big room and whose pipe sliced a hole in the roof. Don decided immediately that it would have been more efficient to have built the felt-lined house a little tighter. The hole in the roof was much larger than the pipe, and bitter wind flowed in constantly.

Their camp was in the Gobi Desert, "A 100 hundred miles from nowhere," but Don was pleased to learn he could buy supplies which were not included in the package; i.e., vodka, whiskey and Coke for his guides. The gesture was unnecessary; he learned later that the Mongolians rarely drank. But given the fact he had generously given away his sleeping bag, he would relish a few belts of bourbon over an open fire after a long day on the trail.

Their track would encompass some 200 to 300 miles on horseback or in a jeep, which at first sight appeared to be in "mint condition." Appearances were deceiving. The vehicle had no starter and had to be parked on a hill every night. Most days, they pushed it a long way before it roared into action. The Mongolians had never heard of anti-freeze, and during the bitter, windy nights, they had to drain the radiator to keep it from freezing.

For 11 days the group moved across the Gobi sands and into the mountains, which were some 2,000-feet high. Don said, "In my book those aren't mountains at all." It was extremely cold and the wind relentless. The fires were fueled with dung from herds of wild camels and horses which were sighted constantly. And, except for them and the game they shot, they never encountered another living thing.

The hunt was expensive—$12,000—not a paltry sum for getting a sheep and "freezing your ass off." So Don willingly joined in the daily search for camel dung.

Evenings, the woman cook served goat stew with potatoes and carrots. It was followed by coffee which the hunter happily laced with bourbon over and over again.

The hardship paid off. He shot a beautiful argolis which went well over 325 pounds. For an added bonus, he got a gray, long-horned Mongolian ibex weighing about 275 pounds and a sleek black buck.

Guides universally wanted bullets for souvenirs. Don was amused by the count. He had used up all four boxes of shells, one way or another, and had given the help $500 in tips. Then as a parting gesture, he left all his hunting clothes and the suitcase for Purka, whose companionship had made all the difference.

The guide and the hunter celebrated over dinner in Ulan-Baton the night before he left Mongolia. At the conclusion of the meal, Don ordered a lunch packed for the long flight to Moscow the next day. By now he was used to brown-bagging it. There was a picnic-like atmosphere on all Russian flights, which were usually filled with soldiers. Don thought it quite pleasant to join in the fun where vodka and food was readily shared.

In Moscow after saying goodbye to George and collecting his gun, he flew to Munich. Of course, there was a short visit with Peter Eltz, who was now a successful art broker in that city.

Within days he headed for Austria, visiting along the way. In that country, Don was always welcomed as if he was a long-lost relative. There were hunters, gunsmiths and friends who actually fought over who would house him. The long evenings were filled with camaraderie and "Schnapps" for toasts to past hunts, future hunts, friends, America, Austria and anything else his convivial companions could think of.

Don said after that trip, "I stayed in Europe long enough to vote." But the ultimate pleasure was picking up the gun he had ordered from H. Dirnberger of Ferlach. The obliging master gunsmith had spent 900 hours making Don a magnificent rifle inlaid with gold, which is reputed to be valued at $125,000 and boasts the finest scope in the world.

The gun was later exhibited with a huge gun collection in Las Vegas, Nevada, from which the maker hoped to acquire many orders.

Eventually, in December, Don headed for Alaska. He was feeling tired.

After arriving home he rested, but Don still felt bone-tired. Ignoring the symptoms he was experiencing, he left for Bear Lake to pick up a Super-Cub. It needed new points, and the flight home took five hours. He began noticing chronic pain in his left arm which was typically not mentioned to anyone. On March 4, 1983, Don had a heart attack, followed almost immediately by a second one. Warren Johnson rushed him to the runway and flew his father to Providence Hospital in Anchorage, where the doctors decided he needed a quadruple-bypass operation. The surgery went well. For a time he seemed to be following a normal recovery, then suddenly he relapsed and was put into ICU where he lingered near death for several weeks. The bypass had failed. His doctors could see no other recourse but to operate, and again, survival seemed doubtful. Flowers from concerned friends worldwide filled his room and an adjoining one while the bush pilot's subconscious will-to-live prevailed. He would cheat death again, but this time the road back would be long and arduous. He said he passed the months reading and counting bush planes passing over the hospital.

Don really believed he would never fly again; he gave the Kenai Float Plane Service to his son.

The confinement allowed time to consider inherent heart problems in the Johnson family. His eldest brother, Clair, had died at age 52 long before bypass surgery was available; a second brother, Dwayne, was already a heart-attack victim; and now, Don was beginning to worry about Quinten. Before two years would pass, all three Johnson brothers would have successful bypass operations. The others returned to health and normal lives, but for Don the road ahead was decidedly unpleasant.

Finally he was allowed to go home. That news raised instant excitement which was quickly dampened by his weakness. Trying to overcome the physical inability to do simple things aggravated Don, but the combination was potentially lethal. In a short time the pilot was depressed. Sylvia Johnson, Don's wife, filed for a legal separation, and he was surprised by a restraining order which forced him out of his home. He took up residence in the hangar on the homestead where he had a makeshift apartment. Eventually, he suffered a stroke. His daughter, Audry, and her husband, Mark Hodgins, brought him home to recuperate. From 1983 on, Don's life seemed to disintegrate; he became a victim of despair—the fight had gone out of him. In June 1984, his doctor and a nurse flew him to Bear Lake where once more he could see the land he loved. The trip was the needed tonic, and by September he was airborne again skimming the tundra in his bush plane. Of course, he could no longer fly passengers.

In November he flew to Europe to see his old friend, Dr. Wechselberger. The doctor wanted to try a new procedure on Don, one with which they were having success in Europe. Don's friends rallied around him, each offering their special talents. Among them was an Austrian woman whose father was a forester. Christina Loidl had known Don for many years while the bush pilot hunted on her father's preserve. After his stroke, she visited him in Alaska, and upon hearing he would be having surgery in Lenz, Austria, Christina, who was an interpreter, offered her services during the hospital visit. The surgery helped somewhat but failed to relieve the circulation problems. Don thanked everyone and returned home, but not before deciding to alter his lifestyle.

Don filed for a bifurcated divorce in August 1987. He and Christina decided to marry. Plans for their new life together and the calming influence of a partner lifted Don out of his despair. Christina encouraged the pilot to reopen his lodge. He still wasn't well but much happier. The wedding, a quiet ceremony in Kenai, took place in November of that year. Don's luck would return, but the dark days had not yet passed. The newlyweds moved into a log cabin deep in the Alaskan woods, a gift from Don's close friends, Jim and Trina Doyle.

Of course, there was always the need to fly. Pilots Keith Hersh, Jim Doyle and Bill Sullivan offered their skills as well as their planes. Bill Sullivan, a retired Western Airlines pilot, lives in Southern California most of the year, but was willing to head for his home in Palmer, almost anytime, to pick up his plane and come to Kenai to help out Don. All of these men flew down chain when they were needed. Don had earned something not many people have—good and lasting friendships.

Don and Sylvia's marriage had been stormy for many years. Don's divorce was quick and devoid of a property settlement. Eventually, and regardless of negotiation, a protracted and bitter legal battled ensued which seriously affected his health. In 1989, he suffered another stroke. Just prior to that time, he flew to Bear Lake and organized construction on a huge building in which he planned to house some 80 people, and which included a reading room, pool room, laundry, showers and baths.

Each stroke left some damage, but Don overcame it with an iron will. To this day there is no visible evidence of any disability.

The new construction at Bear Lake stimulated Don; he felt his old drive coming back. Always ingenious where business was concerned, he knew the future demanded crude, and the oil companies were beginning to drill in the nearby Bering Sea. There are no hotels in that part of the world, but now there was a suitable facility at Bear Lake, half-way down the Aleutian chain and just adjacent to the Bering Sea.

Accomplishing that considerable feat seemed to bring back his spirit, but there was another problem: the artery in his neck was clogged, and the pain in his right arm grew more intense each day. Christina prevailed upon him to go to a specialist in Houston. Eventually even Don knew it was the only course to follow; he had been warned the next stroke would be his last. But at this juncture, the pilot hated doctors and hospitals, the mention of which brought on real anger.

The surgery in Houston was difficult. He said later he honestly believed he would die. Shortly, in true Don Johnson fashion, he checked himself out of the hospital and took a jet to Anchorage. Although she opposed his actions, Christina followed. In Anchorage, he went to the home of Danny Lynch for a day, then, even though he was extremely ill, he demanded to go home. That night he chartered a plane for a flight to Bear Lake the next day. During that flight, Don turned ghostly pale and became very ill, but, as was his norm, he never uttered a complaint.

However difficult that surgery was, it turned the tide for him. Within several months, Don took his pilot's physical and passed

New addition at Bear Lake built to house incoming oil company employees.

Pilot-friend Bill Sullivan with a prize salmon catch.

it. He had fought a valiant battle with the odds against him and still he prevailed. The victory was reflected in his smile—he'd won.

That fall, Christina and Don purchased a home on the Kenai River in Soldotna where they had decided to build a fishing camp. It would take some time to get Bear Lake up and running again, but the future was bright.

This year, the fall of 1991, Bear Lake Lodge will have a full season for moose and caribou in September. Prince Bandar Bin Sultan of Saudi Arabia will arrive for his October bear hunt.

Hunting site in Russia, 1982.

Russian guides preparing for the search for the Tur.

The Tur.

Chapter 32

The Way of It

During June, the salmon are running. That call sparks activity up and down the Bering Sea coast. Hundreds of fishermen pull out from 16 canneries dotting the horizon up and down the Aleutian Chain and lower peninsula. With the fleet is Lori Johnson Gunderson, Don's daughter, manning the Misty, which the enterprising young woman has been sailing since she was 22. Tenders steam up the coast to receive the day's catch; hundreds of down-jacketed men and woman labor in the packing sheds while gulls shriek overhead.

At Bear Lake Lodge the radio crackles incessantly, "Bear Lake, Bear Lake, this is the Misty calling."

"Misty, Misty, Bear Lake," the lodge answers.

A pilot, hungrily spooning fresh-baked salmon and Bear Lake's famous homemade bread, listens to a request for a flight to Cold Bay for three men. Stuffing the last of the bread in his mouth, he reaches for a charge book, down covering and hat, then leaves. And, as the fog rolls in from the sea, helicopters carrying oil company geologists flutter back to earth with their crews. They will not continue to work, while Bear Lake pilots race through the dense air daily.

Three-or four-hundred pilots a year are available to Don Johnson to fly the bush and the coast. "There aren't three of them who can handle the weather," he says with remorse. Fog, mist and rain often travel with the winds, further complicating flights over the glacier, mountains, tundra and the sea.

Occasionally, the winds rest. The sun seeps through heavy clouds warming the tundra which explodes with color: purple warthog and yellow mountain paintbrush open in the bogs mingled with bluebells and heliotrope. The tundra-carpet rolls up the mountains like a lime blanket meeting with tangled alders whose clumping mounds are dark green. At the summit, tiny patches of snow spear the sky, more often than not filled with racing gray-blue tinged, puffy clouds. The scene is dazzling under the sun, and the lake, devoid of wind, mirrors the entire scene.

As bears begin to migrate to the upper end of the lake during July, hundreds of thousands of salmon who have come into the Bear River from the Bering Sea will spawn and die. Sand cranes and loons sing lofty songs floating overhead before landing on the eight-mile lake where swans float lazily by. On occasion, a haughty American eagle soars low, coming close enough to be appreciated. Its white, terra-cotta and brown wings stretch wide, allowing flight from great heights, and, as if by eminent domain, it searches for food.

Early salmon, dead in a heap; their dark-red and silver bodies wash onto the shore near Bear Patch. Lumbering, plump-coated bruins on a nocturnal stroll dot the shore, gorging themselves on fish, fattening for the long winter's sleep. A red fox, whose tastes are more pedestrian, sneaks past the lodge's garden in search of a rabbit for dinner.

Honking geese, waddling through bear grass, are trailed by six goslings; tiny miniatures waddling to the river where, one-by-one, they effortlessly float upstream. They are careful to avoid the fishermen in high waders, recently arrived, eager for a singing line cast into tumultuous water.

Upriver, the small red-and-white fishing cabin sitting close to the bank shadows a young man taking samples of fish which entered his fike with the salmon. His partner climbs a weathered tower with binoculars, and in 10-minute sequences, counts the fish crossing the white net in the river below. Later, hurrying to the cabin radio, he will alert Fish and Game in Cold Bay. That collective count determines escapement for Alaska and will control the length of the fishermen's working days.

As summer fades, the workers at the lodge will cease fileting the salmon and hanging it in strips on hooks in the smokehouse. The attic will contain sacks of newly-dried squaw's candy; that treat will await incoming hunters. Blustery winds herald winter, but not before fading the riot of color on the muskeg. The green carpet turns ochre and dark under threatening clouds deepening as they fill with rain, and later, with snow. A million baby salmon, voluminous in a pink mass, will teem into the Bear River, headed for the sea and life. The bears will dig deep under alder bushes where soon, they will sleep away the winter. And, with all of this will come the sounds of airplanes bringing hunters carrying rifles, knapsacks, down and boots.

The caribou herds will move closer to the sea, passing trophy moose trailing the irregular gullies on the tundra. The duck hunters, in search of the emperor goose flying in from Russia, will appear packing shotguns over the windswept coast. Ptarmigan, whose brown-and-white bodies are beginning to fade, are alert to man while sandspits are already cluttering with gray-and-white screeching gulls cawing near the black-cave nests.

And, finally, as the temperature drops to below-zero in blustery, tearing winds, and the lake stiffens into a silver sheet, snow will fall on deserted Bear Lake Lodge, ghostly on the misting tundra.

A silence will overcome the landscape. Only a few trappers, who will run their lines for 10-mile stretches, will arrive on snow-shoed feet, absorbing the stillness of the great white Aleutian world awaiting spring and a rebirth of life at Bear Lake—visible proof of a hunter's dream.

Christina Johnson at home in Austria.

A rare windless day at Bear Lake.

Aleutian Fox waiting near the lodge runway for a chance at a rabbit.

Don Johnson wishes to acknowledge the years of professional services by the Klineburger Brothers. B. Klineburger International Hunting Consultants Inc., San Antonio, Texas and Klineburger Worldwide Travel & Taxidermy, Seattle, Washington.